Peter R. Neumann is Professor of Security Studies at King's College London and Director of the International Centre for the Study of Radicalisation (ICSR). He is a leading expert on terrorism and radicalization, and has advised governments and international institutions on both sides of the Atlantic. He frequently appears in the media.

RADICALIZED

NEW JIHADISTS AND THE THREAT TO THE WEST

PETER R. NEUMANN

I.B. TAURIS

LONDON · NEW YORK

Published in 2016 by
I.B.Tauris & Co. Ltd
London · New York
www.ibtauris.com

ISBN: 978 1 78453 673 2
eISBN: 978 1 78672 089 4
ePDF: 978 1 78673 089 3

A full CIP record for this book is available from the British Library
A full CIP record is available from the Library of Congress

Library of Congress Catalog Card Number: available

Text designed and typeset by Tetragon, London
Printed and bound in Great Britain by T.J. International, Padstow, Cornwall

The translation of this work was supported by a grant from the Goethe-Institut which
is funded by the German Ministry of Foreign Affairs.

To Zora

Contents

Maps   viii
List of Illustrations   xi
Acknowledgements   xiii
Preface   xv

INTRODUCTION   I

PART ONE: THE FOUR WAVES OF MODERN TERRORISM

I. ANARCHISM, ANTI-COLONIALISM AND THE NEW LEFT   9
2. THE RELIGIOUS WAVE   32

PART TWO: THE NEXT WAVE

3. THE ISLAMIC STATE   55
4. FOREIGN FIGHTERS   85
5. SUPPORTERS   110
6. THE AMERICAN EXCEPTION?   136
7. AL-QAEDA   152
8. COUNTERTERRORISM   172

Appendix A: Fighters from Western Europe   189
Appendix B: Relationship with the Islamic State   190
Names and Organizations   196
Notes   203
Further Reading   227
Index   229

TERRITORIES HELD BY THE ISLAMIC STATE
IN SYRIA AND IRAQ, LATE 2015

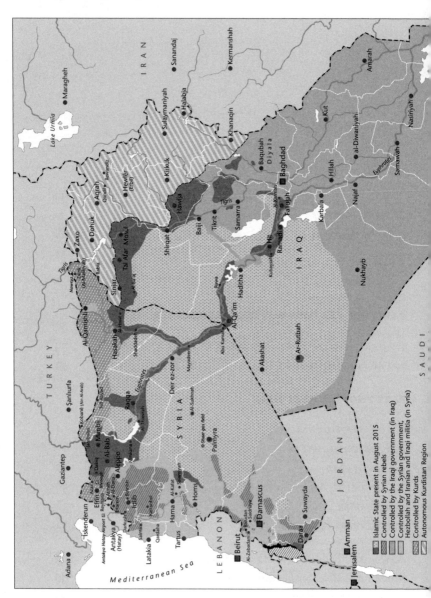

© Peter Palm

ORIGINS OF FOREIGN FIGHTERS
IN SYRIA AND IRAQ, FEBRUARY 2015

Where do foreign fighters in Syria and Iraq come from?
Number of foreign fighters per origin country

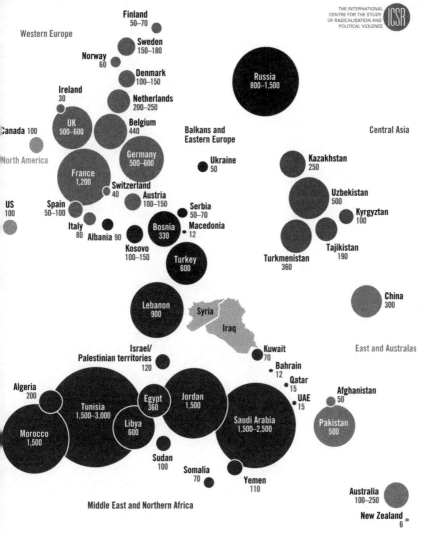

THE INTERNATIONAL
CENTRE FOR THE STUDY
OF RADICALISATION AND
POLITICAL VIOLENCE

ICSR

Western Europe

Finland
50–70

Sweden
150–180

Norway
60

Denmark
100–150

Ireland
30

Netherlands
200–250

UK
500–600

Belgium
440

Canada 100

Germany
500–600

North America

France
1,200

Switzerland
40

Austria
100–150

US
100

Spain
50–100

Serbia
50–70

Italy
80

Albania 90

Bosnia
330

Macedonia
12

Kosovo
100–150

Turkey
600

Lebanon
900

Syria

Iraq

Israel/
Palestinian territories
120

Kuwait
70

Bahrain
12

Qatar
15

UAE
15

Algeria
200

Egypt
360

Jordan
1,500

Tunisia
1,500–3,000

Libya
600

Saudi Arabia
1,500–2,500

Morocco
1,500

Sudan
100

Somalia
70

Yemen
110

Middle East and Northern Africa

Balkans and
Eastern Europe

Ukraine
50

Central Asia

Kazakhstan
250

Uzbekistan
500

Kyrgyztan
100

Tajikistan
190

Turkmenistan
360

China
300

East and Australas

Afghanistan
50

Pakistan
500

Australia
100–250

New Zealand
6

Note: Except for data from the Middle East and Africa, which could last be updated in late 2013, all the estimates below are based on official or semi-official figures. All figures are aggregates, reflecting the overall totals of people who have travelled to Syria and Iraq as Sunni fighters since 2011/12. They include fighters who have died and those who have returned to their home countries.

Source: International Centre for the Study of Radicalisation and Political Violence, 2014; 2015 Munich Security Report, p. 38.

List of Illustrations

FIG. 1.1 The German anarchist Johann Most, who published his *Little Handbook* for "lone wolves" (Wikimedia)   14

FIG. 1.2 The American Weatherman and subsequent professor of education Bill Ayers (FBI)   27

FIG. 2.1 The Egyptian teacher and school inspector Sayyid Qutb, who turned Islamism into a revolutionary ideology (k. A.)   38

FIG. 2.2 Abdullah Azzam, the architect of the "Afghan jihad" in the 1980s (mymfb)   42

FIG. 3.1 The Jordanian jihadist Abu Musab al-Zarqawi, who created a prototype of the Islamic State (Wikimedia)   60

FIG. 3.2 Self-proclaimed caliph and leader of the Islamic State Abu Bakr al-Baghdadi, pictured in Mosul's al-Nuri Mosque, July 2014 (k. A.)   63

FIG. 4.1 Ifthekar Jaman, from the English city of Portsmouth, who wanted to defend Syrian Sunnis against an "existential threat" (k. A.)   92

FIG. 4.2 Jean-Edouard, from Paris, who found a sense of recognition and security in the Islamic State (Facebook)   95

FIG. 5.1 London lawyer Anjem Choudary, the driving force behind the European megaphone jihadists

(By http://www.flickr.com/photos/snapperjack/
[CC BY-SA 2.0 (http://creativecommons.org/licenses/
by-sa/2.0)], via Wikimedia Commons)   117

FIG. 5.2 Bertrand Nzohabonayo, a supporter who became a
"lone wolf" (Facebook)   134

FIG. 6.1 Shannon Conley was radicalized via the internet
and wanted to become a nurse in the Islamic State
(Facebook)   137

FIG. 6.2 Mohammed Hamzah Khan spent many hours a day
watching jihadist videos and chatting to "fanboys"
(Facebook)   148

FIG. 7.1 The Yemeni jihadist Nasir al-Wuhayshi, leader of
AQAP and member of the al-Qaeda high command
until his death in June 2015 (k. A.)   161

FIG. 7.2 The *Charlie Hebdo* attackers Chérif and Saïd Kouachi,
who trained with AQAP in Yemen (Private, undated
passport photos)   169

FIG. 8.1 The division of responsibilities in counterterrorism   178

Acknowledgements

THIS BOOK WAS WRITTEN IN A DOZEN PLACES: ON AN EXPRESS train from Boston to New York, in hotel lobbies in Singapore, Saudi Arabia and Qatar, on the fringes of the Munich Security Conference, in the café at the European Parliament in Brussels, on flights to Oslo and Switzerland, during court proceedings in Northern Ireland and Scotland, in the reading room of the theology faculty at McGill University in Montreal and – of course – at my desk at home in London. The fact that it was finished is not to my credit, but to that of a great number of colleagues and friends who helped me with the research and the writing.

My greatest thanks go to Aymenn Jawad al-Tamimi, a young colleague with encyclopaedic knowledge of global jihadism, who let me bother him at all hours with questions about the Islamic State. Particular thanks are also due to my colleagues and collaborators at the International Centre for the Study of Radicalisation and Political Violence (ICSR), my institute at King's College London, who helped me with the research and also freed me up to work on it. They include Shiraz Maher, Joseph Carter, Aaron Zelin, Alexander Meleagrou-Hitchens, Melanie Smith, Nick Kaderbhai and Katie Rothman. An equally important role was played by students and former students: at King's, Samar Batrawi, Camille Rives, Andrew Ehrhardt, Haakon Sørvald and Viraj Solanki; at Georgetown University, David Sterman;

and at Sciences Po in Lyon, Ronald Hudak. Many thanks also to Pieter van Ostaeyen in Belgium, Thomas van Linge in Amsterdam, as well as Seamus Hughes and Lorenzo Vidino at George Washington University, and David Schanzer at Duke University.

I would also like to mention the sponsors who have enabled my institute to conduct its research into jihadism. They include Brett Kubicek from Public Safety Canada, who has been supporting our research into Syrian foreign fighters for two years, and Michael Hanssler of the Gerda Henkel Stiftung, as well as Nadia Schadlow of the Smith Richardson Foundation, who made it possible for us as early as 2011 to examine the effects of the Arab Spring on the jihadist movement. I am also grateful to Palantir Technologies for making their platform available to ICSR, which has enabled us to perform complex analyses and identify links and connections that would otherwise have gone amiss.

Those who've supported my work from Germany include Georg Mascolo, Julian Reichelt, Volkmar Kabisch, Georg Heil, Florian Flade, Yassin Musharbash, Michael Manske, Behnam Said and Daniel Heinke. Many thanks also to Tim Gürtler and Adrian Oroz from the Munich Security Conference as well as Eveline Metzen from Atlantik-Brücke. Equally important was the help from my parents, who read the manuscript several times, from all the interviewees and the editors, Moritz Kienast and Ulrike von Stenglin (Ullstein) as well as Alexander Starritt and Joanna Godfrey (I.B.Tauris), who accompanied the whole genesis of the book from start to finish with great enthusiasm. For any mistakes that have crept in regardless, I alone am responsible.

Preface

IN THE SUMMER OF 2016, EUROPE EXPERIENCED WHAT WAS
described as a "wave" of jihadist terrorism: first the lorry attack in
Nice, then attacks in the German towns of Würzburg and Ansbach,
the beheading of an elderly priest in Normandy and the stabbing
of two policewomen in the Belgian city of Charleroi. The largest
and most consequential attack, however, took place the previous
year, on the evening of 13 November 2015, when jihadists struck
in Paris. Beginning at 9.20 pm, suicide bombers struck at four different locations in the French capital: a football match, a café, a
restaurant and a rock concert. They killed 130 people; nearly 400
were injured. It was the worst terrorist attack in Europe in over
a decade.

   Few had expected this kind of attack at this time. Many experts
believed that the Islamic State, the group to which the attackers
belonged, wasn't capable of, or interested in, large-scale operations
in the West. Its strategy was different, they said: instead of organizing complex, externally coordinated operations, Islamic State relied
on "lone wolves" – enthusiastic but unaffiliated Western supporters – who would launch shocking but small-scale attacks that didn't
require much planning or direction. There would be occasional
shootings and knife attacks, perhaps even beheadings, but large-scale
"spectaculars" – such as the ones in London and Madrid during the

mid-2000s – weren't going to happen until the group had consolidated its territory in Syria and Iraq.[1]

In reality, the Islamic State had long started organizing such attacks, viewing them as part of a wider campaign aimed at targeting Europe as a whole. As early as February 2015, Harry S., a 27-year-old convert to Islam who had grown up in the northern German city of Bremen and joined the Islamic State as a foreign fighter, witnessed firsthand how the group's "secret service" recruited Europeans for "international operations". Those who signed up received financial support, new passports, as well as "training in... building bombs, explosive belts, [using] weapons, and how to remain undercover".[2] "I was asked twice," he told a journalist: "[When I said no,] they asked me if I knew someone [else] from Germany or the UK." France, he said, was no longer a priority: "They said that France is easy for them... They have enough people [from France]".[3]

The attacks also exposed the lack of preparedness and cooperation among European security agencies. Like Harry, nearly all the attackers were European citizens who had left their home countries, joined the Islamic State in Syria, and become foreign fighters. Their names were known to European security agencies, but none of them had been stopped or identified when they returned.[4] The most shocking example was Abdelhamid Abaaoud, a 28-year-old Belgian who joined Islamic State in the spring of 2013. Nine months before the attacks, he gave an interview to the group's online magazine in which he openly bragged about his travels to and from Europe:

> I was able to [come and leave as I wished]... despite being chased after by so many intelligence agencies... My name and picture were all over the news yet I was able to stay in their homelands, plan operations against them, and leave safely when doing so became necessary.[5]

At the time of the attacks, many in the French and Belgian intelligence services believed that Abaaoud was still in Syria. They only realized that he had returned when they identified his dead body.[6]

The failures of prediction and prevention, which became apparent in the wake of the attacks in Paris – and, more recently, Brussels – reveal a lack of intellectual rigour in dealing with the jihadist threat. On the one hand, the newspapers are filled with stories about Western fighters, jihadi brides and beheadings. Yet in practice, the analytical engagement with these phenomena has remained superficial. Despite years – if not decades – of fighting jihadist terrorism, Western decision makers are often baffled by the movement's actions, its strategy and ideology. Now that jihadist groups, especially the Islamic State, are once again regarded as serious threats, this must change.

Any effort aimed at countering jihadist terrorism must rest on three very basic premises.

First, jihadism is a movement, not a group. For too long, Western governments have conceptualized their terrorist adversaries as organizations. As a result, "Wars on Terror" have revolved around the destruction of groups, the killing of their leaders and dismantling of their affiliates. Yet organizations such as al-Qaeda and the Islamic State have only been the manifestations of a wider social, political and religious movement, a movement whose ideas and networks have spread and taken root in countries around the globe. Even if Islamic State can be defeated, this will not be the end of jihadism, just like the killing of Osama bin Laden didn't mean the end of al-Qaeda. Truly defeating jihadism requires a sustained engagement with ideas and the political conflicts and social cleavages that make them resonate.

Second, terrorism hasn't fundamentally changed. What Islamic State and its supporters do looks different and is more shocking than the actions of the Irish Republican Army, the Red Army Faction or even al-Qaeda. Given that Islamic State controls territory, communicates via the internet, and acts like a proto-state, it may also have more impact. But the underlying logic remains the same. The "propaganda of the deed", "lone wolves", and the idea of violence as symbolic and cathartic, are neither new nor unprecedented – even if its organization and modes of expression have taken full advantage of the opportunities offered by globalization.[7] In short: the new jihadists have turbocharged terrorism, but they didn't invent it.

Finally, just like previous waves of terrorism, this one will take years – if not decades – to play out. As the American historian David Rapoport demonstrated, terrorism is linked to political movements that tend to be generational. Whatever happens in Syria and Iraq tomorrow, the future veterans of this conflict have already emerged. Some of the networks that have formed over the past five years will remain active and be used to facilitate acts of terrorism – just like the networks that came out of the Afghanistan conflict in the 1980s paved the way for al-Qaeda during the 1990s and 2000s.

As a result, Paris and Brussels are not likely to remain isolated events. And they may not be the worst. The new jihadist wave of ter-rorism has only just begun.

Introduction

THE FIRST OF MAY 2011 IS VIVID IN MY MEMORY. IT WAS A Sunday and I was in Nashville, Tennessee, the home of country music, where the following morning I was to give a lecture to police officers from all over the United States on the subject of radicalization. The conference was in a giant hotel complex, the Gaylord Opryland, and I'd just settled into my room when the American news channels interrupted their normal programming. President Barack Obama would be making a statement at 10 pm, they said. The timing was unusual and none of the commentators, who were otherwise so well informed, knew what was going on. Many of my Facebook friends believed that it was about the Libyan dictator Muammar al-Gaddafi (1942–2011), with whom the West was then at war. But Obama had a different villain in mind. Two hours later, the president stepped in front of the cameras and announced that Osama bin Laden, the leader of al-Qaeda and mastermind of the attacks on 11 September 2001, had been killed by American special forces.

His speech hadn't even ended when my phone started to ring. But the first people to hear my opinion were the 200 or so police officers to whom I gave my lecture the following day. In a conference room decorated with guitars, cowboy hats and gold discs, I explained that the significance of the operation against bin Laden was primarily symbolic. He had had hardly any practical role to play in recent years. His death would not lastingly weaken the jihadist campaign. Although it would be wrong to fear-monger or predict apocalypse – as happened in the months after 9/11 – terrorism and especially jihadist terrorism still presented much the same danger as before. The threat was "serious, but not existential", in a formulation coined by my colleague David Schanzer of Duke University, which I often used in lectures.[1]

In spring 2011, this cautious appraisal put me in a minority almost of one. On both sides of the Atlantic, politicians and experts had established a firm consensus: the era of jihadist terrorism was coming to an end. Even before bin Laden's death, 20 of his closest comrades had been killed in drone strikes. And the peaceful demonstrations of the Arab Spring – first in Tunisia and Egypt, then in almost all other states of the Arab world – promised to usher in a new era of freedom and democracy in which jihadist violence would be a thing of the past. Leon Panetta, the American secretary of defense, was already talking about the "strategic defeat" of al-Qaeda.[2]

Four years later, that prognosis sounds absurd. There are more jihadist groups today than ever before. In a study published in 2014, the researcher Seth Jones, from the American RAND Institute, counted 49: from al-Qaeda and its subsidiaries in Somalia, Yemen, North Africa and Syria through to Nigeria's Boko Haram, the Pakistani Taliban and a whole range of obscure groups almost entirely unknown to the West, in Bangladesh, in the Philippines, in the Russian-controlled northern Caucasus and elsewhere. According to Jones, 19 of those groups have emerged since the year 2010. Among them is the "Islamic State", whose leader in mid-2014 proclaimed a caliphate that now stretches more than 500 miles – from the Syrian city of Aleppo to the gates of the Iraqi capital Baghdad – and that recruits fighters from all over the world. (The acronyms ISIS and IS refer to the same organization.) Jones estimates that the number of jihadists has more than doubled in the same period, and now comes to between

45,000 and 105,000 – most of them from the countries of the Arab Spring.[3]

The growth of the jihadist movement since 2011 has been remarkable and, although the majority of these groups and fighters are operating in the Middle East, this development will not be without consequences for the West, and especially Europe. My thesis is that the attacks in Paris in 2015 were not isolated incidents, but rather the first, very dramatic indications of what will be played out over the coming years and decades on our streets. I argue that Europe in particular now stands at the beginning of a new wave of terrorism that will occupy us for a generation. The situation is so dangerous because the number of jihadists is much higher than in the past; because we're dealing with new recruits, some of them very young; and because the jihadist movement has developed an internal rivalry that encourages attacks on the West.

The resulting terrorism will cost many people their lives. But there is also a second danger, which is just as great, if not greater: that our societies will become polarized; that Far Right parties and militant groups will gain in strength; and that ultimately it will become more difficult for people of different faiths and origins to live together. The new wave of terrorism will also threaten minorities like European Jews and – not least – Western Muslims, whose social integration, political status and physical safety all hang in the balance. The new jihadists that this book describes present a challenge to the West's security services but also present an even more serious one for our form of democracy and the European social model.

ABOUT THIS BOOK

My book consists of two parts. In the first I try to put the phenomenon in its historical context. Terrorism existed before the jihadists, and "waves" of terrorism are not new either. The wave concept comes from the American historian David Rapoport, who used it to categorize the development of modern terrorism. According to Rapoport, there have been four waves since the late nineteenth century, namely the "Anarchist", "Anti-Colonial", "New Left" and "Religious" waves. Each began in one country but led to terrorism in many others, and each lasted for approximately a generation, 25 to 30 years. In Rapoport's model, terrorism is not separate from political ideas, but the result of them. Each of the four waves is inextricably bound up with a radical political movement, some of which made the "long march through the institutions" and some of which went underground. The new wave discussed in this book fits seamlessly into that pattern.

It's also telling that Rapoport limits himself to revolutionary, non-state terrorism. I myself, as a professor who leads a master's course on the subject of terrorism, am well aware how disputed the concept is and how frequently the term is misused to discredit political opponents or radical movements. I also know that there is no international consensus on the definition of terrorism and that states are just as capable as non-state actors of employing terrorist methods.[4] And for the jihadists in the Middle East, terrorism – the use of shocking, often symbolic violence to achieve political ends – is no longer the only means available. But it will nonetheless define the imminent conflict in the West.

In the second part of this book I explain what this new wave consists of. Its emergence is inseparably linked to the Arab Spring and – very particularly – to the conflicts in Syria and Iraq. For the jihadists, the Islamic State that has embedded itself in those countries represents a utopia, an inspiration and a logistical hub. It is the centre of a new totalitarian movement that has convinced tens of thousands of young Muslims to leave their homes and go to war. Among them are at least 5,000 Western Europeans, some of whom will form the elite of the new jihad when they return to the countries they grew up in. The foreign fighters are supported by thousands of European Salafists, over whom the Islamic State has cast its spell in recent years. Whether as "lone wolves" or as part of more tightly knit organizations, they embody the threat of relatively straightforward but highly shocking attacks. Another element in this new wave consists of the remnants of the old one: al-Qaeda's networks, which now have to compete with the Islamic State and to assert that they still exist by mounting spectacular operations in the West and elsewhere.

The reason my prognosis sounds menacing is that is the reality. But inciting panic is as far from my intentions as is whipping up anti-Islamic sentiment. On the contrary, Rapoport's wave concept reminds us that not all terrorism has been Islamic, and that a religion which has existed for more than 1,400 years – and now has more than 1.5 billion followers – cannot be sweepingly accused of being prone to violence. I would not argue that the new jihadists have nothing at all to do with Islam, but it would be just as false to present their extreme interpretation as the sole, true version of the faith, as many so-called critics of Islam are now doing. Anyone who reads this book through to the end will understand that the target audience from whom the new jihadists do their recruiting is not "Muslims"; it is a shrill but numerically tiny minority: the Salafists. The "average Muslim" is as unreachable for the jihadists as the "average German" is for violent neo-Nazis.

That does not mean that the integration of Muslim minorities is without its problems nor that there are no troubling views among European Muslims. The resultant social tensions and conflicts provide background noise to the radicalization of young European Muslims. But anyone who goes looking for potential terrorists will find them among the Salafists – not among the "mainstream Muslims".

The last chapter of this book contains suggestions for what can be done about it. The most important of these is the expansion of preventive work, which is still conducted without either enthusiasm or strategy even in major European countries. We can no longer ignore that the young men who appear in the Islamic State's videos, speaking in unaccented German, English or French about the merits of the caliphate, are products of our societies. Their radicalization began not in Raqqa or Mosul, but in Dinslaken, Portsmouth, Nantes and Denver. Anyone who wants to fight the next wave of terrorism will have to work from where it started: here in the West.

PART ONE

The Four Waves of Modern Terrorism

1

Anarchism, Anti-Colonialism and the New Left

MY FIRST ENCOUNTER WITH DAVID RAPOPORT WAS IN JANUARY 2006 at a symposium on suicide bombers in the Israeli city of Haifa. Rapoport kept to himself on the first day of the conference, sitting in the audience and occasionally scratching his white beard – a sure sign that he didn't agree with what the speakers were saying. Rapoport was the conference's star speaker. Everyone knew who he was: a founding father of research into terrorism; someone who had been writing books on the subject before many of us had even been born and whose work we all cited frequently in our own articles.

Rapoport's keynote speech was in the evening, and the University of Haifa, which had organized the conference, invited a group of Israeli officers to come and learn something. But instead of a gripping presentation on the origins and development of terrorism, Rapoport talked for almost an hour about the Macedonian independence movement of the early twentieth century – a topic so obscure that my colleagues began to glance impatiently at their watches (to say nothing of the soldiers). Even I don't remember precisely what Rapoport said that evening. But his encyclopaedic knowledge and his passion for the subject were obvious. Rapoport is not someone who is merely interested in terrorism – not someone who would go on television to speak about terrorism and then come back the next day to speak about something else. I know that he has dedicated his life to the study of terrorism and that is something for which I have the deepest respect.

After the 9/11 attacks, Rapoport formulated a new thesis by pulling together more than three decades of study and research.[1] The four waves that he postulated amount to a concise history of modern terrorism. They describe its historical development and make clear that the new terrorism that befell the United States on 9/11 did not appear out of nowhere. The logic and mindset of terrorism – including the justification of extreme brutality – had been seen before under the aegis of other, non-Islamic campaigns. Terrorist groups, Rapoport argued, were always the product of much broader radical social and political movements and, although many had succeeded in plunging their countries into chaos, almost none had been able to try and build their version of utopia. According to Rapoport, terrorism was a generational phenomenon: as soon as the original wave broke, a movement had to either reinvent itself or be replaced by another.

This chapter describes that recurring cycle of rise and fall for the first three of the four waves. It closes with a brief look at Far Right terrorism, which Rapoport – for good reasons – did not consider a wave of its own.

ANARCHISM

The first of Rapoport's waves is anarchism. Between 1880 and 1905, anarchist terrorists murdered the empress of Austria, the king of Italy and the presidents of France and the United States, as well as dozens of innocent people who were suspected of being part of the bourgeoisie. No other movement has had so much success in carrying out terrorist attacks and yet achieved so little. The international revolution they hoped for did not come off in any country. Nevertheless, the anarchists exerted an important influence. They formulated tactics and a strategy that were still being used decades later as a guide and inspiration for terrorists all over the world.

The name of this strategy was "the propaganda of the deed" and its inventor was Carlo Pisacane (1818–57), an impoverished Neapolitan aristocrat who fought throughout his life for a unified socialist Italy. Pisacane had been part of the liberal revolutions that broke out all over Europe in 1848. But after they had been suppressed he lost his trust in the thinkers and intellectuals who had instigated them. "Ideas spring from deeds and not the other way around," he wrote in his *Political Testament* (*Testamento Politico*), which was published the year he died.[2] His intellectual legacy was the belief that revolutionary action was more important than philosophizing and that revolutionary deeds had a greater effect on supporters than any political tract ever could. A decade later, this idea became accepted doctrine, first among Italian anarchists, then among anarchists all over Europe.[3]

For Pisacane, the propaganda of the deed was not primarily about violence. It was Pyotr Kropotkin (1842–1921), a Russian anarchist, who transformed the concept into a terrorist strategy. Kropotkin, a Russian prince who had converted to socialism at the age of 12, was one of the most influential anarchists and his articles and books were read across the continent. He was convinced that the revolution would begin with single deeds – "acts of individual heroism" – that would persuade like-minded people of the need for urgent action, inspire them to further revolutionary deeds and so start a chain reaction. For Kropotkin, the assumption that these deeds were violent – and had to be violent – was beyond doubt. The act of destruction, Kropotkin wrote, "is natural and just... and [for the revolutionaries involved] deeply satisfying".[4] Kropotkin was also sure that society's elites would respond with state-sanctioned violence. But rather than crushing the rebellion, he believed that oppression would drive new followers into the arms of the revolution.[5]

The first to implement Kropotkin's strategy were the Russian revolutionaries of the Narodnaya Volya ("People's Will"). Starting in 1878, they carried out attacks on prominent aristocrats and leading functionaries of the Tsarist regime. They hoped that other revolutionaries and anarchists would follow their example. The most important and most difficult target was the Tsar himself. In the first three years, the group made eight attempts to kill Alexander II (1855–81), all of which failed. Even the ninth and ultimately successful attempt, on the 1 May 1881, almost went awry. Four revolutionaries had each been equipped with four bombs and were to attack the Tsar's coach from every direction at once. When the first missed his target, the Tsar cried, "Thank God, I'm not wounded!" But one of the other assassins came closer and blew up both himself and the Tsar.[6]

The attack was Narodnaya Volya's greatest success, but also the beginning of its end. The Tsarist regime mobilized the entire state apparatus, including the feared secret police, to destroy the group. The result: a year later there was practically nothing left of Narodnaya Volya. Even Kropotkin, who was closely following the situation in his home country, distanced himself from the group – and thus from his own strategy. In 1891 he wrote:

> Revolutions are not made by heroic acts. Revolution is above all a popular movement. That was the mistake made by the anarchists in 1881. When the Russian revolutionaries had killed the Tsar... the European anarchists imagined that, from then on, a handful of fervent revolutionaries, armed with a few bombs, would be enough to bring about the social revolution. A structure founded on centuries of history is not going to be destroyed by a few kilos of explosive.[7]

One of the most influential violent anarchists was Johann Most (1846–1906), a bookbinder born in Augsburg, Germany. Most was already an active socialist in his youth, organizing strikes and getting himself elected to the Reichstag at the age of 28. But even then he had little commitment to parliamentary democracy. He was arrested several times for inciting violence and, in 1878, Bismarck's government forced him into exile – first to France, then on to London. After the British first incarcerated and then ejected him, the only route left was that across the Atlantic. And in America, too, Most soon established himself as a central figure in the anarchist scene.

His most significant role consisted as before in lobbying for the propaganda of the deed. In 1885, Most published a pamphlet with the laborious title: *The Science of Revolutionary Warfare: A Little Handbook of Instruction in the Use and Preparation of Nitroglycerine, Dynamite, Gun-Cotton, Fulminating Mercury, Bombs, Fuses, Poisons, Etc., Etc.*[8] The brochure was a manual for "lone wolves" who were not part of formal organizations but still wanted to fight for the anarchist cause. Most's approach was identical to that of the Yemeni preacher Anwar al-Awlaki, who published the al-Qaeda online magazine *Inspire* 100 years later. But in contrast to Awlaki, who favoured the internet and home-made explosives, Most printed his *Little Handbook* on paper and was an enthusiastic fan of dynamite, which Alfred Nobel had invented two decades earlier:

> Dynamite... is a formidable weapon against every kind of paramilitary, policeman or detective who suppresses the cry for justice. It can be employed against both people and property. Using it against people is better than against bricks and mortar... A pound of this stuff beats a whole bushel of ballot papers.[9]

FIG. 1.1 The German anarchist Johann Most, who published his *Little Handbook* for "lone wolves"

And yet Most was not a mass murderer. His understanding of the propaganda of the deed was violent but nonetheless strategic. Violence was not an end in itself but served the cause. And so he consistently argued against attacks on ordinary citizens: "The higher-placed the victim of the assault and the more targeted the operation, the greater its effect as propaganda."[10]

ESCALATION

Not all anarchists were so disciplined. The most brutal attacks of the anarchist wave took place in France between 1892 and 1894. They were triggered by the execution of François Claudius Koënigstein (1859–92), an unemployed musician known as Ravachol. After a May Day rally in which the police shot nine demonstrators, Ravachol had carried out a series of attacks on the police and judiciary. From the anarchists' point of view, Ravachol was a charismatic hero who had been systematically demonized by the press. After he was arrested and executed, the violent anarchists directed their fury at the whole system – not just at its highest representatives.[11]

Ravachol's fate inspired a series of "lone wolves", who, although they belonged to the anarchist milieu, were not members of any particular group. Among them was Léon-Jules Léauthier (1874–94), who strolled into an expensive Parisian restaurant in November 1893 intending to murder the first five members of the bourgeoisie he encountered. (In the end he stabbed a Serbian diplomat who happened to be there.) Less than a month later, Auguste Vaillant (1861–94), a comrade of Léauthier's, stormed into the French parliament and hurled a bomb into the chamber. "The deafer they are," Vaillant said in court, "the louder your voice must thunder."[12]

Émile Henry (1872–94), a 21-year-old anarchist from an aristocratic family, carried out what was perhaps the most dramatic attack. On the evening of 12 February 1894, he went into the Café Terminus in Paris and threw a home-made bomb at a band that was playing for the patrons. Although the restaurant was nearly full, only one person was killed. And yet this attack incited more panic than its predecessors, because the Terminus was not an upper-class restaurant, but one frequented by ordinary white-collar workers and the middle class. In the subsequent trial, Henry justified his deed with the words: "There are no innocents!" For him, all members of the bourgeoisie were part of the system and therefore guilty of oppressing the working class and those who fought on their behalf. There was no difference, said Henry, between the government, the police and the bourgeoisie, "and that is why I chose my victims at random".[13] His closing argument was a precis, as dramatic as it was eloquent, of the thinking behind the propaganda of the deed, and could have been formulated the same way – or very similarly – by the terrorists in the waves that were yet to come:

In this war that we have declared against the bourgeoisie, we do not ask for mercy. We bring death and we know that we will have to suffer it ourselves. So I await your judgement with equanimity. I know that my head will not be the last to roll. But I also know that the hungry now know the way to your grand cafés and restaurants... And that their names will be the next on the bloody list of our dead.[14]

The anarchist wave claimed victims in almost every European country and in the United States too. Between 1894 and 1900, Italian anarchists murdered the French president, the Spanish prime minister, the empress of Austria and the king of Italy. In Spain, a bombing in Barcelona's opera house in November 1893 killed 20 people. And in the United States in 1901, an anarchist murdered President William McKinley.

There was a good deal of contact between the anarchists of different countries. They met at conferences, and exiles such as Most spread ideas from one national group to another. But the anarchists were not a transnational terrorist network like al-Qaeda. Communication across borders was still difficult and, despite a shared internationalist ideology, there were almost no transnational operations. Anarchist terrorism remained the sum of many national campaigns.

And of course the anarchist wave came to an end. Many historians believe that was due to harsh laws that took the most dangerous activists out of circulation. Others argue that the social reforms enacted in many European states around the turn of the century pulled the social and political rug out from under the anarchists' feet.[15] As often, there is a grain of truth in both explanations. But it is also true that the anarchist movement had run out of steam everywhere by the start of the twentieth century. The generation that had agitated for terrorist violence in the 1880s was getting long in the tooth and the next generation lacked the (often naive) enthusiasm of their predecessors. The first wave had completed its cycle.

ANTI-COLONIALISM

Compared with the anarchist wave, the anti-colonial wave, which began in the 1930s and reached its peak in the 1950s, was more effective and of larger political significance. The violent groups that belonged to it tended to be more firmly anchored in the population than the anarchists had been and were therefore less reliant on the propaganda of the deed, "lone wolves" and individual attackers. But they were not always successful. Their aim was to create a situation in which colonial powers like Britain or France concluded that the "felt costs" of keeping a colony were greater than the benefits. But the strategy only worked when the struggle was truly about foreign rule.

Colonialism had been on the road to obsolescence since the end of World War I. In the preceding decades, nationalist movements had emerged in every part of the world to resist foreign domination and champion a return to their own cultures, languages and traditions. And in February 1918, the American president, Woodrow Wilson (1856–1924), elevated each people's so-called right to self-determination, a right many of these movements claimed, to the guiding principle of international politics. According to Wilson, it was "not a mere phrase", but "an imperative principle of action which statesmen will henceforth ignore at their peril".[16] What exactly a people was and how the principle was to be implemented were questions Wilson left unanswered. And yet the Americans managed to popularize the idea even among the British, who stood to lose the most by it. The Atlantic Charter, which British prime minister Winston Churchill (1874–1965) signed in August 1941, included "the right of all peoples to choose the form of government under which they will live" as one of eight principles that were to determine the international system after the defeat of Nazi Germany.[17]

Churchill and Wilson may well have been thinking mainly of the peoples occupied by Germany and its allies in the two world wars. But both men must have clearly seen that nations not yet recognized as such would also adopt the principle. Almost all independence movements made self-determination their slogan and many used it to legitimize violent struggle.

The man who took that to its furthest extreme was the Martinique-born French psychiatrist Frantz Fanon (1925–1961), whose radical analysis of liberation struggles provided the ideological basis for many anti-colonial groups. Fanon considered colonialism to be a racist system, which persuaded the "natives" to accept that it was right for them to be oppressed and to think of themselves as inferior. Liberation, according to Fanon, was not about solving a political conflict, but about successfully processing a mental trauma. Actual psychological liberation from colonialism therefore necessitated the use of force. In his most influential book, *The Wretched of the Earth* (1961), he wrote: "At the level of individuals, violence is a cleansing force. It frees the native from his inferiority complex and from his despair and inaction."[18]

Fanon's equation of colonialism with racism made him popular not only with nationalists but also with the Left and the growing student movement in Western Europe and North America. This meant that during the second wave of terrorism there was already a bridge to the Western Left, which campaigned on behalf of independence movements in the developing world and a few years later used Fanon's ideas to justify terrorism of its own.

ALGERIA

At the time Fanon wrote *The Wretched of the Earth*, the British were involved in costly wars in Malaysia, Kenya and Cyprus, and had recently lost their mandate in Palestine. But the most significant conflict of this wave took place in Algeria, where colonial France fought the National Liberation Front (FLN) from 1954 to 1962. Algeria had been under French rule since 1830 and had been seen as an integral part of the French republic since the mid-nineteenth century. That was most obviously manifested by the French settlers, who numbered a tenth of the population when the conflict broke out. Initially, however, the FLN had little success. Basing their strategy on the guerrilla doctrine that Mao Zedong (1893–1976) had employed to seize power in China, they intended to work their way forward from the mountainous hinterland and then advance into the cities. But the self-proclaimed freedom fighters met with resistance before they'd even left the mountains, and the French were able to keep them in check without too much difficulty.[19]

At the start of 1956, Abane Ramdane (1920–57), an influential commander who grew up in the mountains and joined the FLN early in the campaign, proposed an entirely new strategy. Instead of guerrilla warfare he called for terrorism. And this was to take place not in the backwoods but right in the middle of the Algerian capital, Algiers. Ramdane precisely understood how this kind of campaign worked: it achieved its ends not through direct confrontation with the enemy, but by psychologically manipulating their perceptions and interests. By carrying out dramatic attacks on French colonists, settlers and collaborators, the FLN's terrorist campaign was intended to attract attention, polarize Algerian society, disconcert the settlers, provoke a French overreaction and use that to force the government in Paris to withdraw.[20] Fanon, who had gone to Algeria as a psychiatrist at the start of the 1950s and joined the FLN as early as 1955, was one of Ramdane's most enthusiastic supporters.[21]

The campaign that Ramdane organized was brutal. It targeted ordinary Algerians in cafés and marketplaces; even women and children were killed. But the French reaction was just as brutal. During the so-called Battle of Algiers, the French army obeyed the principle that you could defeat terrorists only by using their own methods against them. French paratroopers transformed the Algiers old town into a kind of prison camp, where torture and executions as well as the "disappearing" of suspects were routine. At first, the French initiative seemed successful: by October 1957, the Battle of Algiers was over, the FLN had been defeated and most of its commanders were either dead or in prison. But in the longer term, the French backlash brought about the opposite of what it had intended. Given the choice of which type of "terrorism" they preferred – French or Algerian – more and more Algerians opted for the latter. And French public opinion followed suit. The military's excesses unleashed heated debate about the purpose and legitimacy of the French presence in Algeria. Many French people found that they were not prepared to pay such a high moral, political and financial price for keeping Algeria in their empire.[22]

In other words: Ramdane's strategy worked exactly according to plan. Despite military inferiority, the FLN had created a situation in which France was politically and psychologically no longer willing to hold on to Algeria. Less than five years after the Battle of Algiers, President Charles de Gaulle (1890–1970) released the colony into independence.

PALESTINE AND IRELAND

The FLN's success became a model for independence movements all over the world. Yasser Arafat (1929–2004), the leader of the Palestine Liberation Organization (PLO), flew to Algiers in 1963 – only a year after independence – to study the FLN's strategy.[23] Until then, his comrades had stuck to Mao's guerrilla tactics, but in the 1960s they, too, switched to terrorism. Their initial focus was on aeroplane hijack-ings, which usually claimed few victims but made headlines all over the world. The first took place in July 1968, when a Palestinian com-mando group hijacked a plane from the Israeli airline El Al, diverting it from Tel Aviv to Algiers, from where they negotiated for almost six weeks about the release of Palestinian prisoners. Three years (and half a dozen hijackings) later came the most spectacular operation: the kidnapping of 11 Israeli athletes during the 1972 Olympic Games in Munich, in which all the Israelis were killed.

By that point, there was no one who hadn't heard of the Palestinian struggle for independence, but that did not mean that these opera-tions amounted to an effective strategy. The PLO had no clear idea of how gaining attention for the Palestinian cause would lead to the "destruction" of Israel, which remained the organization's official goal until 1974. In contrast to Algeria, Israel was not a colony – not a dispensable possession held by a foreign power – interested only so long as it stood to benefit. The Israelis' entire existence was on the line and their pain threshold was therefore much higher than it had been for France with Algeria.

Attempts to deploy the FLN's strategy against a rival ethnic group were equally problematic. According to the strategists of the Irish Republican Army (IRA), the conflict in Northern Ireland was about liberation from British colonial rule and, from 1969 onwards, they copied the Algerian model in fighting the British "occupiers" and their supposed local stooges, the Protestant unionists, who were very disproportionately over-represented in the administration and the police. But in reality, Northern Ireland was not primarily a colonial conflict. The right to self-determination on the part of the Catholic minority, many of whom wanted unification with the rest of Ireland, was opposed by a right to self-determination on the part of the Protestant majority, who wanted to remain in the United Kingdom.

The British government had given up long ago on the idea of extracting strategic or economic benefits from Northern Ireland and held on to it only because they feared the consequences of a civil war.[24] It took two decades for the IRA to recognize that its interpretation of the conflict was false. "This requires a more complex response than simply the imposition of one nationality over another," said the republican chief negotiator Gerry Adams (*1948) at the start of the 1990s. "This is a divided community."[25]

But despite all their problems, anti-colonial groups mobilized a broad following. That was because they could draw on ideas – and identities – that were deeply rooted in their supporters and needed no justification: patriotism and the right to self-determination were not remote values for which a revolutionary consciousness had first to be created.[26] That did not mean, however, that groups of this type were always victorious. The anti-colonialists had their greatest success during a broad era of decolonization, when it was relatively simple to influence the colonial powers' cost–benefit analyses by means of terrorist attacks. Later on, however, terrorism proved unable to help even (comparatively) popular movements like the PLO or the IRA to get what they wanted.

THE NEW LEFT

In contrast to the nationalist and anti-colonial groups of the second wave, which often recruited ordinary people, the New Left's members were drawn almost exclusively from the upper middle class. Intellectually, as well as personally, the terror groups of this wave came out of the student movement that emerged all over Western Europe and North America during the 1960s. They enjoyed some sympathy in these circles, but had practically no support among the rest of society – least of all among the working classes whose interests they claimed to represent. And although they presented a serious challenge to the state in Germany and Italy, they never got anywhere near achieving their aims. By the 1990s at the latest, most of these groups had dispersed.

The origins of the student movement lay in the "stuffy" 1950s and a new generation, which turned radically against inherited constraints, conventions and hierarchies. For many, as in every counterculture, it was not initially about politics, but about clothes, music, experimenting with new ways of living and revolt against anything felt to be authoritarian. "Sex, drugs and rock 'n' roll" were superficial markers and soon commercialized – but each in itself represented the breaking of a taboo, a conscious provocation. The movement was intellectually underpinned by French existentialists like Jean-Paul Sartre (1905–80) and members of the so-called Frankfurt School, particularly Herbert Marcuse (1898–1979) and Theodor W. Adorno (1903–69). These thinkers also influenced its gradual politicization. The student movement's supporters included anarchists, libertarians, Maoists, more or less traditional Marxists and naturally a whole lot of people who had no interest at all in ideological debate.

And yet, as the years passed a kind of basic political consensus did emerge. They were against capitalism and the West's supposed imperialism, but generally also against authoritarian socialism as practised in the countries of the Eastern Bloc. Their aim was a new, socially just and anti-authoritarian society, which, though founded on socialist principles, would be different from the "actually existing socialism" on the other side of the Iron Curtain. As a political movement, the New Left reached its highpoint in 1968, when millions of people took to the streets all over Western Europe and North America. But the desired change of system did not take place and, while the majority made their peace with it in the following years, a minority opted for armed struggle.

For inspiration, the New Left's terror groups looked not just to Algeria, but also above all to Latin America. Fidel Castro (*1926) and the Cuban revolution of the late 1950s had shown the way, galvanizing imitators across the continent. Among them was Carlos Marighella (1911–69), the leader of the Communist Party of Brazil, who was an activist throughout his life and often suffered arrest and torture. Marighella had a deep interest in revolutionary strategies and systematically studied the campaigns of other groups and movements to learn from their successes and failures. In his most important publication, the *Minimanual of the Urban Guerrilla* (1970), he formulated a strategy that was supposed to guide even small movements – such as his own – to victory.[27] Only a few months after he had begun to implement his ideas, he was shot dead by the military. But his ideas survived him and were rapidly translated into dozens of languages. For the militant New Left in Western Europe and North America, Marighella's *Minimanual* became required reading.

In contrast to Castro and Che Guevara (1928–67), the architects of the Cuban revolution, Marighella was convinced that the overthrow of the state had to begin not in the countryside but in the cities. The revolutionaries' aim should be to carry out spectacular attacks on the government and other representatives of the "system", and so provoke the state into overreacting. When the state responded with curfews, death squads, roadblocks and shootings, the fascist character of the capitalist system would be revealed. State repression would be so massive and the true face of the system so ugly that the people would blame not the insurrectionaries but the state itself. Just like in Algeria, Marighella sought to militarize the conflict:

> The political situation in the country is transformed into a military one, in which gorillas [the state security forces] are more and more

clearly shown to be the ones responsible for the mistakes and the use of violence, while the problems in the lives of the people become truly catastrophic.[28]

The group that would profit from this situation, according to Marighella, would be the revolutionaries: in the end, the rebels would be so strong and so popular that even a dictatorial regime would no longer stand a chance against them.

THE WEATHERMEN AND THE RAF

A good example of the New Left's thinking and strategies is provided by the American Weathermen, who mounted a series of attacks on the judiciary, Congress and government in the early 1970s. Ideologically and politically, the Weathermen were almost indistinguishable from the student movement from which they originated. Their pre-occupations were the war in Vietnam, discrimination against black Americans, inequality and imperialism. But by 1968 at the latest, traditional activism was no longer enough for them. Bill Ayers (*1944), one of the group's leaders, who was studying at the University of Michigan and had been participating in protests against the Vietnam War since 1965, urged his fellow students to take firmer, more direct action. He gave them the books by Fanon and Marighella and told them about the propaganda of the deed. And he made clear that the time to act had arrived:

Everything seemed urgent now. Everything was accelerating – the pace, to be sure, but also the stakes, the sense of consequences. Madmen were at the controls, several compartments were already in flames and our future existence hung in the balance. It fell to us – and we were just kids – to save the world.[29]

At first glance, the notion that the fate of the world depended on a few dozen American students may seem presumptuous – if not laughable. But statements of this kind were typical of the revolutionary ecstasy that shaped the New Left's thinking in the late 1960s. This also explains how the students could believe that a few attacks on symbolic targets would force the state to its knees.

Ayers took part in three violent operations, one of which was directed against the US Department of Defense, the Pentagon. The attack, in May 1972, damaged three offices, and the repairs were in the order of a few tens of thousands of dollars. And yet Ayers believed that he had made an important contribution to the collapse of the imperialist system:

> I didn't think that our entire arsenal, 125 pounds of dynamite, would actually count for much in a contest with the U.S. military, but I was never good at math, and I did think that every bomb we set off invoked the possibility of more bombs, that the message... was that if you bastards continue to wage war, we'll go into places you don't want us to go, places like the Pentagon, and we'll retaliate, and soon – who knows? – you might completely lose control.[30]

In truth, the Weathermen's attacks inspired no one. Just like during the anarchist wave almost 100 years before them, the supposedly oppressed population had no interest in being liberated, and even large parts of the student movement distanced themselves from the bombings. The state did react – the FBI created a huge surveillance programme that used illegal means to watch numerous activists, including peaceful ones – but that did not win the New Left the support of the masses. Ayers profited from it nevertheless: because the evidence used against him had been illegally obtained, he was acquitted and spent the following decades working unscathed as a professor of education in Chicago.[31]

FIG. 1.2 The American Weatherman and subsequent professor of education Bill Ayers

It was a very similar story for the Red Army Faction (RAF) in Germany. Just like the Weathermen, the RAF consisted of the sons and daughters of the upper middle class, emerged from the '68 student movement and had only a few dozen members – who were just as convinced that an established political system accepted by the general public could be brought down with only a handful of attacks. Just as for the Weathermen, this conviction was based on the supposedly inescapable logic of Marighella's strategy of provocation, which they used as an instruction manual.[32] But – again just like the Weathermen – the RAF failed because the general public rejected them. Although the group enjoyed some sympathy within the Leftist scene, the rest of the population were never persuaded to turn their backs on the state or the system.

Where the Weathermen and the RAF differ is in the length of the latter's campaign and its influence on politics and society. The Weathermen's campaign was more or less over by 1975 and the only people it killed were three terrorists who blew themselves up while making a bomb in New York in March 1970. The so-called first generation of the RAF – particularly Andreas Baader (1943–77), Ulrike

Meinhof (1934–76) and Gudrun Ensslin (1940–77) – were also out
of action and in prison by 1975. But half the RAF's violence – 17 of
34 killings – was carried out not by them, but by a second generation
who made it their mission to get the first generation out of jail. It was
this second generation that kidnapped Hanns Martin Schleyer, the
president of the German employers' association, and so triggered
the dramatic events of autumn 1977: the hijacking of the Lufthansa
aeroplane *Landshut*, the freeing of the hostages in Mogadishu by
GSG 9 special forces and the subsequent suicides of the first RAF
generation in the high-security prison of Stuttgart-Stammheim. The
second generation was followed by a third in the mid-1980s, but it was
the second generation and the "German Autumn" of 1977 that became
an unprecedented test for Germany's young (and in many ways blame-
less) democracy. In comparison with that, the Weathermen were no
more than a footnote.[33]

A similar story was playing out at the same time in Italy, where the
Red Brigades provoked both a repressive reaction from the authorities and reactive Far Right terrorism, wobbling the Italian state. But
neither in Italy nor anywhere else was the New Left even close to
getting what it wanted. Marighella's strategy was effective at creating
chaos, but the "false consciousness" of the masses, which the New
Left always complained about, especially in connection with the
working classes in Western countries, was more persistent than the
young revolutionaries had imagined.

WHAT ABOUT THE RIGHT?

One criticism of Rapoport's theory is the absence of a Far Right wave.
But Far Right terrorism cannot be limited to a single historical period.
It many cases, it was a reaction to the emergence of other – usually
Left-wing or anti-colonial – movements and therefore an ongoing

phenomenon not confined to a particular era. Moreover, the "Far Right" label encompasses highly varied, partly even contradictory ideas. Far Right terrorism could be fascist and revolutionary, but also reactionary and conservative. Many groups were nationalist, some were explicitly racist and some were both. There was no *single political movement* providing the bedrock for Far Right terrorism and therefore no *single wave* in which it was manifested.

The era of classical fascism is the only one in which Far Right terrorism was accompanied by a broader, ideologically coherent movement. Fascist groups in the 1920s and 1930s did see themselves as mass movements and almost all of them took part in elections. That they also employed terrorist methods – and did so frequently, in a precisely targeted way – is often forgotten. Like the New Left and the Anti-Colonialists who came after him, Benito Mussolini (1883–1945), the founder of modern fascism and leader of the Italian Fascists, had philosophized even in his early years about the "liberating effect" of violence and then made terrorism an integral component of his strategy. He developed a sophisticated understanding of how violence could be most effectively put to political use. Its purpose, according to Mussolini, was to intimidate political opponents and polarize the public, especially "in times of crisis". Anything else was "stupid, reactionary violence", which would do the movement more harm than good.[34]

All over Europe, the fascists set up paramilitary organizations that attracted a mixture of former soldiers and young hotheads. Their official task was to provide security for party officials in meetings and at demonstrations. But in reality they served to intimidate political opponents and carry out targeted acts of violence, some of them terrorist. In the early 1920s, Mussolini's Blackshirts torched swathes of offices, shops and restaurants belonging to their communist opponents and committed dozens of attacks on ethnic minorities, later passing them off as reprisals for the deaths of Italian soldiers.[35] The result was a vicious circle of violence, from which no one profited more than the Fascists themselves. Just like Adolf Hitler's Brownshirts, Mussolini and his Blackshirts presented themselves as defenders of the nation and guarantors of justice and order. That they had produced the chaos from which they wanted to rescue their countrymen was quickly forgotten: within two years, the Blackshirts' membership grew from a few hundred to more than 200,000.[36] Unlike in the case of the New Left, the logic of provocation had paid off.

But not all Far Right terrorists were fascists. The sociologist Steve Bruce categorizes many terrorist groups on the Far Right spectrum as "pro-state". According to Bruce, although these groups also had an authoritarian world view, their aim was not to create a new order, but rather to return to the old one.[37] The example he draws on most often is that of the loyalists in Northern Ireland. Their terror campaign was directed chiefly at Catholic civilians, whom they assumed were all supporters of the IRA. Their attacks were mostly random and, in contrast to the IRA, they rarely made an attempt to justify them. Throughout the conflict, English fascists consistently tried to win the loyalists as their partners. But for all their brutality, the loyalists had no interest in fascism. They saw themselves as unflinching defenders of the Protestant population and a counterweight to the IRA. Notions like "uprising" and "national revolution" ran counter to their whole ethos. Their aim was the restoration of state order – not its overthrow.[38]

Anders Breivik (*1979), the Norwegian terrorist who on 22 July 2011 first blew up a government building in Oslo and then shot dead nearly 70 teenagers on a holiday island, represents another type. Breivik was not a classical fascist either. Rather, he considered himself a defender of "the West" against a conspiracy of "multicultural elites" and Muslim immigrants who he claimed were bent on destroying European civilization. This theory, which he laid out in a 1,500-page manifesto, was not his own invention. It was identical to ideas put forward by so-called critics of Islam on blogs and websites he had been absorbing for years. From them he'd learnt that the Muslim population was growing so large that "real", culturally Christian Europeans would soon be in a minority; that the Muslims wanted to replace European with Islamic law; and that Europe was on the brink of a civil war whose outcome was far from certain. The logic of his attack followed from there. He wanted to ignite this civil war (which he thought was inevitable) while the "patriotic Europeans" were still in the ascendancy. And, very much in the spirit of the propaganda of the deed, he hoped that his act would be a model and inspiration to others. "Conquer your fear," he wrote to his sympathizers, "...[only] then can we free Europe from the grasp of the treacherous, corrupt and suicidal... multicultural elites."[39]

The absence of Far Right terrorism from Rapoport's theory makes obvious that the four waves are not a comprehensive description of every facet and type of modern terrorism. But they provide a good overview of the most important trends, differences and commonalities, and so lend a degree of the historical perspective needed to correctly evaluate the events of today. Anyone who engages with Rapoport's wave theory will know that terrorism is nothing new, that it has been continuously present in modern societies, that for a long time it was only rarely Islamic, and that extreme brutality and the dehumanization of opponents do not require a religious justification. The next chapter shows how, from the 1970s onwards, these principles and methods were discovered by religious groups and deployed for purposes of their own.

2

The Religious Wave

PAUL HILL (1954–2003) WAS A TALL, SLIM MAN WITH THREE children and a friendly face. When the American cable television channel HBO interviewed him for a documentary, he spoke calmly and deliberately with a deep voice that seemed to lend his words extra meaning. He described in detail how he had prepared for the attack that had led to his arrest, sentencing and, eventually, his execution. On 29 July 1994 in Pensacola, Florida, Hill shot an abortion doctor and his bodyguard. His comrades in the Army of God, a network of violent Christian-fundamentalist anti-abortion campaigners, had been calling for attacks of this sort for years. And Hill regretted nothing: "The prospect of dying in service of our Lord Jesus Christ was a big motivation for me,"he told HBO.[1] In a later statement he spoke about the "great reward" waiting for him in heaven.[2] Hill thought of himself as a soldier of God and – like many of his fellow anti-abortionists – would have had no cause for complaint about being described as a "religiously motivated terrorist".

Those who portray Hill as mentally unstable are making it too easy for themselves. The ideology of the Army of God hardly differs from the arguments put forward by non-violent Christian opponents of abortion. They say abortion is murder and that the killing of hundreds of thousands of defenceless babies is a state-sanctioned holocaust. Abortion clinics are likened to concentration camps and the doctors who work in them are said to have committed crimes against humanity. To the Army of God, Paul Hill was a resistance fighter who defended unborn life, and they raised money for his family at an annual benefit that was named the "White Rose Banquet" after a group of German opponents to Hitler. Moreover, his act had a strategic logic. Every attack on an abortion doctor scared off hundreds of others working at one of these clinics. The eight murders, 41 explosions and 173 arson attacks carried out by violent anti-abortionists in the 1980s and 1990s forced hundreds of clinics to close.[3] From the perspective of the Army of God, Hill and the other perpetrators saved the lives of thousands of unborn babies.

But for Hill and the Army of God it was not just about abortion. In an interview with my colleague Mark Juergensmeyer, the group's spiritual leader, Pastor Michael Bray, explained that American society was in a state of "spiritual decay" and that it was necessary to construct a "new moral order" based on "Biblical, not secular principles".[4] Bray's words – or very similar ones – could have come from the mouth of an Egyptian Islamist, because the rationale employed by religious fundamentalists is the same almost everywhere. They all diagnose a moral decline caused by the rejection of religious principles, and argue that the decline can be halted only by returning to those principles. This implies a range of options. For some, the solution is to cut themselves off from society and build their utopia in a small, isolated community. These are the ones who move into the woods, open camps and home-school their children. Others go in the opposite direction: they want to actively engage with society and convert it to their ideas – whether through individual missionary work or participation in the democratic process. A third group choose violence, religiously motivated terrorism. Pastor Bray and the Army of God believed they had no alternative. America was on the edge of an abyss, according to one of Bray's followers, and a civil war was inevitable: "Once blood has been shed, Americans will soon understand that it's not worth dying for abortionists and homosexuals."[5]

The Army of God belongs to the fourth, religious, wave of terrorism, which Rapoport dates as beginning in 1979. But it was more than a decade before the phenomenon was identified and described as such by researchers. One of the pioneers was the American historian Bruce Hoffman, who presented a paper titled "Holy Terror" at a conference held by the US Department of Defense in 1993. Hoffman established that in 1968, no known active terrorist group had been religiously motivated. Twenty-five years later, the proportion was at 20 per cent.[6] Many of the nationalist and Leftist groups who had been around in the 1970s were still active, but almost all new groups were religious in character.

Hoffman's concept of "Holy Terror" was not limited to Islamist groups like the Palestinian organization Hamas or the Lebanese Hezbollah, who were making headlines at the time. And nor is Rapoport's fourth wave exclusively about Islam. The examples he gives include the radical Sikhs who fought to establish a theocracy in the Indian Punjab in the 1980s; Jewish extremists who wanted to blow up Jerusalem's al-Aqsa Mosque in the same period; and members of the Buddhism-inspired doomsday cult Aum Shinrikyo ("Supreme Truth"), which sprayed nerve gas into the Tokyo Metro ten years later.[7] But neither Hoffman nor Rapoport could deny that this new tendency was dominated by groups on the Islamist spectrum. According to Rapoport, Islamist terrorists had carried out the "most important and most deadly" attacks and also had the most highly developed international connections. Islam was "the most important religion in this wave". But why was that the case? Where did Islamist terror come from and why did al-Qaeda become its most prominent representative?

ROOTS

The history of Islamism is not the history of Islam. Islam is more than 1,400 years old, but the phenomenon today called Islamism has only existed for a century. In the opinion of many historians, it was born when Islam encountered modernity – Western-style modernity in particular. For many Muslims, especially in the Arab world, the colonial era was a hard and humiliating experience that threw up many questions about their own identity. Despite their own proud history – including caliphs and empires that had held sway over half the world – things had gone downhill for Muslims since the seventeenth century. Large parts of the predominantly Muslim world were ruled by the West, which asserted its imperial interests and often scrapped social and cultural norms, which had been in place for hundreds of years. In the opinion of many future Islamists, that was possible only because Muslims had neglected their Islamic identity and instead become second-class copies of their Western colonial masters.[8]

What Bernard Lewis simplified as the "crisis of Islam" was naturally not perceived as such by all Muslims.[9] The colonial experience varied hugely from place to place and elicited a wide range of sometimes mutually contradictory responses – from resistance through to total assimilation. The initial reaction was not, as we might expect, resistance to colonialism, but rather an attempt by Muslims to rediscover the essence of their own identity. So, particularly in the second half of the nineteenth century, fundamentalist movements emerged in various parts of the predominantly Muslim world, preaching a supposedly pure and uncorrupted Islam, which was based above all on scripture. In British India, it was the Deobandis, whose religious schools were supposed to protect Muslims from Western influences and lead them back to a strict, purist Islam. In Egypt, some young scholars at Cairo's famous al-Azhar University formed a group propagating a very similar idea: a return to Islam as it was said to have existed during the lifetime of the Prophet Mohammed and his direct successors, the so-called "pious forefathers" (*salaf*). Both movements, the Deobandis and the Salafists, emerged from contact with the West and its colonialism, but neither was explicitly political, to say nothing of revolutionary, at the outset.[10]

That changed in the first half of the twentieth century with the launch of what must be the most significant Muslim organization in the world, the Muslim Brotherhood, in 1928. Its founder was Hassan al-Banna (1906–49), an Egyptian scholar from near the Suez Canal, where British domination was at its most obvious. Al-Banna came from a devout family and from a young age considered the influence of Western ideas to be destructive. In his autobiography he wrote:

> After the First World War and during my stay in Cairo, a tide of atheism and lewdness overtook Egypt. In the name of individual and intellectual freedom, it devastated religion and morality. Nothing could stop this storm.[11]

In response, al-Banna founded Islamic schools, charitable associations, hospitals and professional guilds – every aspect of life in society was to be guided and permeated by Islam. His central idea and message – "Islam is the answer" – fell on fertile ground. A decade after it was founded, the organization had half a million members in Egypt. After another decade, there were supporters and subsidiaries in every country of the Arab world.[12] The ultimate aim was not simply to end colonialism, but to abolish the secular judicial system and introduce Sharia, Islamic religious law. And this meant that the Muslim Brotherhood's activities – no matter how much they were initially focused on purely spiritual matters – eventually resulted in a political conflict.

SAYYID QUTB

The great confrontation came in the 1950s, when Colonel Gamal Abdel Nasser (1918–70) and the so-called Free Officers staged a coup in Egypt. Nasser's anti-colonialism initially appealed to many Muslim Brothers, but it quickly became clear that Nasser did not need the Islamists and was hostile to their religious ideas. One of the many Islamist intellectuals who ended up in prison during this period was Sayyid Qutb (1906–66). A teacher like al-Banna, he reinterpreted the Muslim Brotherhood's relatively pragmatic Islamism into an ideology of violent revolution. From Qutb's point of view, modern Muslim states were analogous to the heathen, "ignorant" (*jahili*) societies of the pre-Islamic era. "People's ideas, their beliefs, habits, traditions, culture, art, literature, rules and laws – all of it is *jahili*," he wrote.[13] Only those who absolutely accepted God's "sovereignty" without any reservations could call themselves Muslims. The small vanguard of true Muslims found itself in conflict with society as a whole – a conflict that had to be won by any means necessary. Jihad, in Qutb's opinion, referred above all to armed struggle, which was crucial for implementing God's authority.[14]

Qutb was hanged in 1966, but the books he wrote in prison are still regarded as classics of what is now called jihadism. Many of Qutb's followers, persecuted by Nasser, found sanctuary in Saudi Arabia, where Qutb's ideas and the locally predominant religious doctrine cross-pollinated each other in the following years. Saudi Wahhabism, named after its founder Mohammed ibn 'Abd al-Wahhab (1703–92), is a particularly harsh form of Salafism. For Wahhabists, it is not just about a return to the Islam of the "pious forefathers", but also about enmity towards every form of unbelief, polytheism and religious innovation. That entails an uncompromising separation of the faithful and the infidels (*kufr*), and the destruction of any reference

FIG. 2.1 The Egyptian teacher and school inspector Sayyid Qutb, who turned Islamism into a revolutionary ideology

to other religions.[15] Many aspects of Wahhabism meshed easily with Qutb's concepts of God's "sovereignty" and the alleged "ignorance" of Muslim societies. Moreover, Wahhabism gave Qutb's followers – including his brother Mohammed (1919–2014), who taught at the Islamic University of Medina[16] – a political and religious programme, a vision of the perfect society they would implement after the revolution. In this light, jihadism – to be more specific, jihadist Salafism – is a combination of Qutb's violent theory of revolution and Wahhabist religious doctrine.

CURRENTS

This short history of ideas demonstrates how many different tendencies there are on the Islamist spectrum. Jihadist Salafism, the subject of this book, is only one of many variations. There are also Salafists who swear allegiance to their worldly rulers and restrict themselves to peaceful missionary work (*dawa*); and now there are even some who have founded political parties and are taking part in the democratic process. All of them in the medium or long term want to create a Wahhabist theocracy, but the means they employ could not be more widely divergent. Then there is also the Muslim Brotherhood, which is religiously conservative too but rejects the zeal and puritanism of the Wahhabists. There are pragmatists who want to achieve this common aim through community work ("Islamization from below") or by contesting elections; and there are those who employ violence and terror (such as the Palestinian group Hamas). There can be cooperation among all these different tendencies, but enmity and violent conflict are just as common.

The various forms of Islamism also spread quickly outside Egypt and Saudi Arabia. In Syria, for example, the Muslim Brotherhood was initially very pragmatic. Its founder there, a preacher called Mustafa al-Siba'i (1915–64), had studied in Cairo in the 1930s and got to know al-Banna. Under al-Siba'i's leadership, the organization took part in elections, entered coalitions with secular parties and, in the late 1950s, provided a defence minister, a parliamentary speaker and even two prime ministers, albeit briefly. A second, more aggressive faction also emerged, rejecting any participation in the democratic process and occasionally employing political violence.[17] A third group was inspired directly by Sayyid Qutb. Just like Qutb, their leader considered his society infidel and preached violent revolution. Just like Qutb, he died in prison and, just as happened with Qutb, a terrorist group was formed after his death to make that revolution a reality.[18] But the campaign waged by the "Fighting Vanguard" – like that of all other militant Islamist groups – was initially limited to their own country. The internationalization and global interconnection of the jihadist movement – and thus the actual start of the fourth wave – only began in 1979.

GLOBALIZATION

The Islamic Revolution that Qutb and his followers were hoping for first took place in February 1979 in a country the jihadists actually had little time for: Iran. The revolution's leader, Ruhollah Khomeini (1902–89), and his followers were Shi'as, a denomination rejected by the (Sunni) Salafists. To the Salafists, the Shi'as were heretics and apostates – even worse than Christians and Jews. But Khomeini had succeeded where the jihadists in Egypt and Syria had failed so far: he had brought down a secular regime that very recently was still being celebrated by the West as a paragon of stability and progress. Khomeini's victory, according to the Islam scholar Guido Steinberg, "inspired not only Shi'ites, but also Sunni Islamists all over the world".[19] For Salafists, the question was no longer whether an Islamic revolution was possible, but only how and when. Indeed, a revolution was attempted that same year in Saudi Arabia. A group of jihadists who had met at the University of Medina stormed the Grand Mosque in Mecca and occupied it for nearly a fortnight. It was only with great difficulty (and the help of French special forces) that the Saudi government was able to put down the revolt. The wave of revolution, so it seemed, had become a danger even to Saudi Arabia, the most religiously conservative of all Muslim countries.

The jihadists, however, only truly became a global movement during the Afghan War of the 1980s. Less than two weeks after the uprising in Mecca, the Soviet Union marched into Afghanistan and installed a pro-Soviet government. The Islamists were incandescent. To them, the invasion and occupation of a Muslim country by atheists was a declaration of war, and violent jihad became not just legitimate but necessary. This time they were supported by a powerful coalition of the United States, Saudi Arabia and Pakistan. It was the Cold War, and the Americans wanted to give the Soviets a bloody nose. For the

Saudis, it was an opportunity to portray themselves as champions of the Islamic cause, and for Pakistan, it fitted into the desire to establish a regional sphere of influence. Despite differing interests, the coalition soon came to an understanding: the Americans and Saudis would pay for the war while the Pakistanis would distribute the money and weapons. Within a few months, the Pakistani border city of Peshawar had become the nerve centre of the Afghan resistance, teeming with fighters, weapons and secret agents.[20]

ABDULLAH AZZAM

Internationalizing the conflict in Afghanistan was the life's work of the Palestinian Islam scholar Abdullah Azzam (1941–89), the founder and "godfather" of global jihad. Azzam joined the Muslim Brotherhood as a young man and fought in the Six Day War against Israel in 1967. But his attention was initially on scholarship – he studied Islamic law in Damascus and earned his doctorate at the al-Azhar University in Cairo. He taught as a professor in Jordan – where he was fired for his Islamist views – then in Saudi Arabia and, from 1980, in Pakistan.[21] Azzam's presence in Pakistan was no coincidence. He saw the Afghan jihad as a personal vocation and argued that the conflict was even more urgent than the one in Palestine.[22] His charisma, matched with his efficiency, organizational know-how and theological credibility, made him a leader among the foreign fighters in Peshawar.

In 1984, Azzam set up the Services Office, which organized the transfer of foreign jihadists to Afghanistan. On innumerable trips to Arab countries – and several to the United States – he worked to convince young Arabs to take up jihad in Afghanistan. He recounted the suffering of the Afghans, the "crying mothers and screaming virgins" left at the mercy of the communists.[23] His most important argument was religious: that it was every Muslim's duty to defend Islamic

FIG. 2.2 Abdullah Azzam, the architect
of the "Afghan jihad" in the 1980s

territory. Anyone who didn't perform this duty – this "most important
of all personal duties" – and let others help in his stead was committing a grave sin and would pay for it in the afterlife.[24] Azzam spoke
often about the afterlife – about the almost certain death awaiting
the fighters in Afghanistan – but also about the "heavenly reward" for
those who sacrificed their lives in the service of God. He was thus the
founder of the "cult of martyrdom" that has become characteristic of
the jihadist movement.[25]

Azzam's efforts paid off. The Islam scholar Thomas Hegghammer
estimates that up to 20,000 jihadists went to Afghanistan between
1980 and 1992, most of them after Azzam set up the Services Office
in 1984.[26] Their motivations varied widely. Many were convinced by
Azzam's rhetoric. They had seen on television what was happening
in Afghanistan and wanted to defend their co-religionists and thus
also Islam as a whole. Doing their religious duty and running the risk
of becoming martyrs was not a burden, it was part of the attraction.
Others had been involved in the jihadist scene for years and wanted
to escape persecution in their own countries by going to Afghanistan.

(Many Arab states let known jihadists travel and then voided their passports.) For recruits from poor countries like Egypt and Algeria, payment was also a motivating factor. And of course there were adventurers and – as in every war – a handful of criminals and psychopaths.[27]

One of the most important recruits was Osama bin Laden (1957–2011), the rich son of a Saudi construction tycoon with excellent connections to the royal family. According to the American journalist Lawrence Wright, bin Laden flew regularly to Pakistan after the conflict broke out, but did not meet Azzam until he was on a pilgrimage to Mecca in 1984.[28] The two were a perfect match. Azzam became bin Laden's mentor and in exchange received access to bin Laden's money and contacts, which helped him finance the Services Office.

Two years after their first meeting, bin Laden brought his family to Peshawar and opened a training camp near the Pakistani border. Military successes were limited, but in spring 1987 there was a three-week battle with Soviet special forces from which bin Laden's troops emerged victorious. The defence of the "Lion's Den" – as the training camp was called – became legendary among the foreign fighters and established bin Laden's reputation and popular appeal. Even years later, he would still appear in video messages with a Kalashnikov, which, according to Wright's research, he had taken from a dead Russian officer.[29]

THE AFGHANISTAN MYTH

Overall, however, the foreign fighters contributed little to the Afghan opposition's victory over the Soviets. That was partly because most fighters arrived in Afghanistan after the end of the conflict. By the time of the Soviet retreat in spring 1989, a maximum of 4,000 foreigners had made it to Peshawar and only a minority of those actually fought in Afghanistan.[30] Linguistic problems hampered their deployment to Afghan units, since very few Arabs spoke Pashto or Dari, and few Afghans spoke Arabic. Moreover, many of the Afghan commanders thought the Arabs were cowardly and spoiled, and treated them like tourists.[31] In the opinion of most experts, the foreign fighters did not make a decisive difference in any theatre of the war and even bin Laden's supposed triumph in the "Lion's Den" was in truth a relatively unimportant skirmish, which only drew so much attention because Azzam's people had so few other successes to tell people about.

This interpretation of events naturally carried no weight with Azzam and bin Laden. They were firmly convinced that they and their comrades had defeated the Soviet Union and so forced a superpower to its knees: the defence of the "Lion's Den" had led to victory in Afghanistan and victory in Afghanistan had led to the collapse of the Soviet Union. That was the message Azzam disseminated in thousands of speeches, on cassettes and in his magazine *al-Jihad*. It was enthusiastically received and, after the conflict had ended, thousands more young men came to Afghanistan to join the seemingly powerful and successful jihadist movement. That the Soviets had already been defeated was unimportant. The foreign fighters in Afghanistan had created their own myth.

But what were they to do next? Azzam imagined a sort of mobile strike force that would fight wherever Islamic territory was occupied. For him, it was about the external enemy. He wanted to fight "infidel" soldiers, not civilians – and certainly not Muslim civilians. Another view was represented by Ayman al-Zawahiri (*1951), an Egyptian doctor who had come to Pakistan in 1986 and who, in the 1990s, became acting head of al-Qaeda in place of bin Laden. His previous group, al-Jihad, had assassinated the Egyptian president Anwar Sadat (1918–81) during a military parade at the start of the decade. Al-Zawahiri's objective was an Islamic revolution inspired by Qutb: a violent uprising against secular rulers in the Arab world and struggle against their unbelieving, "ignorant" societies – making use of terror against civilians if need be.

An agreement was never reached. As Azzam and two of his sons were walking to Friday prayers in Peshawar on 24 November 1989, a bomb went off, killing all three of them instantly. It is still not known who was behind the attack. The chief suspects include al-Zawahiri and his Egyptian comrades, but also Arab and Western intelligence agencies, to whom Azzam was no longer useful – and perhaps even dangerous – now that he had completed his task in Afghanistan.[32] No one can say for certain where Azzam would have led his fighters. But his legacy is beyond doubt. Hegghammer, the world's leading expert on Azzam, quotes a jihadist website according to which there is "today not a single jihad and not a single mujahid who has not been inspired by Abdullah Azzam's life, teaching and work".[33] In a survey that was conducted nearly 20 years after his death, Azzam was still one of jihadism's most read and most quoted ideologues.[34] He brought thousands of fighters from all over the world to Afghanistan, where they trained, fought and prayed together. He created the myth of victory in Afghanistan that gave them the belief that no opponent was too strong, no challenge too great. And last but not least, he left his heir apparent, bin Laden, the most famous Arab mujahid,[35] with a document listing the names of hundreds of fighters. It was titled "the basis" – in Arabic, "al-Qaeda".[36]

RISE

The story of jihadism in the 1990s and 2000s is usually told as the story of bin Laden. That is understandable because the attacks he organized on 9/11 were such a central event in the movement's history. But in reality it was not certain for a long time that bin Laden and his strategy would manage to assert themselves. The latest research shows that although bin Laden was an important figure in the 1990s, he was nowhere near as pre-eminent as Azzam in the 1980s.[37] And even in the 2000s, when bin Laden briefly dominated the jihadist movement, he and his group – al-Qaeda – were too weak to hold the movement together ideologically or strategically. When the Arab Spring presented the jihadists with their greatest opportunity yet, bin Laden's successor al-Zawahiri was taken by surprise and soon found himself out of his depth. The Afghanistan generation were unable to live up to their mythical reputation.

Many of the conflicts and terrorist attacks involving Afghanistan veterans were chalked up to bin Laden and al-Qaeda after 9/11. But the jihadist movement was still quite amorphous, especially in the early 90s. Bin Laden, who paid for many of the training camps, was certainly well known and influential, but he initially had as little to do with the conflicts in Algeria and Egypt as he did with the civil war in Somalia. In Algeria, the local branch of the Muslim Brotherhood – the Islamic Salvation Front – won the first round of parliamentary elections in December 1991, after which the government cancelled the second vote and so prevented the Islamists' presumable victory. This situation led to the creation of the Armed Islamic Group (GIA), which became radicalized in opposition to the state and ultimately waged war against big parts of Algerian society. Its leaders included a large number of Afghanistan veterans, but that did not mean that bin Laden was directing either them or the GIA as a whole. The same applied to Egypt, where the jihadists made a second attempt at bringing down the regime. Veterans of Afghanistan – above all, the leader of the Egyptian Islamic Group – played an important role there, too, but bin Laden had no direct influence over them.[38] Another example is the "Black Hawk Down" incident, when two American helicopters were shot down over the Somali capital, Mogadishu, in October 1993, resulting in the deaths of 18 US soldiers. The American government later laid the blame on al-Qaeda,[39] but in truth those responsible were – again – Afghanistan veterans with no direct ties to bin Laden.[40]

The conflict in which Azzam's idea of a mobile strike force came closest to being realized was the war in Bosnia. Just as in Afghanistan, the fighting was between Muslims and an external enemy: the Orthodox Christian Serbs. Between 1992 and 1996, the war mobilized up to 2,000 foreign fighters, many of whom came to the Balkans straight from training camps in Afghanistan.[41] Although bin Laden helped finance the operation – as he did in many places – the fighters did not report to him, but to a red-bearded Saudi nick-named "Barbarossa". For a short while, the fighters were even part of the Bosnian army and therefore – at least theoretically – under its command.[42]

It was Bosnia that elicited the first significant mobilization of European Muslims, who were shocked by the fate of their co-religionists and the inaction of their European home countries. Among at least 200 Britons was Omar Saeed Sheikh (*1973), a 20-year-old statistics student at the London School of Economics.[43] At university, Sheikh saw a documentary about the suffering of Bosnian Muslims and spontaneously volunteered to take part in an aid convoy. Once he arrived in Bosnia, Sheikh became radicalized and ended up in a training camp near the city of Zenica. Shortly after the 9/11 attacks, Sheikh abducted the American journalist Daniel Pearl (1963–2002) in Pakistan and was involved in his beheading. Asked how he dealt with the brutality, Sheikh told a journalist, "Whenever I have doubts, I remember my brothers in Bosnia."[44]

During the Bosnian War, bin Laden and his closest associates were in Sudan, where the regime offered them refuge in 1992. What precisely bin Laden did there is still disputed. To Western reporters he liked to present himself as an "engineer and agriculturist", but bin Laden had not suddenly become a development worker.[45] Actually, he was building up alliances and working on a new strategy. He was torn between his hostility to the Saudi royal family – whom he considered apostates since they'd formed a coalition with the United States in the Gulf War of 1990 – and another idea: a war against the United States, which he believed supported corrupt Arab dictators in order to divide and exploit the Islamic world.

Bin Laden eventually published two declarations of war. The first, in 1996, was aimed at the Saudi royal family, but two years later – after he'd returned from Taliban-ruled Afghanistan – he set his sights on the West.[46] And his words were soon followed by deeds. Five months after the second declaration had been published, in August 1998, bin Laden's followers carried out attacks on the American embassies in Kenya and Tanzania, killing more than 200 people. All of a sudden, bin Laden was no longer just a financial backer, he was the most wanted terrorist in the world and undisputed leader of the global jihadist movement. Giving up on hopeless civil wars and Qutb-inspired coup attempts, he committed himself to terrorism against the West, especially the United States, and to spectacular, multiple attacks on symbolic targets. The new strategy became al-Qaeda's calling card.

DEFEAT

The 9/11 attacks marked the high point of bin Laden's "career" as a jihadist. To many Muslims, he was not a criminal but a sort of Islamic Robin Hood, who had put one over on the "arrogant Americans".[47] The papers were full of reports about sleeper cells and suicide bombers supposedly just waiting for the order to strike. And the United States reacted with a "global war on terror", which presented bin Laden as America's new arch-enemy and so made him more important than he really was. Actually, bin Laden's influence was still limited. He had a network, but he didn't have an army, and the jihadist movement would follow him only as long as his global reputation was still advantageous for them.

Despite the bombings in Madrid in 2004 and London in 2005, and a long list of ambitious plots that the security services prevented at the last moment,[48] bin Laden never produced another attack like those on 9/11. Rather, he was struggling to bring the movement – which the whole world believed was his to command – under his control. The most extreme example was a group led by the Jordanian Abu Musab al-Zarqawi (1966–2006), out of which the Islamic State later emerged (see Chapter 3). When the Americans marched into Iraq in 2003, Zarqawi was the only one already in the country who could organize jihadist resistance to the foreign occupiers. He swore an oath of loyalty to bin Laden in October 2004, but consistently refused to follow his instructions. Against the wishes of the al-Qaeda leadership, Zarqawi provoked a civil war with Iraqi Shi'as, which became so brutal that it shocked even many jihadists and moved al-Zawahiri to try and call Zarqawi to order. But aside from writing letters there was nothing al-Qaeda's leaders could do.[49]

On top of that, some of the more obedient al-Qaeda offshoots – such as al-Qaeda in the Islamic Maghreb (AQIM) or al-Qaeda in the Arabian Peninsula (AQAP) – mounted local campaigns that ran counter to the global strategy. Even when the attacks struck international institutions, embassies or Western companies, as bin Laden wanted, the victims were often local Muslims. And the less al-Qaeda managed to achieve on the international level, the more attention was paid to the involvement of its regional subsidiaries in civil wars, intra-Muslim conflicts and the killing of Muslims in general. Many of these attacks on co-religionists were unpopular even among those supporters who endorsed struggle against "infidel regimes", and bin Laden and al-Zawahiri were constantly having to justify attacks they'd known nothing about beforehand and that contradicted their own strategy. "Excuse me, Mr Zawahiri," one al-Qaeda sympathizer asked in an extremist internet forum, "who is killing civilians in Baghdad, Morocco and Algeria? Does the killing of women and children now count as jihad?"[50]

New opportunities were, however, provided by the internet. Despite the jihadists' apparently backwards-looking ideology, they have always been quick to embrace new technologies. Since the Iraq War, the internet has become an important forum for debate and the professionally produced videos from Afghanistan, Iraq and elsewhere have convinced many supporters that they are part of a powerful and successful movement. Since around 2008, al-Qaeda has also used the internet to call for terrorist attacks. These messages are directed at supporters in the West who are meant to strike without outside help, as "lone wolves". Even small attacks can be shocking and therefore effective, according to Anwar al-Awlaki (1971–2011), a Yemeni preacher who was born in America and spoke fluent English. In 2010, under al-Awlaki's direction, AQAP began producing the English-language online publication *Inspire*, which was presented like a glossy magazine and printed bomb-making instructions alongside reader letters and colourful accounts of jihad.

Compared with bin Laden's ambitious – but almost always unsuccessful – plots, al-Awlaki's strategy was very effective. Almost every attack carried out in the West in this period can be ascribed to him – including the Boston Marathon bombing in April 2013, which was based on instructions in *Inspire* (see Chapter 6).[51] But the tempo of these attacks was slow and this kind of terrorism was a far cry from the almost apocalyptic events of 9/11.

While al-Awlaki spoke on YouTube about jihad in the West, bin Laden and his aides were hard pressed by America's drone campaign, which was aimed particularly at al-Qaeda's leadership in the Pakistani tribal areas. One bin Laden loyalist described the situation like this:

"They're constantly circling over us, all the time." The jihadists could leave their homes only during bad weather, "but as soon as the sky clears, they're back".[52] As a result, communication between members of al-Qaeda's high command – as well as between them and the regional subsidiaries – became more difficult. And more importantly, in two years of drone strikes, 20 of bin Laden's closest associates were killed. Then, in May 2011, bin Laden himself was killed in an American commando raid on his hiding place in Abbottabad, far from the tribal areas.[53] Al-Zawahiri survived this period and became bin Laden's successor, but the al-Qaeda model – which had been in crisis for years – died with bin Laden.

THE ARAB SPRING

The weakness and helplessness of the jihadist leadership became particularly apparent during the peaceful revolutions that took place in several Arab countries in 2011. Al-Qaeda and the jihadists were in no way involved in these revolutions. A great majority of the demonstrators on the streets of Tunis and Cairo were not Islamists and most of the violence that occurred during the protests came from the state. Nevertheless, al-Qaeda's leaders tried to claim the credit. As early as that spring, al-Zawahiri released a video in which he argued that the 9/11 attacks had laid the foundations for the success of the Arab Spring. He claimed the attacks had given the Arabs confidence and shown them that an uprising could be successful. Moreover, it was only because of the "blessed attacks on New York, Washington and Pennsylvania" that America had changed its Middle East policy and allowed the overthrow of secular dictators like the Egyptian president Hosni Mubarak (1981–2011).[54]

But al-Zawahiri's arguments fell on deaf ears. In Tunisia and Egypt, governments were formed by more pragmatic Islamists who wanted nothing to do with al-Qaeda and the jihadists. And in Libya, the opposition had been helped to victory by (entirely un-jihadist) NATO air strikes. As a result, some of al-Qaeda's leaders attempted to get on good terms with the Muslim Brotherhood, an organization that jihadists had been roundly criticizing for decades. For example, a Libyan ideologue who, only a year earlier, had still wanted to excommunicate all non-jihadists, now invoked "Muslim unity" and appealed to the "kindness and tolerance" of his co-religionists.[55]

A more realistic response came from al-Awlaki, who was to be killed a few months later in an American drone strike. He wrote, "Regardless of whether the new governments are secular or Islamic, our brothers… have some breathing space for the first time in decades." He argued that the jihadist movement must take advantage of this new freedom, but be patient. In the long term, the present chaos would be "very useful" for the so-called mujahideen – the movement's fighters.[56]

Unlike al-Zawahiri and many of the others, al-Awlaki understood that the al-Qaeda model and the Afghanistan generation it created had been made obsolete by the Arab Spring. The 9/11 attacks were such a dramatic success that they had concealed the movement's structural and strategic failings. Though the jihadists had followed bin Laden, he had always been too weak to turn such an amorphous movement into a cohesive fighting force.

But the failure of al-Qaeda did not mean the failure of jihadism. The fourth wave was characterized by al-Qaeda – and not, say, the Army of God – because of the strength of the underlying movement and its ideas. And it was the movement, not al-Qaeda, that managed to reinvent itself in the Arab Spring, enthusing a new generation and inspiring the next wave of terrorism. How that happened is the subject of the second part of this book.

PART TWO

The Next Wave

3

The Islamic State

ABDULLAH ANAS (*1958) IS DEFINITELY AN "OLD" JIHADIST.
The big, powerfully built Algerian is now in his late fifties, has five
sons and, while living in London, runs an Islamist satellite television
channel that broadcasts the message of Algeria's Muslim Brotherhood
back to his home country. In the early 1980s, he was one of the first to
follow Abdullah Azzam's call. He went to Afghanistan to die a martyr's
death but instead ended up making a career among the Arab Afghans,
getting to know Osama bin Laden and becoming a protégé of Azzam
himself. The two men became so close that Anas married his mentor's
daughter. That has made him part of the jihadist aristocracy.

I meet Anas in London, in Trafalgar Square. We've known each
other since 2008 and had a cup of tea together a dozen times. When
some question is preying on my mind, I write to him on Facebook
and usually get a reply within a few minutes. This meeting is about
the caliphate as an institution. What does it mean to him? And how
important is it to jihadists? Anas doesn't hesitate:

> Every Muslim understands the significance of the caliphate. It is a
> vision – and also a political project. The aim is to have all Muslims
> pulling in the same direction and speaking with the same voice. To

get rid of borders and have one market, one currency, one voice, one constitution and one government. So that we're on the same level as America, Europe, Russia and China.[1]

Later in our conversation, it becomes clear that the precise structure of the state, its functions and the person of the caliph are not very important to him. When Anas speaks about the caliphate, he means Muslim power and a striving for unity. The caliphate proclaimed by the Islamic State in June 2014 is something he rejects entirely:

[Abu Bakr] al-Baghdadi's caliphate is just a slogan. What it should be about is education, knowledge, freedom and justice – then the caliphate will emerge of its own accord. Anyone who calls himself the caliph without having laid the foundations for it is just making himself ridiculous. Al-Baghdadi uses phrases that have no practical meaning.[2]

But even Anas would have to admit that al-Baghdadi has achieved what his comrades-in-arms could only dream of: creating a successful and expanding Salafist state in the heart of the Middle East; a magnet for foreign fighters and a point of orientation for jihadists the world over. Even bin Laden never came close to that.

Jihadism and jihadist terror groups existed before the Islamic State, and the Middle Eastern conflicts and fissures it exploits are nothing new, either. But never before had these trends given rise to such an ambitious state-building project.[3] The Islamic State is a would-be global empire, one that has declared all other countries on earth its enemy and – at the same time – attracted followers from all over the world. Even the Iranian revolution had neither that kind of magnetism nor such a grand programme.

Of course, the Islamic State did not appear out of thin air. It was a product of the conflict in Iraq in the 2000s, the Arab Spring and – even more crucially – the jihadist movement that Azzam and bin Laden set in motion in 1980s Afghanistan. It is rooted in – and physically connected with – the fourth, religious wave of terrorism discussed in the previous chapter. Just as happened in the other waves, the Islamic State brought together a whole range of movements and developments that had been in progress for decades. But it also has a character of its own. The movement has reinvented itself. It has mobilized a younger generation, pursued similar but far further-reaching ends, founded new institutions and employed even more extreme methods than were seen before.

This part of the book explains what the new wave of terrorism consists of. The next chapters discuss the foreign fighters who have moved from Western Europe to join the Islamic State's caliphate; the supporters who have stayed at home; the movement's lack of success in the United States; and the growing competition between al-Qaeda and the Islamic State. This chapter examines the Islamic State itself – its origins, character and tactics – as well as the strengths, weaknesses and internal contradictions that will determine its future.

BEGINNINGS

The organization that today calls itself the Islamic State is the political, military and personal legacy of the jihadist Abu Musab al-Zarqawi. His group was the most important within the jihadist movement for several years after the invasion of Iraq in 2003, but foundered in the second half of the decade due to hostility from the Sunni population and the rest of the uprising. The reasons for Zarqawi's failure and the conclusions drawn from it set the course for crucial developments in the following years. On the one hand, the Syrian Abu Mohammad al-Julani (ca. *1975) built up an affiliate group in his home country that seemed more pragmatic and less doctrinaire than its Iraqi predecessor, while Abu Bakr al-Baghdadi (*1971), the current leader of the Islamic State, pursued an even more brutal and hard-line version of Zarqawi's model. Although both interpretations have profited from the chaos and political discord since the outbreak of the Arab Spring, it is al-Baghdadi's vision – and thus ultimately Zarqawi's – that has come to dominate.

ABU MUSAB AL-ZARQAWI

The story of the Islamic State begins with Zarqawi's arrival in Iraq in September 2002. The Jordanian had previously run a training camp in Afghanistan and wanted to make a name for himself in the imminent conflict between the United States and the Iraqi dictator Saddam Hussein (1937–2006). Compared with the privileged origins of the bin Ladens and al-Zawahiris, Zarqawi had come from an unusual background. One of nine children, he could barely read or write and had been in trouble with the police as a teenager. In his early twenties, he was imprisoned for drug dealing and converted to Salafism. He found a mentor in an important jihadist ideologue, the Palestinian Abu Muhammad al-Maqdisi (*1959), and they founded a terrorist group together in the 1990s – which landed him in prison for a second time. Upon his release as part of an amnesty in 1999, he promptly set off for Afghanistan. He had boundless ambition and his idea of jihad seemed more severe, more aggressive and even more uncompromising than bin Laden's. He directed his hatred primarily at the "near" enemies: the Jordanian royal family, Jews, Israel and the Shi'as, all of whom he considered heretics and apostates.[4] The conflict in Iraq served his purposes, but was not his ultimate objective. His idol was a Turk called Nur ad-Din, who in the twelfth century had ruled over "Greater Syria", and his goal was a caliphate stretching from Lebanon across Syria and Jordan, including the territory that was now Israel.[5] "Our eyes are on Jerusalem" was the crucial slogan in many of his speeches.[6]

Zarqawi's hope that the United States would wage war against Saddam and occupy Iraq was realized in spring 2003. The country that had been held together by Saddam's extreme brutality rapidly disintegrated into its sectarian components. The Sunni side developed armed militias, many of which were motivated by nationalism and sectarianism, and some of which were motivated by religion. Zarqawi's group was the most extreme example, carrying out thousands of attacks in the following years, including 200 suicide bombings and dozens of kidnappings, which often ended in the hostages' decapitation. Zarqawi's victims were not exclusively Americans and their allies, but also Sunni collaborators and – above all – Shi'i civilians, on whom he declared "total war" in September 2005.[7] His plan was to unleash a civil war so chaotic and so barbarous that the Americans would leave Iraq and the Sunni parts of the country would break away from the rest. The breakaway didn't happen, but the civil war certainly did: while in 2004 an average of 30 Iraqis were killed in the conflict every day, by 2005 it had risen to 43 and by 2006 it was nearly 80.[8]

Zarqawi made an alliance with al-Qaeda in October 2004, but his relationship with bin Laden and al-Zawahiri was never harmonious. Al-Qaeda's leadership feared that potential supporters would be scared off by Zarqawi's attacks on Shi'as. For al-Zawahiri, the fight against the American occupiers was a greater priority than attacking Shi'as, as well as being less controversial. The same applied to the beheadings, whose brutality distracted from the actual objective and gave the movement a bad name: "The Muslims will not accept it no matter how much you try to explain it to them," wrote bin Laden's representative in a now-famous letter of summer 2005.[9] But Zarqawi would not be diverted.

FIG. 3.1   The Jordanian jihadist Abu Musab al-Zarqawi,
who created a prototype of the Islamic State

What was more dangerous for Zarqawi than al-Qaeda's disapproval was the hostility of Sunni tribes, whom he had offended with his arrogance and religious zealotry. The strict Wahhabi rules that Zarqawi enforced in the areas under his control – no music, no films, no smoking – were as alien to them as were a large section of his troops, which mustered fighters from Syria, Libya, the Gulf and even Europe. Due to their unhappiness with him (among other reasons), 30 tribes and a range of Sunni militias, mobilizing 90,000 fighters, allied themselves with the Americans.[10] Zarqawi had no chance. In June 2006 he was killed by an American air strike and, of the estimated 10,000 followers he had had in 2005, at most a tenth were left five years later.[11] In the West, many thought his group had been wiped out.

ABU MOHAMMAD AL-JULANI

The second part of the story plays out in Syria, where huge crowds took to the streets in spring 2011 to protest against the dictator Bashar al-Assad (*1965). The demonstrations were initially peaceful, but that gradually changed after Zarqawi's successors sent an eight-man delegation over the border. Their leader was Mohammad al-Julani, a Damascene in his mid-thirties, who had made the journey in the opposite direction years earlier to join Zarqawi's jihad in Iraq. His task now was to found a new group in Syria.[12]

That he didn't have to start from scratch was, ironically enough, thanks to his enemy. Assad had opened his borders during the Iraq War to rid himself of his own jihadists and to drive up the cost of the American occupation. At the start of the Iraq conflict, Syrians made up the largest group of foreign fighters in the country, and the smuggling operations developed all over Syria were used by jihadists from around the world. An American government study found that 90 per cent of all suicide attackers in Iraq were foreigners, of whom 85–90 per cent had arrived via Syria. Almost all Syrian fighters joined Zarqawi's group and the many who survived returned to their homeland in the second half of the decade.[13] These survivors were now reactivated by al-Julani.

He had drawn his own conclusions from Iraq and wanted to avoid repeating Zarqawi's mistakes at any price. Rather than copy his former leader, he took up ideas proposed by Abu Musab al-Suri (*1958), a veteran Syrian jihadist who had taken part in an uprising against Assad's father in the early 1980s and then became one of the movement's most important strategists. Al-Suri argued in favour of pragmatic alliances with other insurrectionary groups, expected high standards of behaviour from his fighters and warned against alienating the population with too rapid – and too strict – an implementation of the Wahhabist social programme.[14] Al-Julani's new group, Jabhat al-Nusra ("the support front"), enjoyed great success with this apparently softer strategy. From the end of 2011 onwards, al-Nusra was responsible for the most spectacular attacks on the Assad regime and al-Julani's fighters were respected and popular among the Sunni population, especially in the north-west of Syria. They were so popular that even rival insurrectionary groups worked with them and defended them against attacks from abroad (see Chapter 7).[15]

ABU BAKR AL-BAGHDADI

Al-Nusra was a success story for the jihadist movement, but al-Julani's colleagues gradually became suspicious of it. The most mistrustful was al-Baghdadi, the self-proclaimed caliph and current leader of the Islamic State, who took command of Zarqawi's organization in May 2010. Al-Baghdadi was 38 at the time and unknown even to many in jihadist circles. There are still many myths swirling around his origins, but his personal history has since been reasonably firmly established. Al-Baghdadi was born in Samarra, a mid-sized town north of Baghdad, where he passed his school exams by the skin of his teeth. At the Islamic University of Baghdad he then studied theology and completed a doctorate.[16] After the Western invasion, he joined the uprising – albeit in a relatively unimportant role – and found himself in the American prison camp Bucca in Iraq at the start of 2004.[17] The ten months he spent there proved formative. Al-Baghdadi made contact with other revolutionaries and won a reputation as a reticent but effective fixer. The men he met in this period remain his closest comrades and most trusted confidants.[18] The camp, according to a former American officer who served in Bucca, "was a recruiting office and school for those who we're fighting as terrorists today".[19] When al-Baghdadi was released in December 2004, he founded a militia that was soon incorporated into Zarqawi's organization, which was calling itself the Islamic State in Iraq (ISI). In 2006, he became part of the ISI high command, and four years later he managed to secure the leadership.

FIG. 3.2 Self-proclaimed caliph and leader of the Islamic State Abu Bakr al-Baghdadi, pictured in Mosul's al-Nuri Mosque, July 2014

Al-Baghdadi had run the expansion into Syria as a secret project. But the stronger al-Nusra grew, the more confident and independent became al-Julani – and al-Baghdadi had considered his pragmatic strategy suspect from the outset.[20] On 8 April 2013, he took the bull by the horns. Without consulting al-Julani, he announced in an audio message that al-Nusra was an affiliate of ISI. And he left no doubt about to whom al-Nusra owed its success:

[In summer 2011 we sent] al-Julani and a group of our sons… from Iraq to Syria… We laid plans for them and drew up a way for them to proceed, and every month we gave them half our income and we supplied them with men who had known the battlefields of jihad. This is how the Islamic State [extended] its influence… into Syria. But we refrained from declaring it, for security reasons… But now the time has come to proclaim to the people of Syria and the whole world that the Nusra front is nothing other than an offshoot of ISI and a part of it.[21]

Among al-Nusra's fighters the confusion ran deep. Which group did they belong to? Whose instructions should they follow? Many units initially accepted al-Baghdadi's statement and declared their loyalty to the organization now called the Islamic State in Iraq and Greater Syria (ISIS). But when, two months later, the head of al-Qaeda, al-Zawahiri, came down on the side of al-Nusra and ruled that the merger of the two groups was invalid, some went back on their decision.[22] In short: the movement was split, and for the first time there were two rival jihadist groups that were both part of al-Qaeda operating in the same country.

In contrast to al-Nusra, ISIS controlled territories on both sides of the Syrian–Iraqi border and profited in both countries from the way that Sunnis had been marginalized, vilified and – in Syria – attacked by their own government with barrel bombs and chemical weapons. A jihadist group now had the movement's first opportunity to bring a large, transnational, historically significant area under its control. But although al-Baghdadi had been toying with the idea of a caliphate since the end of 2013 at the latest, the formal proclamation didn't come till June 2014, when ISIS had consolidated its Syrian territory and made large gains in two provinces in the north-west of Iraq.

The "Islamic empire" that al-Baghdadi proclaimed in a Friday sermon at the al-Nuri Mosque in the Iraqi city of Mosul surpassed every previous jihadist achievement. It stretched for more than 500 miles, sat at the heart of the Islamic world, was within striking distance of Mecca, Medina and Jerusalem, the holiest cities of Islam, and – on top of all that – it wiped away the hated Sykes–Picot border, which millions of Arabs considered a symbol of colonial division and oppression. Al-Baghdadi had overshadowed his internal rival, al-Julani, his previous group, al-Qaeda, the great Osama bin Laden and even his role model Zarqawi, all in a single stroke.

PRESENT

Few outside the jihadist movement accepted that al-Baghdadi had founded the true caliphate and was now the "leader of the faithful". In the summer of 2014, dozens of scholars denied al-Baghdadi's legitimacy and asserted that his authority was null and void. This had no effect on his success and even his critics had to admit that al-Baghdadi had created a new reality, as well as that his state – which now called itself simply "the Islamic State" – was not going to disappear any time soon.

A year later, in 2015, the Islamic State is still hard to get a handle on. It rejects the international state system, but behaves like a state. It has global ambitions, but its leadership consists almost exclusively of Iraqis. Its religious doctrine is so extreme that even other extremists don't want to have anything to do with it, but its methods are often (frighteningly) rational. Anyone trying to understand the Islamic State encounters inconsistencies and contradictions. This should be taken as a positive for the group's enemies because the Islamic State is not as unified and cohesive as it likes to suggest.

PHILOSOPHY

The difference between al-Qaeda and the Islamic State does not lie in the aspiration to build a Salafist caliphate. Al-Qaeda, too, always intended to take power in Muslim countries and for al-Qaeda a caliphate was also the ultimate goal. But al-Qaeda pursued a different strategy. Its theory was that secular dictatorships, like Hosni Mubarak's in Egypt, were only so powerful because the West supported them. That was why attacks on the "far" enemy – America and its Western allies – were believed to be of prime importance. What would happen after the West had pulled out wasn't something to which they gave much thought. For Zarqawi and al-Baghdadi it was the other way around: for them, the process of state-building had to come first, not at the end. Their priority was to found a state that would expand in all directions, constantly conquer new territories and become ever stronger until it encircled the whole world. In contrast to al-Qaeda, it therefore had to work out right at the outset how to wage and win a war inside the Islamic world. The result was a philosophy more intensely preoccupied than al-Qaeda's with subjects like sectarianism, the internal cleansing of the faith, extreme violence and even the prospect of apocalypse.

A decisive influence on the thinking of the Islamic State was exerted by a mediaeval theologian called Ibn Taymiyyah (1263–1328), who is also considered an important authority by many other Salafists and jihadists. Taymiyyah spent most of his life in Damascus and lived through the Mongols' invasion and brief reign of terror at the start of the fourteenth century. The Mongols were Muslims, not infidels, but they oppressed the native population nevertheless – a situation that Taymiyyah found unbelievable. His reaction to their regime landed him in prison and after that he formulated a series of legal opinions (*fatwas*) with which he tried to distinguish between "true" and "false" Muslims. According to Taymiyyah, "false" Muslims – like the Mongols – were even more dangerous than the infidel. No punishment was too severe for them. They should be excommunicated (*takfir*), and even killing them was legitimate.[23]

Zarqawi used Taymiyyah to justify his hatred for Shi'as. They were "false" Muslims, and it suited him that Taymiyyah had already described them and their distant Syrian relatives, the Alawites, as the "most dishonest of all sects" – "more dangerous even than the Christians and the Jews".[24] Whether Zarqawi really believed that is hard to say: in his native Jordan there were hardly any Shi'as and sectarian conflict was rare, and nor did the al-Qaeda leadership think that fighting the Shi'as was a priority. But whatever his true beliefs, Zarqawi clearly recognized how useful the sectarian tensions in Iraq could be and how simply he could exploit them for his cause. The same thing would be possible in the Syrian conflict, where Taymiyyah's writings were enjoying a renaissance among jihadists and Islamists.

The other thinker of comparable significance for the Islamic State is Abu Bakr Naji (*1961), an Egyptian jihadist who published a book titled *The Management of Savagery* in 2004.[25] It was completely ignored by large swathes of the jihadist movement, but Zarqawi and his organization were among Naji's first – and most eager – readers.[26] On similar lines to the Brazilian guerrilla strategist Marighella (see Chapter 1), Naji argued that revolutionaries must provoke an overreaction from the state in order to unleash chaos and then present themselves as a force for order. The in-between phase – that is, between the collapse of the old and the construction of the new – was the phase of savagery. Here Naji differed from Marighella by postulating that in this phase practically any means were justified for eliciting terror and panic in the enemy, breaking his will and compelling him to submit. Moreover, the more brutal the methods employed, the quicker would be the transition to a new order. In Naji's eyes, extreme violence was not only acceptable, it was also positive and desirable because it accelerated the shift from chaos to stability.[27]

William McCants, head of Middle Eastern politics at the Brookings Institution in Washington, translated the book into English in 2006 and so made it accessible to the Western reader. To him it seems clear that the Islamic State's grotesque violence – the beheadings and executions and the burning alive of a Jordanian pilot – was inspired chiefly by Naji's theory. When I met him in Washington in March 2015, he told me about reports that the Islamic State had distributed the book to all of its commanders.[28] According to McCants, al-Baghdadi was using Naji's strategy as a "textbook" but Naji's importance was still being underestimated by analysts and policy makers in the West:

> Here in the United States everyone asks: Why the brutality? Where does the cruelty come from? Everyone believes these people are crazy. But in reality they follow a plan – a strategy – that allows them to justify even the most absurd acts of violence as logical and rational.[29]

What Naji proposed was the opposite of what the al-Qaeda leadership had been preaching to its members for years. Unlike al-Suri and al-Julani's group in Syria, Naji and the Islamic State had no interest in winning the "hearts" of Muslims. Their aim was to subjugate them to the new order using every means at their disposal.

Another influence on the Islamic State, albeit one whose significance is disputed,[30] consists of apocalyptic prophecies. There are hundreds of them, but the most important for the Islamic State concerns a dramatic battle that, according to the *Hadith* – the recorded actions and sayings of the Prophet Mohammed – will take place in the village of Dabiq in the north-west of Syria. There, says the prophecy, the saviour's army will meet "the soldiers of Rome", drive out the unbelievers once and for all, and usher in a golden era of Islamic rule. Zarqawi was familiar with the prophecy and believed his group to be the nucleus of the Islamic army that would one day win the battle of Dabiq. "The fire we have ignited in Iraq," Zarqawi said in September 2004, "will burn larger and fiercer until it engulfs the crusaders at Dabiq."[31]

For bin Laden and the al-Qaeda high command, most of these prophecies were hocus-pocus,[32] but Zarqawi turned them into an organizational principle – and al-Baghdadi, too, has been influenced by them.[33] In July 2014, Islamic State troops launched an offensive in the province of Aleppo with the sole aim of bringing Dabiq under their control. From a strategic perspective, the attack made no sense, because the area around Dabiq is militarily inconsequential and only sparsely populated. The fighting led to heavy losses for al-Nusra and the Islamic Front, a coalition of Salafist groups that had been holding the village.[34] For the Islamic State, conquering Dabiq was a triumph far outweighing comparable victories in more strategically significant parts of the country. The group's online magazine, which first appeared that month, was named *Dabiq*. And soon afterwards, the village was chosen as the location for a beheading video. In it, a British-accented executioner declares with great pathos: "Today we are burying the first American crusader in Dabiq... eagerly waiting for the remainder of your armies to arrive."[35]

It is hard to say to what degree this notion and the overall philosophy of the Islamic State can be described as "Islamic", because Sunni Islam has neither a pope nor any other absolute authority who can rule on matters of belief. To assert that the Islamic State has nothing to do with Islam is well-intentioned but misleading. Its members consider themselves Muslims and draw on the same sources referred to by the majority of (non-extremist) Muslims. And its exegeses of religious texts have impressed some observers.[36] But for all that, it is wrong to lump together the Islam of the Islamic State with the Islam practised by hundreds of millions of (deeply observant) Muslims. Not only because there is no such thing as a single, supposedly "true" Islam, but also because the Islamic State's interpretations are considered extreme even by the standards of the jihadist spectrum. If even al-Qaeda brands the Islamic State an apocalyptic sect, it is obvious just how far outside the theological mainstream the group is operating.

That, however, does not mean that the Islamic State is not dangerous or unable to mobilize followers in the name of Islam. Its success in doing just that is plain to see. But using it to make blanket judgements about Islam is both false and ultimately counterproductive, because Muslims – and particularly those who take their religion seriously – will be needed to defeat the Islamic State.

ORGANIZATION

When the German author and former politician Jürgen Todenhöfer returned from a two-week trip to the Islamic State in December 2014, he spoke on every television channel available about its strength and unity. The Islamic State, said Todenhöfer, was a "1% movement with the effect of a nuclear tsunami" – "clever", "dangerous", "almost intoxicated with enthusiasm and confidence of victory".[37] What he reported was precisely the image that the Islamic State wanted to publicize in the West. Todenhöfer had let himself be used. In reality, the Islamic State is not as unified and cohesive as it likes to suggest, and there is no reason why the organization's various components – Iraqi leadership, local foot soldiers and foreign fighters – could not break apart as quickly as they came together.

There is disagreement even over the size of the group. Current estimates range from 20,000 to 200,000 fighters.[38] Which number is correct depends on how you think about it. The core organization – that is, full members who have personally sworn an oath of loyalty to it and belong to no other organization – consists of perhaps 30,000 to 40,000 people. Added to that are so-called helpers, who support the Islamic State on the ground and wear its insignia, but haven't sworn an oath.[39] The same applies to tribal militias and smaller groups with which the Islamic State cooperates. In a best-case scenario (from the group's perspective), the Islamic State might be able to mobilize 200,000 troops, but that does not mean that all of them would be soldiers of the Islamic State, nor that they would all be equally loyal and ideologically aligned.

Structurally, the Islamic State is a hybrid of a state and an insurrectionary group. On the one hand, there are various councils reporting to al-Baghdadi, such as the Sharia Council, which is made up of scholars and sets religious guidelines, or the 30-man Shura Council, which contains al-Baghdadi's most important advisers. On the other hand, there is a "cabinet" with ministers for "finance", "social issues", "explosives" and "suicide bombers".[40] The organization is still strikingly dominated by Iraqis. In 2014, when the caliphate was proclaimed, 19 of the 20 most important positions were in Iraqi hands, and two years later the situation has hardly changed. Moreover, half the Iraqi leadership cadre consists of former army officers who served under Saddam.[41] Among their number are al-Baghdadi's closest confidants, those he met in 2004 in the American prison camp Bucca.[42] In that respect, the Islamic State's brutal methods are also the legacy of decades of secular dictatorship.

In contrast to their leaders, the Syrian and Iraqi foot soldiers are a motley crew. Of course there are some "true believers" who back the Islamic State because they consider its political and religious doctrines to be correct. But ideological resolve is not the only reason for joining. For the book *ISIS: Inside the Army of Terror*, Michael Weiss and Hassan Hassan spoke to dozens of ordinary recruits and discovered a whole range of other motivations. A large proportion of the foot soldiers, they write, joined the organization for "pragmatic" reasons. Many had previously been with other Islamist groups, but thought the Islamic State seemed stronger and more disciplined, and in some places it was the only option. Another tranche is made up of fighters with a sectarian agenda. They are driven above all by hatred for the Shi'i government in Baghdad and the minority-dominated regime in Damascus. A third and final section consists of "opportunists", who have simply adapted to the presence of the Islamic State, think it will last and see in it a chance for personal advancement. According to

Weiss and Hassan, this last category includes both straightforward mercenaries and former commanders of the Free Syrian Army and al-Nusra, who have been "hired" by the Islamic State and gone on to make their careers in it.[43] "Most local fighters have no ideological agenda," says Aziz al-Hamza, a Syrian opposition activist who has a network of informers on the ground. "They go along with it because they get a salary and their families get free accommodation."[44]

A much more problematic group is made up of so-called *muhajirun* – the foreign fighters who make up at least 40 per cent of the core organization, dominate it ideologically and embody its transnational ambitions. Most come from the Middle East and North Africa, especially Saudi Arabia, Tunisia and Morocco. A fifth come from the states of the former Soviet Union and another 20 per cent are from the West, Western Europe in particular (see Chapter 4).[45] Not only have the majority consciously decided to join the conflict and fight for the Islamic State, they were also – with some exceptions – active in Salafist groups before they made the journey. Syria and Iraq are not their home countries; they are not fighting for their families, their friends or their village, but for the concept of the *Ummah* – a worldwide community of Muslims. Just as in previous conflicts, foreign fighters are less willing to accept compromise[46] and participate more frequently in acts of extreme violence.[47] They are the most dangerous part of the organization.

MILITARY

One important reason for the Islamic State's attractiveness used to be its military strength. Far and away the group's greatest success was the conquest of Mosul in June 2014; how could a city of millions of people – Iraq's second city – fall to such a small group in just three days? Why did tens of thousands of Iraqi soldiers simply give up?

Many of the details are still not clear, but it had nothing to do with conspiracy. Of the supposed 40,000 Iraqi soldiers defending Mosul, only a quarter actually existed in the first place, and two of their commanders fled the city within 24 hours of the battle breaking out.[48] Moreover, the attacking force comprised not only a 1,000-strong detachment from the Islamic State, but also a Sunni coalition, which included several thousand former Saddam supporters and the Iraqi jihadist group Ansar al-Sunna.[49] On top of that came the attitude of the majority Sunni population, which the largely Shi'i Iraqi army had been pushing around for months. In their eyes, the Iraqi soldiers were not defenders but occupiers from whom the Islamic State promised to liberate them. The Islamic State troops, for their part, weren't seen as religious extremists but as the old Baathists in new clothes. The British journalist Patrick Cockburn described it as a "Sunni uprising".[50]

But just as decisive an influence was exerted by the innovative tactics that the Islamic State had already used to overrun a third of the country in the preceding weeks. Commentators often underestimate how much work the group puts into preparing for the conquest of a new area. That effort has been demonstrated in documents published by journalist Christoph Reuter in *Der Spiegel*. Written by the military strategist Haji Bakr (1958/64–2014), who – like many of his comrades – was in the secret service under Saddam, they describe how the Islamic State first "infiltrates" a new city, opens recruiting offices, wins followers and then uses them as "sleepers". In the first few months, he writes, it is above all a question of finding out everything about the place and its inhabitants: which families have the power and where does their money come from? What other insurrectionary groups are active? Have their leaders committed any personal indiscretions that could be used to coerce them?[51]

The second phase is destabilization. Opponents are kidnapped or shot, potential allies persuaded or pressured. Car bombs and suicide attacks demoralize the security services. The group puts fear into its opponents. Those with a lot to lose – Christians, Shi'as and other minorities – start packing their bags. The result is chaos, terror and a city whose (remaining) population is ripe for a takeover. When – in phase three – the Islamic State's troops suddenly make themselves known and roll into town in their pickups, there is often no more resistance than a few skirmishes. In the ideal scenario, the Islamic State achieves its military aims solely through coercion, manipulation and classical terrorism.

If it comes to a real battle, the Islamic State's commanders will have spent months getting ready. They can deploy veteran fighters from the Caucasus and Iraq who have been fighting in insurrections for years and are among the most experienced in the world. A prime example was provided by the recently deceased Georgian Abu Omar al-Shishani (1986–2016), who rose to become commander-in-chief in northern Syria – one of the top military jobs otherwise occupied only by Iraqis.[52] When people like al-Shishani sent their troops into battle, it was usually as part of convoys that – before the beginning of American air strikes – were largely made up of pickups that could move rapidly from one position to another.[53] As a result, the Islamic State's elite troops could be very rapidly deployed to where they were most urgently needed.[54] And that confused their opponents: anyone coming up against the Islamic State was in the dark – just as Haji Bakr had planned – about whether they were facing 200, 500 or even 1,000 soldiers.[55] Coalitions with other groups are formed only when there is no other way. And in those instances, such as the conquest of Mosul, the Islamic State will already have a plan for how to control its coalition partners after a joint victory.[56] The tanks that drive in triumph through the cities are often purely decorative. Militarily, the Islamic State is still an insurrection, fighting unconventionally and using conventional means only when that serves its purpose.

The group is, however, far from invincible. "The Islamic State is strong where its enemies are weak," writes Cockburn.[57] Indeed, when the group encounters well-organized resistance, it often comes off second best. As early as spring 2014, the Islamic State was defeated several times by a coalition of Syrian rebels it was then fighting. And since the West's provision of training, intelligence and air strikes, Kurdish forces have scored successes against the Islamic State – as have the Shi'i militias and Iraqi army from time to time. The group made its biggest strategic mistake to date in the northern Syrian city of Kobane, where it sacrificed hundreds of fighters in a full-scale offensive lasting five months. On the Iraqi side of the border, the group took another important city, Ramadi, but lost it again, along with 40 per cent of the other territory it had conquered in summer 2014. If Mosul itself were to fall back into Iraqi government hands, it would be a massive blow to the Islamic State, because Mosul is not just its largest city, it is also the place where the caliphate was proclaimed.

There will be no quick and purely military victory against the Islamic State – the group is now too well equipped and too tightly interwoven with local structures for that – but its propaganda myth of invincibility has long since been exploded.

THE STATE

But the Islamic State is not merely an army. It controls more territory and has a larger population than half the members of the United Nations. For a German television report at the start of 2015, I got access to hundreds of internal Islamic State documents that give an insight into how the group is run. Most were mundane and even boring: invoices, accounts, memoranda and organizational charts. One document described how much the region Baghdad-North had spent on mobile phones and technical equipment in November 2013 ($18,500). Another announced the results of a competition for the best social-media campaign (the winners were the "media knights" of the Iraqi province Diyala, who received a "fully equipped HD camera" and a "wireless HP printer" as prizes).[58] The documents' mundanity reveals an aspect of the Islamic State often overlooked in the West: the Islamic State considers itself a state and behaves like a state – and employs bureaucrats who are not so dissimilar to their Western colleagues as we might think.

On the one hand, the state's objective is to realize a Salafist vision of society, but on the other, the enforcement of strict religious rules is also part of Abu Bakr Naji's strategy for social reorganization. After the *total* chaos in the "phase of savagery", Naji argues that the imposition of *total* order is the best means of convincing people to accept the new system. So wherever the Islamic State comes to power, it immediately institutes Sharia courts. They cost almost nothing, are free from corruption, impose order and arbitrate in disagreements that have been ignored for decades.[59] The next step is the religious police. Its officers patrol the towns and apprehend women who aren't wearing their veils correctly or men who are smoking or listening to music or who don't close their shops during the time of prayer. Where crimes have been committed, they apply the so-called *hudud*, a harsh scale of punishments: whipping those who drink alcohol, cutting the hands off thieves and stoning adulterers.

In the long term, according to Naji, it is about building not just a virtuous but also a "fighting society".[60] In schools, young men are taught about war and young women about how to raise future warriors. Almost all "conventional" subjects – music, art, history, philosophy, geography and chemistry – are scrapped and replaced with religion, military training and marching exercises.[61] From the Islamic State's perspective, this represents progress:

The curriculums are free from homosexuality, evolution, music, theatre, inter-religious dialogue and all the other garbage taught at non-Muslim schools. In the caliphate, children's minds are protected from harmful influences![62]

The situation is similar at universities: eight have been closed and at the others, according to a professor at the University of Mosul, there are now more weapons than students.[63]

The greatest challenge is economic. The Islamic State may be the "richest terror group in the world" with an income once estimated at up to 5 million dollars per day,[64] but it is also a state and thus responsible for between 5 and 7 million people who expect to be supplied with food, water, heating and electricity. In the early stages, the Islamic State received significant donations, but many of its backers in the Gulf states have since got cold feet, and even the supposedly legendary profits from exporting oil have now collapsed.[65] According to Charles Lister from the Brookings Institution, most of the wells have been destroyed and the quantities still being produced are enough only to supply the Islamic State's own population.[66] What's left are primarily taxes, confiscations and fees levied inside the Islamic State's own territory. As sources of income, these are reliable and relatively safe from outside disruption, but they present a medium- and long-term problem insofar as a state that no one wants to trade with and that produces nothing of note will inevitably have less and less to tax and confiscate.[67] The Islamic State is therefore a plunder economy: as soon as its expansion stops, its finances – and the services it provides to its inhabitants – start to falter.

So far, expansion has taken place mainly away from the Middle East. It has come in part through new alliances, because other groups – such as Boko Haram in Nigeria – have sworn loyalty to the caliphate and, after rigorous examination, been accepted into the state by the caliph. It has also come through the founding of new provinces (*wilayat*), for example in Libya, where al-Baghdadi sent a confidant in September 2014 to organize the local jihadists and integrate them into the structure of the Islamic State.[68] The Libyan *wilayah* is now the Islamic State's most successful subsidiary and is used as a safe zone and training area for the group's supporters from neighbouring Tunisia (see Chapter 7). But in Yemen, too, and in Sinai, Pakistan, Algeria and even in Saudi Arabia, al-Baghdadi believes he is in with a good chance. This still in no way amounts to an all-encompassing global empire, but as an idea, a "brand" and a structure, the Islamic State might be able to survive defeat in its home territories.

FUTURE

How well does the Islamic State function? Since the year 2012, the group has published an annual report on its own activities. These are released like the yearly reports of big companies and contain almost as many figures. But instead of profit and turnover, the Islamic State's reports list car bombs and mortar attacks. The most recent report available at the time of writing, from June 2014, enumerates 7,681 operations, including more than 1,000 political assassinations and 250 suicide bombings – a significant increase on the previous year. About the Islamic State's political performance the report says almost nothing, but it is the group's political strengths and weaknesses that will decide its future – and in that field its results, despite its initial military successes, are decidedly mixed.

STRENGTHS

One of the Islamic State's biggest strengths is its relationship with the tribes, which are still the most important social structure outside the cities and determine the status, opportunities and identity of millions of people. For the jihadist movement, tribes have always been a double-edged sword, since in principle, loyalty to anything except Islam is forbidden. Al-Shabaab wanted to destroy the clan system in Somalia, and Zarqawi had little patience for it too. And the Iraqi tribes' decision to turn away from the group in 2006 and 2007 in order to make common cause with the Americans remains a traumatic experience for Zarqawi's successors.

As a result, al-Baghdadi and his comrades paid a lot of attention to the tribes right from the outset. The objective was not to destroy the tribes, but to make them biddable. The guiding principle is that of carrot and stick: tribes that cooperate with the Islamic State, swear fealty and provide troops are showered with privileges and get priority in supplies of grain and oil. Anyone who resists is punished. That is what happened to the Shaitat in the east of Syria and the Albu Nimr in the Iraqi province al-Anbar, both of which fought against al-Baghdadi and paid for it with the lives of hundreds of their people.[69] The example that the Islamic State made of them had the desired effect, and no one now expects there to be an uprising of the kind seen in 2006 and 2007.

Another important strength comes from the imposition of order. Of course, the Islamic State's legal system is brutal and has little to do with liberal notions of equality and justice. But for the Syrians and Iraqis who live under its jurisdiction, those comparisons are irrelevant: their starting point is not liberal democracy, but years of war and, before that, the corrupt and arbitrary dictatorships of Assad and Saddam. In contrast, the Islamic State's Sharia courts seem like progress: they are open to everyone, adjudicate on all kinds of problems, hear witnesses from both sides, publish their sentences – and carry them out at once. The punishments are harsh and the public executions controversial,[70] but crime is nearly at zero. Anyone who doesn't belong to a minority or fall foul of the Islamic State can be confident of getting a form of justice. And anyone who wins their case in a Sharia court has an interest in maintaining that judicial system – and thus also in maintaining the Islamic State. "Total order", as proposed by Abu Bakr Naji, is a plus for the Islamic State – particularly when the only alternatives are chaos or continuing war.

The absence of a political alternative is even more significant than the absence of a judicial one. Many armchair strategists in the West see the dictator Assad as a potential partner who would guarantee stability and protect minorities. But for the Syrian Sunnis, whom his army spent years bombing and attacking with chemical weapons, he is and remains a despot. Nor do the Iraqi Sunnis, who were systematically marginalized and disadvantaged under Prime Minister Nouri al-Maliki (*1950), want to have anything more to do with their government. For them, the Islamic State is the lesser of two evils, and so long as the international community fails to produce a credible alternative, al-Baghdadi will still be able to rely on the support of many Sunnis.

Even the war crimes and atrocities that elicit so much horror in the West are interpreted by the population on sectarian lines. Only very few inhabitants of the Islamic State have any objection to the mass execution of Syrian and Iraqi soldiers. In their eyes, the executions are reprisals for enemy atrocities and therefore often popular. The enslavement of Yazidis and the shocking sexual violence against women are more controversial.[71] Even many militant Salafists baulk at these practices, which may have been mentioned in the Qur'an but have not been seen for centuries and which al-Qaeda itself has never introduced.[72] From an Islamic perspective, the summary execution of Christians is also absolutely forbidden, because the Qur'an affords unconditional protection to the so-called "religions of the book" – Christianity and Judaism.[73] But though this violence hasn't won the Islamic State any friends, nor has it seriously threatened the group's backing among its core supporters, Syrian and Iraqi Sunnis.

WEAKNESSES

The Islamic State's greatest weakness lies not in its atrocities but in the unsustainability of its economic and administrative model. The resultant problems have already become apparent inside the Islamic State. The Iraqi officers who dominate the high command may know how to infiltrate a city, but none of them has ever governed one. Many of the highly qualified professionals – engineers, doctors, teachers – among the population were liberals or belonged to minorities and have fled abroad. As a consequence, the state is groaning under the burden of responsibility only a year or two into its existence. Even the foreign fighters have begun to complain about shortages and rising prices. Only in exceptional cases are engineers given permission to travel to other countries.[74] The appeals in current issues of *Dabiq* for doctors, cooks and mechanics show that there are no longer enough Iraqis and Syrians qualified to do those jobs.[75] The perfect welfare system that the Islamic State promised its citizens – guaranteed provision of basic supplies, free health care and cheap housing – can hardly be realized without them. Nor will the situation improve in the future, since the Islamic State receives almost no support from the outside; and even if the group's next iteration is able to fight, it won't be able to meet the requirements of its own population.

The Islamic State's answer to these problems has always been "expansion". But the territorial enlargement, which took place with such breathtaking speed in summer 2014, has since lost its momentum. Many of the oil fields that the group briefly controlled are back in Kurdish or Iraqi hands and there have been only isolated gains in other places. Even before the American air strikes, the Islamic State was close to reaching the limits of its "organic growth", because its Iraqi territory now borders on majority Shiʻi or Kurdish areas, which the group would not be able to subdue without great difficulty, and its Syrian operations have been facing strong resistance from al-Nusra and a range of other Salafist and Islamist groups for the past 18 months. The incorporation of new "provinces" in Africa and Asia may be an ideological success, but it does nothing to solve the economic problems in the heartland. On the contrary: the more the Islamic State's advance through Iraq and Syria in summer 2014 reveals itself to have been a flash in a pan, the weaker is its attraction for fighters and jihadist groups in other parts of the world. In this way, the problems in the heartland put the entire ideological project in doubt.

On top of that comes the fact that the most important elements of that ideological project – the Salafist social programme – are unpopular among the Islamic State's inhabitants. As in other places where jihadists have briefly become a government, people were initially pleased about the restoration of stability and order, without thinking too much about what kind of society their new rulers sought to create. The longer the peace has lasted and the more the jihadists have dedicated themselves to their actual objective – the construction of a Salafist state – the more their regime has been disliked. Even in conservative countries like Somalia and Afghanistan, the "virtuous terror" of the 2000s turned people against the jihadists. And in the Islamic State, too, there are signs that things are moving in a similar direction. The group apparently held back at first when it came to enforcing religious laws, but it has since begun to impose brutal punishments for even the smallest violations of the rules.[76] Not only liberals and women have been turned off the Islamic State,[77] so too have former supporters. One of these is Issa from Raqqa, whose story is typical:

> I was a member of the Uwais al-Qarani Brigade. Once we'd sworn loyalty to the Islamic State, everything changed. We were suddenly supposed to obey extreme regulations... It started with smoking and by the end we were meant to report our own families for infringing Sharia laws.[78]

A large part of the problem stems from the foreign fighters, who are often responsible for enforcing the strict rules. They are an inalienable component of the Islamic State, define its transnational identity, belong to its elite, are given the best houses and prioritized in supplies of luxury goods, medicines and places at kindergartens. But in the eyes of many Syrians and Iraqis, they are foreigners who don't know the local conventions, have no ties to the area and often don't speak Arabic. Their role in the fight against Assad and the Iraqi government made them briefly popular, but their arrogance, capriciousness and ideological intransigence have transformed many of their previous supporters into enemies.[79] Although native Iraqis and Syrians still make up the majority of fighters, the foreigners are increasingly dominating public appearances and local perceptions. That was already a problem for Zarqawi's group in the 2000s, and it is now creating tensions again. "The Syrians have no say any more," is how Issa puts it. "We've become servants to the foreigners."[80]

But there is no guarantee that the Islamic State's weaknesses will quickly lead to its collapse. As the example of North Korea shows, a totalitarian state can exist for decades even when internationally isolated and economically ruined. Nor is the population's gathering discontent a reliable sign that revolt is imminent. The absence of a credible alternative and the Islamic State's unwavering readiness to brutally suppress any opposition could crush an attempted uprising before it really begins. "A lot of people are now against the Islamic State," says the opposition activist al-Hamza, "but they are afraid and they don't get any chance to organize themselves."[81]

Even if the caliphate disappeared off the face of the earth tomorrow, it would leave an enormous legacy behind. None of the previous waves of terrorism has succeeded in erecting such a potent symbol. And none has convinced so many followers to leave their homes, move to another country and fight for the cause. These followers – the Islamic State's foreign fighters – are the subject of the next chapter.

4

Foreign Fighters

THE PRESENCE OF EUROPEAN FIGHTERS IN THE SYRIAN CON-
flict is something I only became aware of in mid-2012. I was
researching an article about European fighters in previous conflicts – Afghanistan, Iraq, Somalia – and in the conclusion I wanted
to speculate about how the phenomenon would develop. Syria
was an obvious candidate. I Googled for articles and found only
a handful. All of them were about Libyans and Saudis – no trace
of Europeans.

At the end of that year, one of my colleagues, Aaron Zelin, told
me that Europeans were fighting for al-Nusra. I was curious and
asked him to keep me in the loop. Three months later, he came back
with a full set of statistics, which we published at the start of 2013.
We estimated that as many as 600 Europeans had made their way
to Syria, including 100 from the Netherlands, 130 from Britain and
40 from Germany.[1] His article was based on hundreds of reports in
the English and Arabic press, which he had painstakingly evaluated.
Our findings caused a sensation in the media. Zelin and I spent a
whole week giving interviews. Even the European Union's counterterrorism coordinator felt it necessary to make a statement. But as
it turned out, what Zelin had documented was only the tip of the

iceberg. In the course of the following weeks, it became clear that more European jihadists had gone to Syria than to any other previous conflict. The media started talking about an exodus.

Two months after the publication of our first estimates, another of my doctoral students, Shiraz Maher, found the Twitter account of an English fighter. It was entirely new to us to see a jihadist speaking so publicly about himself and his experiences of war. His posts were not just about religion and politics, but also about his everyday life, the situation the foreign fighters found themselves in, his hopes and fears. Many of his photos showed him in action, holding a Kalashnikov at the wheel of a truck, but in others he was posing with cats or having dinner with his comrades. The account and the accompanying Facebook profile were like a public diary – an exclusive insight into the life of a foreign fighter on jihad. His lists of friends and "followers" led Shiraz to the social-network accounts of more fighters. Within two years, our database grew from just a few fighters to more than 700. Shiraz spoke to just under a hundred of them via Skype, WhatsApp and Facebook. We also managed to meet a handful of them in person, near the Turkish–Syrian border.

Never before had it been possible to learn so much about the lives of Western fighters. Many of the stories my colleagues have researched resemble one another, yet the young Europeans fighting for the Islamic State are not a uniform group. What follows here is an attempt to outline an increasingly complex phenomenon in a few short pages. In doing so, the fates of individuals, which we can read about every day in the newspapers, are less important than the processes and structures that allow us to correctly understand those stories. This is not about fear-mongering, it is about realistically evaluating a phenomenon that will define the new wave of terrorism.

ORIGINS

With the help of our data, we can give a good indication of the general picture. The estimates that my institute has been publishing regularly since 2013 are based on a combination of various sources. These include reports in the European and Arabic press, statements from authorities, death notices in extremist internet forums and the writings of the 700 foreign fighters whose accounts we are following on Facebook, Twitter, Instagram and Tumblr. The composite emerging from all this is not precise. We don't know all their names and in many cases we have only vague information about where they've come from and where they are now.[2] But the overview is clear: the conflict has mobilized more foreign fighters than any other. According to our most recent estimate, from January 2015, at least 20,700 fighters had travelled to Syria and Iraq in the previous three or four years.[3] That is more than the figure for the entire 1980s and early 1990s in Afghanistan, and many times that for the conflicts in Iraq, Afghanistan after 2001 and Somalia.[4]

It is also clear that a kind of "jihadist international" has emerged in Syria and Iraq. We know of fighters from more than 90 countries. The largest contingent comes from the Middle East and North Africa. We estimate that they account for more than half the foreign fighters, including 900 Lebanese, 1,500 Jordanians, 1,500 Moroccans, up to 2,500 Saudis and 3,000 Tunisians. Around 15 per cent of the fighters are from the countries of the former Soviet Union, above all Russia (up to 1,500, including many Chechens), Uzbekistan (500), Turkmenistan (36) and Kazakhstan (25). There are around 1,000 from the Balkans and Turkey, and another 1,000 come from East and South Asia (especially China and Pakistan). Our figures for South-east Asia are the least precise, but we believe there to be several hundred fighters.[5] Western states outside Europe – Canada, the United States,

Australia and New Zealand – have provided up to 500 fighters, half of them from Australia.

The Western Europeans whom this chapter examines are also well represented. In most Western European countries, the mobilization of jihadist fighters has surpassed not only that for any previous conflict, but also that for all previous conflicts put together. We estimate that up to 4,000 foreign fighters have come from Western Europe, 20 per cent of the total. France (1,200), Britain (up to 600) and Germany (also 600) have supplied the largest groups, but are also the largest states. When measured against population size, smaller countries are more seriously affected, particularly Belgium (440), the Netherlands (250), Sweden (up to 180), Denmark (up to 150) and Austria (150). Even Spain (100), Italy (80), Finland (up to 70), Norway (60), Switzerland (40) and Ireland (30) have fighters in Syria and Iraq (see Appendix A).[6]

Not all the foreign fighters have been involved from the start. The first arrived over the course of 2012, when the situation in Syria was becoming more and more extreme. A big influx came in summer 2013, when it became widely known that the Syrian army was being supported by the Lebanese Shi'i militia Hezbollah. For Assad's opponents, this was proof of a Shi'i conspiracy, and the radical preachers who had agitated against Assad from the outset now called their followers to make *hijrah* – emigration to Syria. The second big influx came in summer 2014, when al-Baghdadi proclaimed his caliphate and overran large parts of Iraq. This time, it was a matter not of defence, but of expansion – the creation of a global Salafist empire. Anyone who had been living in Europe and dreaming of a caliphate now wanted to be in the Islamic State. That summer, dozens of Europeans travelled to Syria and Iraq every week – a year later, the figure had dropped to four or five.

But not all foreign fighters immediately joined the Islamic State. Initially, there were many who fought with the (relatively) secular Free

Syrian Army. But as early as 2012, the dynamic changed. Fighters from the Persian Gulf and North Africa gravitated towards Salafist groups such as Ahrar al-Sham, which were sponsored by the Gulf states and had a stricter religious orientation. Many Europeans ended up with al-Nusra.[7] By the time the Islamic State split from al-Nusra, the Free Syrian Army had lost the competition for recruits. The foreigners who came to Syria from spring 2013 onwards wanted to join the Islamic State, and the Islamic State welcomed all new arrivals with open arms – even those who didn't speak a word of Arabic. Of the Western Europeans who went to Syria and Iraq in 2014, fewer than a fifth joined al-Nusra, and by now the great majority of Western Europeans in the conflict are part of the Islamic State.

MOTIVATION

In the photos from Syria and Iraq, the foreign fighters look much like one another: young men with long beards and Kalashnikovs, broad grins and tremendous self-confidence. But behind those pictures lie a wide variety of stories. Most of the fighters may be in their twenties, but the age range is far broader than in previous conflicts. In the Belgian contingent, for example, the youngest fighter is only 13, the oldest 69.[8] A large majority grew up with Muslim parents, but 15 per cent were born Christian or in other religions.[9] Some take their faith very seriously, but just as many are almost completely ignorant about it. And for the first time, as many as 15 per cent of the arrivals are women – an entirely new development in the jihadist movement, and one described in more detail in the next chapter.

Socio-economic origins vary from country to country. In Germany, Belgium, France and Scandinavia, a large majority come from deprived backgrounds and have neither school qualifications, professional training nor any prospect of a decent job. A study by the

German Interior Ministry found that half the German fighters had criminal records.[10] In Britain, however, a majority were studying or had completed their studies when they decided to leave – one was even a doctor who had graduated from the University of Cambridge.[11]

What unites them is not some demographic or socio-economic marker, but their lack of identification with the Western societies they (or most of them) were born and grew up in. Based on our data set of 700 fighters, they break down into three types.

DEFENDERS

For the first "generation" of fighters, who travelled to Syria in 2012 and 2013, it was often about protecting the Sunni population. At that point, the conflict was still chiefly a dispute between the (minority-dominated) Assad regime and the (mainly Sunni) opposition, whom the regime was brutally repressing. From the fighters' perspective, the events in Syria were an "existential threat" – an argument for mobilization, which the political scientist David Malet already identified in many previous conflicts.[12] Muslim identity was crucial because it fostered strong identification with the suffering of the Sunni civilian population. Many of the defenders were devout but very few considered themselves religious extremists. A great number came to Syria as part of aid convoys and were so shocked by the conditions they encountered that they stayed and joined the uprising. For them, it was not about America or the West. On the contrary, many explained that this was the first time that they'd found themselves on the same side as the West, since America and Europe also demanded an end to Assad's dictatorship.[13]

A good example of this is Ifthekar Jaman, a then 22-year-old from the English city of Portsmouth who joined Islamic State in summer 2013. Ifthekar had been privately educated and then worked in customer support for a British television channel. He wasn't a high-flyer, but he had a steady job, was popular and seemed to his friends to be well integrated. His parents had moved to Portsmouth from Bangladesh four decades earlier and opened a restaurant there. Religion had not been important in Ifthekar's upbringing: as a teenager he read Harry Potter and was a keen guitarist. His transformation into a Salafist began two years before his departure for Syria, but Ifthekar continued to think independently. Islam was important to him, but his relationships with his parents, (non-Muslim) friends and colleagues all remained intact. He was critical of the West, but did not hate it. It was the Syrian conflict that radicalized him.[14]

When the war broke out, Ifthekar was already a Salafist. He and his friends met every evening, watched videos about the Assad regime's atrocities and discussed the situation until late at night. How should a good Muslim react? Going to Syria himself and becoming part of the uprising was an option that he initially rejected. "Everyone said it was a civil war between Muslims," Ifthekar told my doctoral student Shiraz Maher via Skype, "and that was something I didn't want to have anything to do with."[15] But as the conflict escalated, his opinion began to change. Assad's forces became more indiscriminate and more brutal, and increasingly targeted (Sunni) civilians. The internet was full of *fatwas* (Islamic rulings) declaring Assad and his supporters to be "false Muslims", and proclaiming a jihad. The Saudi preacher Mohammed al-Arifi (*1970), one of the most prominent Salafist scholars, harangued his followers:

> Think of a child that has been killed, and imagine that it is your child, that the girl is your sister, the woman your mother and the old sheikh your own father. Feel their pain, their injuries, their fear. "The faithful are your brothers," says the holy Quran... Does this brotherhood have no practical meaning?[16]

FIG. 4.1 Ifthekar Jaman, from the English city of Portsmouth, who wanted to defend Syrian Sunnis against an "existential threat"

Ifthekar had found his justification. In May 2013, he flew to Turkey on a one-way ticket, determined to defend his co-religionists against genocide. "Muslims were being slaughtered," Ifthekar told the BBC. "I had to do something."[17]

Ifthekar made his own way to Syria. He knew no one there. When he presented himself to al-Nusra, they didn't want to take him, because he had no contacts inside the group – no one who could vouch for him – and his Arabic was far from fluent.[18] He didn't want to go to the less religious groups and so all that remained was the Islamic State, which was still calling itself ISIS and welcomed all comers. "I didn't know about them," Ifthekar told Maher, "but I had a look at what they had to offer, and I liked it."[19]

Ifthekar had had no military training of any kind and at first was only allowed to do guard duty. During the long hours at his post, he published thousands of tweets and photos, which made him a kind of local celebrity in his hometown. In December, four months after he had been accepted into the Islamic State, the group let him actually join the fighting. He was killed in his first skirmish.[20]

SEEKERS

The second type – those searching for meaning – are chiefly motivated by neither politics nor religion, but are part of a booming jihadist counterculture that meets their need for identity, community, power and a feeling of masculinity (see Chapter 5). The best evidence of this is provided by the photos they themselves have posted online. They show young men who only a few months ago belonged to the European underclass: denied any chance of a good job, pigeonholed by the media and ostracized by the rest of society. Now, in the Islamic State, they are strong, confident, armed and charged with an important mission. Nobody cares about their past, background or skin colour; anyone who makes the profession of faith and follows the rules belongs to the community. What they're doing is exciting, dangerous and – for the first time in their lives – meaningful. "[US president Barack] Obama has no idea about what a 25-year-old shop assistant in Primark is up to," says Maher, "but if he goes to Syria and joins the Islamic State, the whole world knows who he is."[21] Seekers are often the socially deprived jihadists, the ones with criminal records, the ones who have been humiliated in the West, and in the heroic foreign fighter they see an idealized version of themselves. They tend to be theologically illiterate, albeit familiar with Salafist rituals and slogans, and only superficially engaged with Islam. For them, being a fighter is the adventure of their lives, a way out, a fresh start and – at the same time – an answer to gnawing questions about identity, meaning and self-worth.

"Jean-Edouard", a 20-year-old Frenchman who travelled to Syria with a friend in summer 2013, is a typical case. He was born in Haiti and grew up in the suburbs of Paris, where criminality and hope-lessness go hand-in-hand and a large majority of the residents come from economically unstable immigrant families. His parents were evangelical Christians and tried to bring up their son in that tradition. But Jean-Edouard didn't want to subordinate himself to his parents' will. The French journalist David Thomson, who researched his story, describes an enthusiastic and ambitious young man who wanted to make something of himself, but quickly realized that in France he would never get the chance to do so. First he fled into the world of music, posting rap videos on the internet, then he converted to Salafism. His life changed drastically. He cut himself off from his parents, stopped rapping and quit his job, because as a trainee chef he had to prepare pork. After less than a year in the Salafist scene, he decided to become a mujahid – a jihadist fighter.[22]

As soon as he had arrived in Syria, he posted pictures of himself online. They show a clean-shaven and bespectacled young man with braces on his teeth.[23] In many of the photos, he is posing in a circle of his new comrades. "There are English people here, Bosnians, Somalians, Japanese, even Chinese," he wrote on Facebook. "We're the EuroDisney of the mujahideen."[24] Once he'd begun military training, the ungainly Frenchman injured himself within only a few days. In many of the photos after that, he has bandages on his shoulder and his right leg, but his injuries seem to have done nothing to dampen his enthusiasm: "No problem at all. The brothers are looking after me," he told his friends in Paris.[25] He used this unwanted hiatus to propagandize for the Islamic State. "Jihad is compulsory," admonished one of his tweets – before going on to describe its perks in the same breath: "We offer slaves, pizza and martyrdom."[26]

Only a few of his messages are about religion. Instead he continuously predicts the Islamic State's inevitable triumph: his Twitter feed is full of maps documenting the spread of the caliphate. Any victory is enthusiastically celebrated, no matter how small. He is excited about the ideological and political project that the group represents. Only the caliphate is in a position to protect Muslims, he says.[27] Posts like

FIG. 4.2 Jean-Edouard, from Paris, who found a sense of recognition and security in the Islamic State

this make clear just how strongly Jean-Edouard identifies with his new homeland. In less than two years, the Islamic State has given him what France did not give him in 20: acceptance, a feeling of strength and recognition, and an important role to play. He hates France ("the country of Allah's enemies"),[28] but he does not want to go back as a terrorist: Jean-Edouard thinks of himself as a citizen of the Islamic State; he wants to fight for its expansion – and die for it.[29]

HANGERS-ON

The hangers-on – the third type – also often come from precarious backgrounds and have similar issues and needs to the seekers. What makes them different is their tight social connection to a (small) group and its leaders – a phenomenon that the terrorism researchers Donatella Della Porta and Marc Sageman have observed for decades in a wide variety of movements.[30] If hangers-on go to Syria or Iraq, it is not because of political events or because they themselves have looked for an opportunity to do so, but because their leader has decided it.

For them, home is not a physical place, but instead wherever their group is. Inside their community, they feel safe and accepted, and if their group goes to Syria, they go too. Their motivation is not primarily religious or political, but social, that is: an imperative desire to maintain an emotional connection with their leader and the other members of the group. Which means that in Syria and Iraq, too, they tend to live in the same place.

There is a good example in Bremen, Germany. For years, it had a so-called Cultural and Family Association, a mini-mosque on an industrial estate with around 70 members before it was banned in December 2014. The association was founded in 2007 and emerged from a split in the Salafist scene. Its leaders were so extreme that they considered even the well-known German Salafist preacher Pierre Vogel (*1978) an apostate. In the following years, the association became a point of contact for foreign extremists – including a Belgian who took part in an unsuccessful attack in Denmark.[31] Those inside the mosque formed a committed group that communicated less and less with the outside world. Their parents called it brainwashing and went to the mosque several times to confront its leaders – in vain.[32]

Practically all the fighters from Bremen now in the Middle East were members of this association and almost all of them left for Syria at the same time.[33] The first departure, documented in the Bremen state government's application to ban the group,[34] happened in January 2014. It was the group's leader, who flew from Bremen to Istanbul and then Skyped home a few days later from Syria. His successful arrival was the signal that his followers in Germany had been waiting for. In the following eight weeks, there were another 20 departures, including women and children – entire families made their way to the Islamic State. Within a few months, Bremen went from being a federal state with no foreign fighters among its citizens to having the greatest number relative to its population. The group was reunited in

Syria: the 20 hangers-on who had followed their leader all met up in a town near the Syrian city of Aleppo and live next door to each other to this day.[35]

The dynamic was similar in Wolfsburg, a town in the north-west of Germany from which another 20 people travelled to the Islamic State. Here, too, there was a group whose members were so deeply bonded that they would have followed one another anywhere. They knew one another from school, met at night in a kebab shop or played pool in the local mosque's recreation room. At first, only a few of them were religiously conservative, let alone Salafist. But their leader pushed through the new doctrine step by step – and anyone who wanted to stay had to accept it. The 26-year-old Ebrahim B., who left the group and has since returned from the Islamic State, described the situation in an interview with German broadcaster ARD:

> These weren't strangers, they were old classmates, old friends…
> [Earlier] the fashion was that everyone had a boxer's haircut and
> Bushido [a rapper] on their phone… If you did that, you belonged to
> the group. And in 2014, it was that you grew a beard, dressed differ-
> ently and went to some meetings. Then you belonged to the group.
> That's exactly how it was.[36]

Ebrahim was poorly prepared for life in the Islamic State. After only three weeks in a training camp, he decided to go back to Germany. Following his friends to Syria was something he now calls "the biggest mistake of my life".[37]

DEPARTURE

The most immediate problem facing many "emigrants" is a practical one: how do I get to the Islamic State? In most cases, would-be jihadists depend for their travel planning on contacts or chats with those who have already made the journey successfully and are willing to answer their questions on websites like Ask.fm. Since March 2015 there has also been an official English-language online handbook called "Hijra to the Islamic State", which comprehensively describes each stage of the process. The first 13 pages are devoted exclusively to packing. Essential items include a sleeping bag, an MP3 player ("for lectures and the Qur'an") and a solar charger, "because there's only power four hours a day, but the sun's always shining". The instructions for the journey itself are just as detailed: which ticket to buy, how to behave at the airport, making contact with the Islamic State.[38] Everything is set out down to the smallest detail – emigration to the Islamic State has become a well-oiled machine.

Practically all these journeys go via Turkey, which shares its southern border with the Islamic State. Those wanting to become fighters book a ticket to Istanbul, Ankara or Antalya and pretend to be tourists if asked at the airport. The brave ones fly straight on to Gaziantep, Adana or other regional airports near the Syrian border. But the paths actually taken can vary widely. Whereas, at the start of the conflict, most fighters booked direct flights to Turkey, many have now become more careful. The handbook recommends disguising the journey to Turkey by flying there in several legs, for example: first flying to a neighbouring country or to North Africa, then on to Turkey with a separate ticket.[39] Germany plays an important role in this, because it has the most (and the cheapest) flights to Turkey, which means that many would-be fighters from France, Belgium and the Netherlands first drive to Frankfurt or Düsseldorf and start their journey to Turkey from there.[40]

On my team's last visit to the Turkish–Syrian border area in April 2014, we interviewed numerous fighters and the people smuggling them across. It was not difficult to find them, because at that point the jihadist groups still operated more or less openly on the Turkish side. Every taxi driver knew which guesthouses the "foreigners" were staying in. In a café in Antakya, the capital of Hatay Province, we met Abdullah, a 25-year-old Syrian who had been doing his military service when the conflict broke out, but went over to the opposition and finally fled into Turkey at the start of 2013. Since then he'd been earning money as a smuggler. When he found out I was German, he spoke to me excitedly about Burak Karan (1987–2013), a Turkish–German footballer who had played for the under-17 national side. "I took him to Syria," he told me proudly. According to Abdullah, the foreigners travelled in groups and anyone who arrived at the airport in Gaziantep was collected by him personally: "Then we go to a guesthouse or a safe house and the brothers stay there until we've checked them out." Those who passed the security checks could go to Syria. "The border is full of holes," said Abdullah. "I know dozens of ways to take people into Syria."[41]

What Abdullah told me was mirrored in German court papers. For example there is the story of Ismail Issa, a 24-year-old Lebanese–German who was tried in Stuttgart in mid-2014. Issa was a typical "seeker": an apprenticeship broken off, odd jobs here and there, drugs, constant trouble with the police, then conversion to Salafism and emigration to Syria shortly thereafter.[42] In August 2013, the time had come: together with a friend he flew from Düsseldorf to Istanbul and then on to Gaziantep. They were met at the airport and driven in a minibus to the little town of Kilis – right on the border with the Syrian town of Azaz, which was then in the hands of the Islamic State. They spent the first few nights there in a safe house, where they were checked and cleared for transfer.[43]

But even the Islamic State admits that the situation has grown more complicated since the end of 2014. Instead of Gaziantep, the handbook now advises would-be fighters to fly to the town of Şanlıurfa, which is further east and thus closer to the border with the Islamic State. "The conditions have become more difficult." The handbook ascribes this to the Turkish security services: "The Turkish intelligence services are in no way friends of the Islamic State. If they suspect someone of being part of the Islamic State, they will try to arrest him." But that does not make it impossible to get across. "The Turks are afraid of attacks," says the handbook, "so many of our members can [still] live in relative freedom in Turkey."[44]

Another factor that has made it more difficult to get into the Islamic State is its fear of spies. Anyone wanting to move to Syria must, as a rule, have a recommendation, called a *tazkiyah* in Arabic. Only rarely, say the smugglers and fighters, will jihadist groups still accept people who have made their own way to one of the border areas. Anyone totally unknown is not trusted.[45] The Islamic State's handbook recommends that would-be recruits without contacts inside the group introduce themselves to a fighter on Twitter before they leave.[46] The Wolfsburg defector Ebrahim B. corroborated that that is how the process works:

> Because there are so many foreigners arriving, everyone is now seen
> as a spy... What saved me was that they asked who my recruiter was...
> And then they asked him, is it true that Mr Such-and-such came via
> you? He confirmed it. I was lucky he did.[47]

Those who make it to a safe house on the Syrian border have to submit to further checks. To start with, their passports, laptops and phones are confiscated and the recruits have to give up the passwords to all their accounts. The "security officers" read through every email; look at every Facebook picture. Anyone whose profile only goes back a month or two doesn't stand a chance. It's just as problematic if they find party photos with alcohol or cigarettes, rap songs or WhatsApp chats with women.[48]

Issa, the Lebanese–German from Stuttgart, passed all these tests. From the safe house in the Turkish town of Kilis he made it into a refugee camp in Syria. There was no more suspicion of his motives, but what was the group supposed to do with this young man from Germany? Where could he be used? Issa was relatively fit, but had no military training. He wasn't stupid, but had no qualifications. At least he could speak Arabic – unlike most of the Western Europeans. A commander decided that he was suitable for simple military tasks and sent him to a training camp, where he learnt to shoot. It wasn't like in *Rambo*, but Issa was happy, because the training culminated in what he had been looking forward to for months: the oath of loyalty. He was now a mujahid, a soldier of the Islamic State.[49]

DUTIES

The term "foreign fighter" is disputed because not all recruits to the Islamic State are deployed militarily and only a minority of the Western Europeans are on active combat duty or involved in war crimes.[50] In contrast to other jihadist groups, the Islamic State presents itself as a state and so offers foreigners a plethora of opportunities for service that extend far beyond the purely military. The online magazine *Dabiq*, which is aimed primarily at Western jihadists, explicitly calls on its readers to start a life in the Islamic State, inviting women and families and devoting almost as much attention to the construction of a "new society" as to the war against infidels and apostates. The invitation to move to the Islamic State is directed not only at fighters but also equally at engineers, tradesmen and nurses.[51] Many foreigners are put in the religious police (*hesba*), patrolling the streets and ensuring that the strict rules are adhered to.[52] Others work in professions that they previously practised in Europe. Someone who was a mechanic at home can repair the vehicles of the Islamic

State and someone like Jean-Edouard, who trained as a cook, can prepare meals for the fighters. In particularly high demand are foreigners who know their way around software and social media. They produce the group's propaganda and take care of publishing *Dabiq* in half a dozen European languages. Deso Dogg (1975–2015), a German former rapper who swore allegiance to the Islamic State in April 2014, was said to be responsible for video production.[53]

Nonetheless, that does not mean that the term "foreign fighter" is completely inaccurate. Although the Islamic State considers itself a state, it is not a peaceful member of the international community. It is a "fighting state" and wants a "fighting society" (see Chapter 3), so the organization does remain primarily military. Even civilian jobs serve a military need: someone cooking for the Islamic State is supporting its military efforts just as much as someone repairing its cars and armoured vehicles. Just as in other armies, uniformed mechanics are ultimately soldiers, who can be mobilized and have to fight if ordered to do so. The crux is the oath of allegiance: those who have sworn it are part of the army. For most of the Western European recruits, that is neither a problem nor a burden: if they have left Europe and made their way to Syria and Iraq, it is not for cooking but for combat.

MILITARY DUTIES

Only very few of the Europeans have any military training or know how to handle a weapon. Many are physically unfit or struggle to cope with the climate. Compared with the Chechens or Iraqis who have been fighting in insurgent groups for years and have mastered the art of soldiering, they are militarily worthless. So why is the Islamic State still interested in having them as part of its fighting contingent?

For one thing, it's a question of ideology, prestige and attention. The Islamic State considers itself a global empire uniting Muslims from all over the world. Western faces are desirable because they underscore the group's global ambitions and demonstrate that it has supporters deep in enemy territory. So Americans, French and Britons receive privileges and get better accommodation.[54] The other reason is that Western recruits are obedient. In contrast to the Syrians and Iraqis making common cause with the group for opportunistic reasons (see Chapter 3), most of the Western Europeans come out of a Salafist scene, do not have to be persuaded to accept the extreme ideology and have already travelled far to become part of the caliphate. When they arrive, they often understand very little about the conflict, speak no Arabic and know no one outside their group. In short: they are almost entirely dependent on the Islamic State, support its ideological project and have no opportunity to orient themselves on anything else. Whether they want to be or not, they are the Islamic State's most loyal troops.

The Western Europeans mainly perform simple tasks. The most common of these is guard duty. It requires no special training; anyone who can use a Kalashnikov and a radio is qualified. That is a far cry from the action promised in the Islamic State's propaganda videos. But most accept their assigned role without complaining. Many convince themselves that their job is important and quote *Hadith* (traditions from the life of the Prophet) supposedly showing that *ribaat* – guard duty – was considered a serious responsibility during the first caliphate 1,400 years ago, and that the caliph entrusted it only to his most devoted troops. On YouTube there are dozens of videos in which jihadist scholars give reasons for the significance of *ribaat* and extol its advantages,[55] and the online magazine *Dabiq* recently published a six-page article on the subject.[56] Those who get bored nevertheless use the time to take pictures and write journals that they send to their friends at home via Facebook or Twitter in the evenings.

A more disturbing use for the foreign fighters is as "cannon fodder". Those who have no military training or combat experience and who cannot make some other meaningful contribution to the construction and expansion of the caliphate are "expended" in big battles. That became most readily apparent during the battle for the northern Syrian town of Kobane at the start of 2015, where after five months of fighting the Islamic State suffered its most significant defeat to date. According to my colleagues' estimates, around 100 – perhaps even 200 – Western Europeans were killed, many on kamikaze missions with no clearly defined strategic purpose. Practically every Western fighter we were in touch with on Skype and WhatsApp during the siege told us about comrades who'd been "martyred" in Kobane.[57] From Sweden alone, 12 fighters were killed. At least five French fighters blew themselves up in suicide operations.[58] None of these "martyrs" will return to Europe but their fate illustrates the negative influence that foreign fighters have on the conflict itself: they make the struggle harder and costlier for everyone.

Another use for foreign fighters is in committing the atrocities and war crimes local fighters don't want to get involved in.[59] That includes torturing prisoners as well as carrying out beheadings and – again – suicide attacks. Already during the Iraqi uprising in the 2000s, practically all suicide operations were performed by foreigners, because no Iraqis could be found to do it.[60] That pattern is repeated in the present conflict. My colleague Aymenn Jawad al-Tamimi, who has been documenting the jihadists' operations in meticulous detail, estimates that 70 per cent of the Islamic State's suicide attacks can be attributed to foreigners – many of them Europeans.[61] The same goes for beheadings and mass executions, in which Western Europeans are also disproportionately represented. The fighters who do these things are essential for the Islamic State: they project the power, strength and ideological determination that are then described on the evening news.

RETURNEES

Not everyone who goes on jihad will come back. An estimated 10 to 15 per cent of foreign fighters have already been killed, and that proportion will rise as the conflict goes on. Moreover, many of the fighters want to stay in the Islamic State; in contrast to Afghanistan in the 1980s or Bosnia in the 1990s, fighting for the Islamic State is about realizing a utopia, constructing a new society. Neither Osama bin Laden nor Abdullah Azzam ever thought of burning their passports, but for the Islamic State's fighters it has become a ritual.[62] A greater number than in previous conflicts will fight to the bitter end. And others will try to make it through to one of the overseas "provinces" or to find a place on some new jihadist battlefield.

It is hard to predict what shape these things will take, since no one knows how long the conflict will last. But there is no doubt that there will be returnees, since many foreign fighters have already come back. In November 2014, the British government cited a figure of 300 people.[63] In Belgium, the internal security services put the number at 120.[64] And in Germany, the number in each state is between 25 and 40 per cent of those who originally left. The argument put forward in autumn 2014 by the Bavarian minister of the interior, Joachim Herrmann, that would-be fighters should be deported to Turkey as a means of ridding Germany of the problem, has already been superseded.[65] And although not every fighter comes back from Syria and Iraq, nor do all of them want to stay there or die in battle.

It is also clear that not all returnees become terrorists. Two academically credible studies on this subject have examined the phenomenon from a historical perspective. The Norwegian jihad researcher Thomas Hegghammer looked at nearly 1,000 Western returnees from the conflicts in Somalia, Iraq, Afghanistan and Pakistan in the 1990s and 2000s. One in nine of them (11 per cent) were charged and/or sentenced for terrorist crimes in their home countries after going back.[66] Jytte Klausen from Brandeis University in the United States conducted a similar examination that yielded a higher result: of the nearly 900 foreign fighters in her sample, approximately one in four (26 per cent) became active terrorists after returning home.[67] The difference is striking and indicates the weakness of the methods and the data collection – hardly surprising when you bear in mind how difficult it is to conduct the research. And yet, both agree that the great majority of returnees (74 per cent or 89 per cent respectively) do not become terrorists.

THE TRAUMATIZED AND THE DISILLUSIONED

The conclusion that not all returnees become terrorists fits with the observations my team has made among the foreign fighters in Syria and Iraq. We differentiated four groups. The first group were the "traumatized", those whose participation in the war had damaged them psychologically. These are usually "hangers-on" and rarely have a solidly ideological world view. They could become a danger to their European home countries if their traumas remain untreated and others incite them to acts of violence. Crazed individual acts of terror – rampages or shooting sprees – are also possible.

The second group consists of the "disillusioned", whose experiences in Syria and Iraq have distanced them from jihad. We know from numerous sources that there are fighters like this. The initial lead came via my colleague Shiraz Maher, whom an English jihadist contacted in August 2014 claiming to speak for two-dozen compatriots – all "defenders" who had gone to Syria at the start of 2013. He told Shiraz:

The truth is: many people left to help the Syrian people, but then we got labelled as terrorists, and now people want to come back, not to attack but because they found out jihad isn't what they thought... We all saw videos... and they hyped us up. We saw the suffering of the Syrians. But right now Muslims are fighting Muslims. Assad's forgotten about. The whole jihad was turned upside down.[68]

Shortly afterwards, reports emerged about French and English jihadists who had defected and made it over the border into Turkey,[69] as well as about dozens of their comrades whom the Islamic State had executed as deserters.[70] In spring 2015, the founder of the Syrian opposition network Raqqa Is Being Slaughtered Silently told me about some Belgian girls who had travelled to Syria half a year earlier and now wholeheartedly wished they could go back to Europe.[71] Around the same time, Claudia Dantschke from the defectors' network *Hayat* ("Life") was in contact with several Germans who wanted to flee the Islamic State,[72] and she has since managed to bring one back to his homeland.[73]

Of course it would be naive to believe these individuals' accounts without putting them to the test. The security services are right to warn of fakers, double agents and opportunists.[74] And it's also clear that those who turn away from the Islamic State don't automatically become supporters of liberal democracy. But there is no longer any doubt that at least some of the returnees are frustrated and disappointed.

THE DANGEROUS AND THE UNDECIDED

At the other end of the spectrum are the "dangerous", whose conviction has only been strengthened by fighting for the Islamic State. Even Hegghammer, who estimated that only 11 per cent of returnees were terrorists, considers that terrorists with foreign experience are especially dangerous. Being deployed in battle, says Hegghammer, has given the returnees military know-how, desensitized them emotionally and secured them access to new (and international) networks allowing them to mount larger and more sophisticated attacks. This theory can even be statistically confirmed: terror plans made with the help of foreign fighters are one-and-a-half times as likely to be actually carried out as plans made without them, and twice as likely to lead to fatalities.[75] Simply put: terrorists with foreign experience are better – that is, more deadly – terrorists.

That returnees from Syria and Iraq will try to carry out attacks in Europe has already been demonstrated – not least in Paris in November 2015 and Brussels in March 2016. The first known case, which preceded Paris and Brussels, was that of Mehdi Nemmouche, a 29-year-old Frenchman who fought for the Islamic State for nearly a year before going home via Frankfurt in March 2014. He is now on trial for an attack on the Jewish Museum in Brussels in which four people were killed. Other examples include plots to carry out an attack in the south of France (February 2014), a suburb of Paris (October 2014), the Belgian city of Verviers (January 2015) and Oberursel in Germany (May 2015), all of which the police were able to prevent.[76]

The last group – and by far the largest – is that of the "undecided", those whose actions are still entirely unpredictable. After returning home they often take up contact with their old circles, but keep a low profile and neither embrace terrorism nor explicitly distance themselves from it. The security services' fear is that they could be "reactivated" at an opportune moment, or that they, as veterans of jihad, will attract new recruits.[77] It's just as possible that they will subside into obscurity, reintegrate themselves into their former surroundings and try to lead a "normal" life. This argument is put forward by the American researchers Daniel Byman and Jeremy Shapiro, who propose in a report for the Brookings Institution that the fear of returnees may turn out to be exaggerated. They give the example of the Iraq conflict in the 2000s, in which up to 5,000 foreigners took part – including several hundred Europeans – without it leading to attacks afterwards.[78]

I am less optimistic. The number mobilized for the present conflict is already four times what it was for Iraq and looks as if it will continue to rise. Even if we assume 30 per cent killed or permanently "emigrated" and even if Hegghammer's relatively low conversion rate of one in nine turns out to be true, we would still end up with 300 "dangerous" returnees, who are motivated and networked and have learnt their "profession" from the most brutal terror group of all time. It is impossible to judge yet what damage they will do, especially since not all of the dangerous ones can already be identified as such and since many of the undecided are still in the process of defining what role they will play in future. Which returnees are "dangerous" and which are not will become apparent only with the passage of time – a challenge that will occupy the European security services for a generation.

5

Supporters

THE SECOND DAY OF MY TEAM'S APRIL 2014 RESEARCH TRIP
to the Turkish–Syrian border began in a café in the centre of Antakya,
an elegant Turkish provincial capital with a history going back more
than 2,000 years. We had arrived in Gaziantep the night before and
didn't yet have any clear idea of what awaited us, nor of how easy
(or difficult) it would be to speak to fighters. We had just turned
on our laptops and ordered something to drink when my doctoral
student Joseph Carter noticed a small group of bearded men walking past the café in the direction of the old town. He grabbed my
shoulder and said excitedly, "I bet those are jihadists!" But what
were we supposed to do about it? Joseph and my other colleague,
Shiraz Maher, who was also on the trip, stared at me as if I were
their general and had to give the order to attack. I had no choice:
"After them!"

Joseph was the most enthusiastic. He was first to catch up and
brought the three men to a halt. "Hey, how's it going? Where are you
from?" he asked in English. "From England," said the oldest one.
"Great," Joseph carried on. "Us, too. What brings you to Antakya?"
The answer consisted of a single word – "Holiday" – and the rest of the
conversation was not much more revealing. After a couple of minutes,

the three of them turned and walked off. Joseph went after them for a while, calling out more questions – with no answer. It was our first, and shortest, encounter with foreign fighters.

That the three men really were fighters was something we were able to establish three months later, in January 2015, when the British media published reports about a 32-year-old jihadist from Luton, a town on the outskirts of London, who had gone to join the Islamic State. Abu Rahin Aziz had a round face, was short and stocky and looked exactly like one of the supposed tourists we'd met in Antakya. The dates matched, too. What we hadn't known was that Aziz had been convicted of grievous bodily harm in Britain and skipped bail to head for Syria.

Moreover, Aziz was no newcomer to the jihadist scene. For several years he had been part of a group that made the headlines with shrill demonstrations against America, British soldiers and cartoons of Mohammed. Even the grievous bodily harm had been an act of conscience: he stabbed a football fan in the head with a biro – allegedly because he'd insulted the Prophet.[1]

Aziz – who was killed by an American drone strike in July 2015 – is an example of how the Islamic State's foreign fighters don't materialize out of thin air. No one is radicalized overnight and no one strapping on a suicide vest has been a supporter of liberal democracy any time recently. For the Islamic State as much as for any other jihadist organization, European supporters are recruited from a Salafist counter-culture that has grown both larger and more radical in the past five years. You come across it in the centres of European towns, and on the internet. Its supporters are not only angry young men like Aziz, but women, too. It is a breeding ground for foreign fighters and has recently also begun to incubate the "lone wolves" who further the Islamic State's military strategy by carrying out terrorist attacks in Europe.

SALAFISTS

As in all previous waves of terrorism, jihadist terrorism is inextricably connected with an extremist counterculture – a "scene" or a "radical milieu" from which sympathizers, supporters and members are recruited.[2] The terrorists and this counterculture share fundamental ideological convictions and often also agree on their objectives, though not always on the (violent) methods used to achieve them. Those who become jihadists in Europe were usually Salafists first or found their way into a jihadist group via connections in the Salafist scene. That does not mean that every Salafist becomes a jihadist, but the converse statement – that practically all European jihadists are Salafists, or closely connected to them – is essentially correct.[3]

Today's Salafists have little to do with the Salafist reform movement that developed in nineteenth-century Egypt (see Chapter 2). European Salafism is no longer just a (very) conservative faction within Islam, but a modern movement whose language, symbols, rituals and arguments owe as much to life in a developed Western society as to the example set by the "pious forefathers" of 1,400 years ago.

What this movement offers its supporters is threefold:

Firstly, it is about *rebellion*: Salafism is against everything that Western societies stand for – not only their foreign policies but also democracy, equality and human rights. It preaches active "enmity" towards the "unbelievers".

Secondly, Salafism provides *order*. It is a perfectly closed system of rules and injunctions with an answer for any situation. Everything is black or white, true or false. Those who follow the rules go to Heaven – those who break them go to Hell.

Thirdly, Salafism offers *community*. Those who subordinate

themselves to its system are accepted 100 per cent by the others – regardless of skin colour, origin, past or education.[4]

Even though some well-educated and well-integrated people stray into Salafism – as has happened in England, for example – the Salafists' pitch is aimed squarely at the stranded, the directionless and the left behind. Their "market" consists of people who feel ignored or marginalized by society and who are searching for a new identity, a new home. They are often young people with an immigrant background who don't know where they belong, children from broken homes, petty criminals, drug addicts and outsiders.

The susceptibility of these people to a movement preaching the renunciation of every kind of freedom is not at all contradictory. "In a time when [even] politicians have tattoos," says the political scientist Aladin El-Mafaalani, "the greatest provocation and the most radical self-separation is… abstinence."[5] In this model, Islam functions as a symbol, a justification and a promise of salvation, but the problem would be more easily overcome if it were only a matter of religion: in Europe, Salafism has become a youth culture whose attraction extends far beyond people who grew up as Muslims or those interested in religion as such.

JIHADISTS: FROM THE PERIPHERY TO THE CENTRE

Compared with traditional Islamic communities, the Salafists remain a marginal phenomenon, albeit one that is growing rapidly. Their numbers have jumped in every European country over the past five years. In 2014, there were 7,500 in Germany alone – nearly twice as many as in 2012.[6] This figure, however, conceals a variety of trends and tendencies. The literature often differentiates between "quietists", "activists" and jihadists.[7] That is a little simplistic, but does help us understand where various Salafists stand in relation to the state and society.[8] The "quietists" advocate absolute loyalty to the authorities, the "activists" believe in peaceful agitation and the jihadists are in favour of violence and martyrdom.

The borders between them are not as hard and fast as this categorization suggests. There is a lot of crossover between these groupings and those who fought yesterday may collaborate tomorrow. And while the divisions run deep on certain topics, there are pragmatic alliances on others. Put simply: Salafism is like any other social movement in which there are ideological and tactical differences of opinion, but in which the intersections between different strands of thought are often quite fluid.

It is also true, however, that while the "quietists" used to dominate, the jihadists are increasingly coming to set the tone. One explanation for this is that state repression has become harsher, often creating greater solidarity and prompting many "activists" to go over to the jihadists.[9] The conflicts in the Middle East have been just as important, especially the war in Syria, which has been so traumatic for many Salafists that non-violent advocacy for Islam (*dawa*) – to which many "quietists" and "activists" had restricted themselves – has come to seem like cowardice. Even Ibrahim Abou-Nagie (*1964), one of the founders of the German scene, was shocked by the extent of the radicalization:

> At our meetings, we're [suddenly] seeing brothers who are intoxicated by jihad, intoxicated by Syria, who simply have no sense of responsibility for their actions. They're coming with t-shirts that say al-Qaeda on them, they're coming in combat clothes.[10]

Syria gave the jihadists access to parts of the scene that had previously ignored or rejected them, and their unwavering answer to the question of what to do – violent jihad – suddenly came to seem the only plausible response.

Supporters were given two options: either go to Syria and fight or assist the struggle from European soil. Indeed, many of the organizations established to deliver humanitarian aid to the Syrians – Helfen in Not (Help in Need) and Help4Ummah in Germany, for example – provided the jihadists with an entry point into less radical parts of the Salafist scene.[11]

MEGAPHONE JIHADISTS

Four years ago, when my team first started to examine the international network of Salafist groups, we quickly noticed that European jihadists all operated on the same pattern. We labelled them "megaphone jihadists" because they were so shrill.[12] Wherever they appeared, you saw signs with the same slogans: "Sharia will come", "Your soldiers are murderers" or "Voting is a sin". Another thing they all had in common was a strong presence on the internet: even groups of only 20 members were active on every social network, posting videos of every meeting on professionally designed websites. Jytte Klausen and her colleagues from Brandeis University soon provided proof that the European jihadist groups were all interconnected, copying one another's online materials and keeping one another up to speed with their campaigns.[13]

This network was the brainchild of Anjem Choudary (*1967), a 49-year-old lawyer and the leader of the English group al-Muhajiroun ("The Emigrants"). Choudary went to school in London in the 1980s and then studied law in Southampton, a city on England's south coast. He didn't take his religion so seriously at that point: there are photos of him drinking in his student days and former classmates have said he had girlfriends and wild parties. This ended when he went back to London in the early 1990s. Choudary turned to Islam, changed his life and became the right-hand man of Omar Bakri (*1958), a

Syrian preacher who had fled to London and was proselytizing jihad from there. The two men founded al-Muhajiroun, in which Bakri took the role of charismatic frontman while Choudary worked in the background.[14]

Al-Muhajiroun had an estimated membership of around 100, but many more came to their events because Bakri and Choudary did their best to provoke British public opinion. On the third anniversary of 9/11, Choudary organized a conference praising the terrorists as the "magnificent 19". His supporters protested against the Mohammed cartoons wearing mocked-up suicide vests.[15] And Choudary blamed the July 2005 attacks in London on the victims. "When we say 'innocent people', we mean Muslims," he told the BBC.[16] For a short while, al-Muhajiroun maintained an office in Pakistan that connected British jihadists to the Taliban.[17]

But overall, Choudary was careful not to be linked to anything actually illegal. He expressed sympathy for those caught plotting attacks, justifying and defending them – but emphasized that he was not actively involved. His position was always that although he did know the suspects, he hadn't seen them for a long time. And even though his followers have been implicated in half of all attacks planned in the UK, the British authorities have never yet managed to prove that he was lying.[18]

EXPANSION

At the end of the 2000s, Choudary began to export his group's strategy and methods to other parts of Europe. Of course most countries already had Salafists, jihadists and terrorist plots. But Choudary brought together the most radical people in the scene and professionalized their public profile. After Choudary had visited a country, new groups would often be founded that employed the same methods and

FIG. 5.1 London lawyer Anjem Choudary, the driving force behind the European megaphone jihadists

had almost identical names: in France, there was Sharia4France,[19] in Belgium, Sharia4Belgium and in the Netherlands, Sharia4Holland.[20] The Norwegians called themselves Profetens Ummah ("The Prophet's Community") and the Danes Kaldet til Islam ("Call to Islam").[21]

Just like al-Muhajiroun, these other European groups focused on provocation and publicizing their cause. They distributed Qur'ans, posted YouTube videos and burned American flags. But they also functioned as a relay for a great number of those who went to Syria as fighters after 2012. Everywhere that the megaphone jihadists were active and attracted new followers, people left for Syria. In Vilvoorde, a little town north of Brussels, for example, Sharia4Belgium established a presence in 2010, organizing a series of demonstrations. Their leader prophesied that the "black flag of Islam" would wave "over the palaces of Europe".[22] The first of their followers made his way to Syria at the start of September 2012. At the end of the same month, there were another three, in January another ten.[23] Two years later, the number of foreign fighters from Vilvoorde stood at 28.[24] A similar process took place in Antwerp, from where nearly 70 fighters have gone to Syria – many of them with connections to Sharia4Belgium. The head of the Belgian secret service described the group as an "incubator" for Belgian jihadists.[25]

The pattern is identical in Germany, although Choudary has had less direct influence there.[26] The group that provided the breeding ground for foreign fighters called itself Millatu Ibrahim ("Abraham's Way") and was led by Mohamed Mahmoud (*1985), a 31-year-old Austrian who had propagandized for al-Qaeda in his home country and spent four years in jail for doing so. After his release in September 2011, he moved to Berlin and made friends with the German former rapper Deso Dogg.[27] Like Bakri and Choudary in England, the two men combined charisma and organizational talent. Millatu Ibrahim attracted supporters all over the country – in big cities like Berlin and Frankfurt, but also in small places like Solingen, Dinslaken and Kempten. In Wolfsburg a group was formed by Tunisian–Germans who worked for a subcontractor of Volkswagen, played football together and, from the end of 2013, handed out Qur'ans at the railway station. First one went to Syria, then two – in November 2014, the Constitution Protection Office counted a dozen,[28] and by mid-2015, the *Süddeutsche Zeitung* was reporting that 20 people from Wolfsburg were now with the Islamic State.[29]

As in Vilvoorde, the fighters from Wolfsburg were part of the jihadist scene and supported the Islamic State long before they made their way to Syria. What set them apart from the comrades who stayed at home was not the degree of radicalization, but how easy it was for them to get to the Islamic State. So the phenomenon of foreign fighters cannot be examined in isolation: the Europeans fighting for the Islamic State are a manifestation – and a consequence – of this hyper-radicalized Salafist scene.

WOMEN

The presence of women in the jihadist scene was hardly recorded before the conflicts in Iraq and Syria. Ten years ago, when I was researching my first report on the subject of radicalization in Europe, that was still accurate. The only women involved with jihadism were married to jihadists. The only example I can remember was the wife of Mohammad Sidique Khan, who had led the attacks in London. Until the Syrian conflict, she was the only female jihadist ever to go on trial in Britain. There may have been cases elsewhere, such as the Belgian al-Qaeda recruiter Malika el-Aroud, but I know of no European country in which women were actively and visibly participating in the jihadist scene in any numbers in the mid-2000s.

That has changed in the past six or seven years. Up to 15 per cent of emigrants to the Islamic State since 2013 have been female. That has come as a shock to many, but – as is the case for foreign fighters overall – the high number of women joining the Islamic State is not a cause but a consequence: it reflects stronger and more active female participation in the Salafist scene, something that has developed over several years.

Already at the end of the 2000s, there was a series of reports about women in the jihad movement, and security services all over Europe issued warnings about this "new phenomenon".[30] In Germany, these were principally the wives of fighters who had followed their husbands to the tribal areas of Pakistan. The journalist Wolf Schmidt documented some of their stories and dubbed them "the widows of Waziristan" because many of their husbands had been killed in battle. The most famous of these widows was Luisa S. from Bonn – a convert in her early twenties who before her radicalization had worked in the transport department of a local council on the Rhine. After her husband was killed, she appeared in a propaganda video in which she first thanked God that her husband had been granted "this honour" and then called on her "dear sisters" in Germany to follow her example: "Nowhere else," she said, "will you get to experience the freedom and dignity of being a woman as fully as here."[31]

Whether this appeal had any effect is impossible to tell. Then as now, the majority of women active in the jihadist groups arrived in the scene via a male contact.[32] That is often the husband, but in many cases also a brother, cousin or other family member. This has often been ignored in the reporting on the (sometimes very young) women who have gone to Syria since 2013. A good example of this is the case of Salma and Zahra Halane, 16-year-old twins from Manchester, who went to the Islamic State in summer 2014. The British press portrayed them as "the terror twins" – two teenagers who had made it all the way to Syria on their own initiative.[33] But in truth, their elder brother Ahmed was already there, in Raqqa, and had organized the journey. They were in contact with Ahmed throughout the trip and were met by him at the Turkish border. If their brother hadn't "incited" them to come, the twins probably never would have done so.[34]

This doesn't mean that no women join the movement of their own volition. On the contrary: the increase in the number of female activists is due above all to the influx of women who have come to jihad without any male connections. This has been made possible by the internet, since most jihadist events are men-only and there are no separate female groups. Online, women can move more freely and take part in discussions without necessarily identifying themselves as female.

Schmidt reported on female "Online Holy Warriors" who were preaching jihad in extremist chat rooms at the end of the 2000s. The most active at the time was Filiz Gelowicz, who was married to the leader of the so-called Sauerland Group, which planned attacks in Germany in 2007. In court, Gelowicz admitted posting "more than

1,000 videos, articles and comments" online – in addition to running her own YouTube channel and sending countless emails to women interested in jihad.[35]

Gelowicz was not an exceptional case. In 2009, a team of researchers from Dublin City University showed that female jihadists used the internet more than their male counterparts and that they expressed more hard-line opinions.[36] This was demonstrated during the attacks on Paris in January 2015, when hundreds of women tweeted their approval. "May Allah help the mujahideen to kill as many [unbelievers] as possible," wrote one British woman.[37] "Hats off to the mujahideen," said another.[38] Even the "terror twins" from Manchester were enthusiastic: "Jihad in the [land of the enemy]!!! God is great!!!" tweeted Zahra.[39] "May Allah protect the mujahideen in Franceeee!!! Shooting was maad!!" added her sister.[40]

My colleague Melanie Smith believes that the internet acts as a kind of release valve for female supporters of jihad:

> Many of them are frustrated that they're not allowed to fight. So they spend a lot of time on the internet and try to be even more aggressive than the men. That's their way of contributing to jihad.[41]

"WARPED FEMINISM"

When the media report on female jihadists, they are usually presented as victims. The young women have "strayed" into the jihadist scene, been manipulated by men or fallen in love with pictures of "rugged fighters". That female jihadists can also be intelligent and highly motivated and that they play an active role in the dissemination of jihadist ideology is something these reports don't mention. "When I open the paper," says Smith, "the men are terrorists and the women are 'jihadi brides'."[42]

But defectors' accounts of their time in the Islamic State show that female jihadists are often just as harsh and ideologically severe as their "brothers". One difference is the far greater importance of their clothing, namely the full veil. Those who refuse to wear it are quickly accused of treachery. "I was told that I didn't have enough knowledge about the religion," reports a convert from near Frankfurt, who went to meetings of Millatu Ibrahim: "And from that they concluded that I must be a spy or a journalist." A whole year later she was still being bullied on Facebook by her former "sisters". "'You're really sick', [said one]. When I asked what her problem was, she said: 'People like you are my problem.'"[43]

It is difficult to say whether the "emancipation" of female jihadists will eventually reach the point where women play a full part in carrying out attacks. Of course, there have already been female suicide bombers and Roshonara Choudhry, a then 21-year-old student from London, stabbed a member of parliament in May 2010. But the current jihadist doctrine is that women are not fighters and should concentrate on supporting the cause in other ways. This does not mean that female jihadists are unimportant, let alone undangerous. The women who have joined the Islamic State play an important role in its propaganda and see it as their mission to promote jihad and the group's ideological project. They have already issued warnings: "Live in fear," threatened one female British jihadist after the attacks in Paris. "Sleepers and lone wolves are everywhere!"[44]

It is striking just how confident the female jihadists are – and it is also puzzling: what prompts intelligent women from European societies to take part in something like this? Reports on and interviews with female jihadists show that their motivations do not fundamentally differ from those of men. For them, too, it is often about structure and order, a longing for community and meaning. On top of that comes what Melanie Smith and Erin Saltman have called "warped feminism":

many women see jihad as a liberation from the sexual expectations of Western societies. "Women are valued in the Islamic State's propaganda," the two researchers write, "not as sexual objects, but as the mothers of the next generation and protectors of the ideology."[45] The street worker Berna Kurnaz, who looks after north German families whose daughters have gone to Syria, confirms this: "The girls and women aren't weak. The emigration, the radicalization, is a conscious, a confident act – a form of emancipation."[46]

ONLINE

The fact that the Islamic State has so many supporters – women and men – is not solely due to the situation in Europe nor to conflicts in the Middle East. Equally important is the Islamic State's presence on the internet. Never in the history of terrorism has a group communicated so much and never has a terrorist campaign been so defined by how it is perceived online.[47] The Islamic State uses the internet as a weapon of war, intimidating its opponents and promoting itself and its ideological project. But behind this apparently cohesive facade is a plethora of people and groups among whom the Islamic State is only one of many – and by no means the most influential.

The first feature of the Islamic State's online presence is the content it produces itself. That includes highly professional 90-minute documentaries described by journalists as "cinematic";[48] shorter clips that show the everyday life of fighters or report on current events; handbooks, texts, photos and – of course – the online magazine *Dabiq*, which appears in half a dozen European languages. In order to disseminate this content, the Islamic State has created a sophisticated system that manages thousands of social network accounts, giving the impression that its supporters are everywhere. The most important network used to be Twitter, on which most of the social-media campaigns began. For a while there was even an app with which supporters could synchronize their accounts to the Islamic State's.[49]

But not everything ascribed to the Islamic State is actually produced by it. The most influential elements of its online presence are only partly under its control, if it all. That includes fighters who post pictures on their private Facebook, Twitter and Telegram accounts and communicate with supporters in Europe via Twitter or WhatsApp; radical preachers who distribute their lectures on YouTube and present themselves as religious cheerleaders; and simple "fans" who spend their days and nights on the internet, tweeting the newest information and rumours and so exerting influence on the network of supporters. Often it is not the Islamic State that is promoting the Islamic State online, but rather its followers, supporters and those it has inspired. They all belong to an online jihadist ecosystem, which is more complex and far less centralized than is usually assumed.

FIGHTERS

The most important part of this system are the hundreds of fighters documenting themselves and their experiences in the Islamic State on Facebook, Twitter, Telegram, Instagram and Ask.fm. The conflict in Syria and Iraq is the first in which it has been possible to communicate with hundreds of fighters personally and in real time. Many don't mind that their home countries' security services are watching their profiles, because they see themselves as citizens of the Islamic State and want to live and die there. They use the internet to persuade comrades who've stayed at home to come and join them. They speak the same language as their audience, answer every question, make jokes and present themselves as friends. Their photos are often wobbly and out of focus, but they convey a feeling of strength, community and adventure better than any glossy publication. Their viewers see in them a confident, idealized version of themselves.[50] The fighters are not heroes, but friends and role models. What you see on their profiles is not Hollywood, but reality TV – and that is precisely why it is so attractive.

The Norwegian jihadist Kim André Ryding is typical. He was born in 1989 in a small town south of Oslo and mutated into a "gangsta" as a teenager. His life was stormy for several years: women, alcohol, drugs, a dozen car thefts and burglaries, constant trouble with the police. As late as February 2012, he was mixed up in a manhunt in Oslo, which ended with a wild gun battle. Shortly afterwards came the complete switch. After his girlfriend left him he became depressed and began to question his whole existence. He fell in with Profetens Ummah, the jihadist group that Anjem Choudary had helped set up. Ryding converted to Islam, renamed himself Abdul Hakim and cut off all contact with his former friends. Less than a year later, he got on a plane to Istanbul and then drove a rental car to the Syrian border. In April 2013 he swore allegiance to the Islamic State.[51]

Ryding has since become a star of the jihadist internet. His Facebook posts are in Norwegian and English, but his fans come from all over the world. Ryding posts pictures of his everyday life: they show him at the computer in his dormitory, swimming in the Euphrates or posing with children. He is devout but also muscular and tattooed, with broad shoulders and bulging biceps. In many of the pictures, he is wearing camouflage and sitting at the wheel of an off-road vehicle, or standing in front of tanks that used to belong to the Iraqi army. He answers questions patiently and makes no secret of his turbulent past:

I hope you are ready to meet the Angel of Death. There is no way back. And when it is time, many will regret that 50 Cent, Eminem, 2Pac, Drake, football, parties, girls, friends, drinking and clothes were more important to us than the Creator.[52]

The fact that Ryding is in Iraq as a soldier of the Islamic State and still takes the time to advise his comrades back home is something that many of his admirers consider an honour. Many want to be like him.

CHEERLEADERS

The second group consists of spiritual authorities. Because many supporters are Islamically illiterate, they place a high value on religious legitimacy and so the internet has become home to a whole host of self-appointed sheikhs, who take the Islamic State's side, defend its project and act as authority figures. What matters is not the qualifications these preachers have, but how convincingly – and personably – they come across. That lesson was learnt early by Anwar al-Awlaki, the American–Yemeni preacher who inspired many "lone wolves" in the 2000s and communicated with his audience almost exclusively online. Many of the new spiritual authority figures emulate his example. In April 2014, my institute in London examined which preachers were most influential among the fighters we'd collected into our database. The result was surprising, because the two most popular preachers – liked by more than half the fighters – were citizens of Western countries and in no way affiliated with the Islamic State. We called them "cheerleaders" because they had taken up the Islamic State's cause on their own initiative and rapidly become unofficial but nonetheless important online spokesmen for the group.[53]

One of these was a 29-year-old Australian called Musa Cerantonio, who was from an Irish-Italian family in Melbourne and had grown up a Catholic. He converted as a teenager and became a well-known Salafist while still a student, roaming the campus of Victoria University in white robes and speaking to strangers about Sharia. His rhetorical talent was already evident: he expressed himself clearly and had a gift for explaining complex issues in simple terms. But his degree was not in Islamic theology, it was in media and history, and nor did he in the following years ever formally study the faith that he preached with such authority, first in obscure mosques, then on an Egyptian satellite channel and finally on the internet.[54]

He owed his popularity to countless YouTube videos in which he discussed a wide variety of topics. Like his role model al-Awlaki, Cerantonio didn't talk exclusively about jihad, also dealing with non-political topics, questions of identity and everyday problems. But whenever he did come to speak about jihad, his position was uncompromising: jihad means armed struggle, he argued, and is obligatory. He supported the Islamic State from the beginning. In February 2014, he wrote on Facebook:

> I have been very clear about why ISIS are the best forces on the ground and that is because they are doing what the others do not...
> I have stated this before and I will state it again – As a Muslim I will pledge my allegiance to any man who establishes himself as the valid [Caliph] of the Ummah [global community of believers].[55]

Cerantonio had more than 11,000 fans on Facebook before his page was deleted in May 2014. For a young convert from Australia with no qualifications as a preacher, his ascent was unprecedented.

FANS

The third part of the jihadist internet consists of ordinary supporters, who follow the fighters' accounts and translate, comment on and disseminate news from the Islamic State. Some are also active offline in groups like Millatu Ibrahim or Profetens Ummah, but many are only involved in jihadism online. The American author Jarret Brachman identified this phenomenon years ago and labelled the particularly active ones "jihobbyists":

[They] do it from the comfort of their home computer or their local coffee shop, but they are still actively seeking to move forward the jihadist agenda. By hosting jihadist websites, designing propaganda posters, editing... videos, recording soundtracks (nashids) for those videos, compiling speeches from famous jihadist sheikhs and packaging them into easily downloadable files or writing training manuals, [they] help to form the base that keeps the movement afloat.[56]

Indeed, much of what journalists attribute to the Islamic State actually comes from fans, who although they enthusiastically support the group are not members and have never been to Syria or Iraq. They are important for the Islamic State and how it is perceived online because there are so many of them and because they help to translate texts from Arabic into English or from English into other European languages, but also – and especially – because they Westernize these texts and ensure that they will resonate with a European audience. They are the ones who combine messages from the Islamic State with rap stars, Western brands and advertising slogans, and so make the group appear "cool".

A good example of this is the "five-star jihad" campaign advertising the Islamic State in mid-2013. The idea came not from the Islamic State itself, but from fans who wanted to use pictures of fighters splashing about, playing billiards and driving big cars to show how glamorous and simultaneously "normal" life was in the Islamic State. The campaign was a huge success, but the Islamic State had mixed feelings about it. That summer, the group issued several official videos in which fighters made plain that jihad was not a luxury holiday, but a serious undertaking. Anyone looking for adventure and big cars would be coming to the wrong place. "Brothers! When you come here, you're representing Islam," scolded one British fighter, "and that's how you have to act."[57]

The most important "jihobbyist" to date was called Shami Witness, an English-speaking blogger whose Twitter account had 20,000 followers at the last check. Shami provided the latest news, official statements, photos and rumours. He was the central hub where all kinds of information came together. His fans included supporters and sympathizers who'd stayed at home, but also hundreds of foreign fighters who got updates from his account about other parts of Syria.[58] Shami did not mince his words: he openly propagandized on behalf of the Islamic State and poured scorn on its enemies – not only Westerners and Shi'as, but also supporters of al-Nusra, whom he decried as "sick in the head".[59] When it emerged in autumn 2014 that Islamic State fighters had taken Yazidi women as slaves, Shami first passionately denounced the reports as "lies" and "propaganda",[60] then had to correct himself when *Dabiq* itself mentioned the practice and defended it as "Islamically correct".

For a long time, everyone assumed that Shami was English. But a team from the British television station Channel 4 discovered at the end of 2014 that he had previously changed the name on his Twitter account and that the former name matched that of his Facebook profile, which belonged to a software manager from Bangalore in southern India.[61] The "real" Shami was called Mehdi Masroor Biswas, a 24-year-old who, aside from making propaganda for jihad, had an entirely normal life, a family and a well-paid job, and liked to throw pizza parties with his friends.[62]

LONE WOLVES?

It is nothing new for terrorists to incite their followers to attacks without helping to carry them out. The anarchists in the late nineteenth century hoped that this would provide a simple means – without their needing to do anything – of unleashing the chaos they thought was necessary for bringing about a revolution (see Chapter 1). The Far Right discovered the same idea 100 years later: at the start of the 1990s, the American neo-Nazi ideologue Louis Beam (*1946) formulated the idea of "leader-less resistance" and so inspired the attack on a government building in Oklahoma City that killed 170 people.[63] Anwar al-Awlaki, the jihadist preacher who in the late 2000s called on his followers to perpetrate attacks in the West, was thus not the first to encourage "lone wolves". What differentiated him from his predecessors was the number of channels through which he could disseminate his thinking. He gave lectures first on VHS, then on DVD and – finally – on YouTube. He had a blog, was always available via email and published al-Qaeda's online magazine *Inspire*, which told readers how to "make a bomb in your mom's kitchen".[64] Thanks to the internet, al-Awlaki reached an audience of millions – and practically for free.

But even al-Awlaki's success was limited. Although almost every al-Qaeda-inspired attack on the West in the years before the Syrian conflict could be ascribed to his influence (see Chapter 2), the big breakthrough never came. Despite his popularity in the jihadist scene, by 2013 he had persuaded only a few dozen of his American followers to actually mount attacks – and most of them went awry or failed to make the headlines.[65] (The *Charlie Hebdo* attack in Paris, which took place four years after his death but was "encouraged" by him, may have been his greatest success; see Chapter 6.)

An important reason for this was that al-Awlaki's strategy seemed born of desperation. Al-Qaeda at the time was trying to carry out large-scale attacks: a second 9/11 or at least another London or Madrid. Any jihadist with ambition wanted to get to a training camp in Pakistan, become a "soldier" and then join a big, important operation. Lone wolves were seen as losers, wasting their lives on acts that no one would remember. Al-Awlaki expended a lot of energy on trying to change this perception. "She hasn't wasted her life," admonished

Inspire after Roshonara Choudhry stabbed her MP: "She has per-formed a service for the religion of God... All men sitting around at home should be ashamed of themselves!"[66]

Nevertheless, lone wolves only became heroes with the rise of the Islamic State – three years after al-Awlaki had been killed by an American drone. The beheadings of American and British hostages in summer 2014 showed that the group didn't need months of planning, highly complex operations or exploding buses and falling towers to terrorize the whole world. Even though "Jihadi John" was not a lone wolf and the beheadings took place not in Europe but in Syria, the message was clear: one man with a knife had humiliated America, forced a world power to its knees and placed its citizens in a state of fear. From that point on, lone attackers were no longer second-class terrorists, and everyone understood that a knife could be just as potent a weapon as a ton of explosive.

DOCTRINE

Ideologically, the Islamic State has always considered Western "crusaders" its enemies. The Islamic empire that it wants to create is a riposte to the West – and even the Arab states against which the group does most of its fighting are ideologically only a staging post on the way to the final confrontation described in the apoc-alyptic fantasies of Abu Musab al-Zarqawi and his followers (see Chapter 3). It would therefore be naive to imagine that the West could simply have avoided confronting the Islamic State: it is an aggressive, expansionist and anti-Western project with which con-flict was inevitable.

But it is true that the confrontation came earlier than the Islamic State itself had planned and that the group's original strategy did not envisage launching attacks in the West as early as became the case. Until mid-2014, its entire rhetoric was aimed at attracting young Western Muslims into the Islamic State and there had been no systematic call to assault Europe or America.

That changed with the start of the Western air strikes in August 2014. Within a few weeks, the Islamic State published a speech in which its spokesman Abu Mohammed al-Adnani (*1977) for the first time explicitly called for attacks in the West. Unlike al-Qaeda's strategy, the emphasis was not on big, spectacular operations, but on very simple, easily perpetrated acts of raw violence:

> If you can kill a disbelieving American or European – especially the spiteful and filthy French – or an Australian, or a Canadian, or any of the other disbelievers waging war [against us], including the citizens of the countries that entered into a coalition against the Islamic State, then rely upon Allah, and kill him in any manner or way however it may be. Smash his head with a rock, or slaughter him with a knife, or run him over with your car, or throw him down from a high place, or choke him, or poison him.[67]

The Islamic State's leadership understood that these kinds of attacks would incite just as much terror as the more sophisticated operations in which al-Qaeda once specialized (and which the Islamic State was also working on). It was aware that this type of strategy would lead to more results more quickly than large-scale plots, which required months of planning and were therefore easier for the security services to disrupt. In short: the lone wolves who had been derided only a few years earlier were now placed centre stage.

Two years later, nothing about this doctrine has changed.[68] In an audio message in May 2015, al-Baghdadi gave his followers two options. The emphasis was still on *hijrah* – emigration to the Islamic State – but if that were impossible, devout Muslims had to take up arms and fight the enemies of the Islamic State "wherever they may be".[69]

For al-Baghdadi, these appeals are not about "conquering Rome" or raising the black flag of Islam above Downing Street. That is all supposed to happen later. Rather, they are part of a strategy of asymmetrical warfare with which the group wants to hit Western governments where it hurts, that is, at home. With these and the more complex, al-Qaeda-style operations that we have witnessed in Paris and Brussels, it seems the Islamic State's aim is to provoke a Western overreaction, so that America and its allies either retreat from the conflict entirely or intervene on such a massive scale that it would give the Islamic State the opportunity to fight "Western occupiers" in Syria or Iraq.

IMPLEMENTATION

This doctrine was first implemented outside Europe. The first attacks took place in Canada: on 20 October 2014, a lone perpetrator tried to run over two soldiers near Montreal; two days later, there was a shooting at the Canadian parliament in Ottawa. In mid-December, a jihadist took hostages in the Australian city of Sydney; the perpetrator was a self-appointed preacher who had converted to Sunni Islam only a few weeks before. None of the attackers was a member of the Islamic State, nor had any fought in Syria or Iraq – but all were enthusiastic supporters.

At the end of the year, there were attacks in Europe, too. On 20 December, a 20-year-old Frenchman called Bertrand Nzohabonayo stormed a police station in a suburb of Tours, shouted "God is great" and stabbed three officers before he was killed. His story is almost identical to that of jihadist supporters and fighters elsewhere in Europe: the son of African immigrants, Bertrand had problems in

FIG. 5.2 Bertrand Nzohabonayo, a supporter who became a "lone wolf"

school and was in constant trouble with the police. Bertrand first tried to become a rapper and started his own YouTube channel, like many of his comrades, but ultimately converted to Islam and renamed himself Bilal.[70] He had little to do with the traditional mosque-centred Muslim communities around Tours. Instead he found information about Islam on the internet, became an active "fan" and made the Islamic State's black flag his Facebook profile picture.[71] Whether he knew about al-Adnani's statement cannot be established. But only a few days after his death, the online magazine *Dabiq* published an obituary praising Bertrand's actions and warning that there would be more attacks: "Others will follow his example."[72]

Indeed, within the next few days there were attacks in Dijon and Nantes – both attempts to run over pedestrians. Here, too, the perpetrators shouted, "God is great", but both had psychological problems and were therefore not categorized as terrorists by the French authorities.

At the start of January 2015 came the first attacks in Paris: jihadists stormed the editorial offices of the satirical magazine *Charlie Hebdo*, killing 12 people, and two days later another jihadist took hostages in a kosher supermarket, where four people died. In February, the pattern was repeated: a Danish supporter of the Islamic State attacked a podium discussion and a synagogue in Copenhagen. Then, too, people were killed and – shortly afterwards – the attacks were praised in *Dabiq*.[73]

With the exception of the *Charlie Hebdo* attackers (see Chapter 7), all these were carried out by supporters of the Islamic State, though none of them had been to Syria or received specific instructions from the group. They were labelled "lone wolves", even though many of them acted in twos and threes, were known to the police, had been part of the jihadist supporter scene for years and had at various times been under observation by the intelligence services. Lone perpetrators like Bilal, who became radicalized entirely on his own, remain the exception.[74]

The fact that ordinary supporters who were not deeply integrated into any jihadist group have been mobilized for terrorism so quickly and in such great numbers is a new and worrying phenomenon that will complicate the work of the security services. The "career paths" of supporters are hard to predict. Moreover, the "old jihadists" of al-Qaeda have not gone away: they are part of the new wave, too.

6

The American Exception?

ON THE MORNING OF 8 APRIL 2014, SHANNON CONLEY LEFT HER home in Arvada, just a few miles north of Denver, Colorado. When she arrived at Denver International Airport, everything seemed normal. The 19-year-old trainee nurse printed the boarding pass for a United Airlines flight to Frankfurt, Germany, and checked her baggage. After making her way through security, she sat down at her gate and waited until the flight was called. But Conley never boarded the plane. As she was walking down the jetway, FBI agents stopped and arrested her. It was the sudden end of her *hijrah* to the Islamic State – a trip she had planned for months.[1]

Conley was a tall, skinny girl with short hair and geeky glasses who didn't have many friends and liked to keep things to herself. One of her friends at college said she "tried out" several religions before "settling on Islam".[2] But even her parents didn't know what kind of Islam she adopted. Nor did they know that Conley was watching Anwar al-Awlaki's sermons. Or that she had fallen in love with a 32-year-old Tunisian man who was fighting for the Islamic State. Conley wasn't part of a mosque community, and she didn't hang out with other Muslims. Speaking to her FBI interrogators, she admitted that "her knowledge of Islam was based solely on her own research that she conducted on the Internet".[3]

Conley's idea of what jihad involved seemed to change over time. Initially, she told police interrogators that she had no intention of harming civilians, but that "defensive jihad" was legitimate, and that she would "assist Jihadi fighters in whatever manner is needed". Later, she talked about "guerrilla warfare" and lone wolves, saying that she was attracted to this way of fighting because she could "do it alone". After making contact with the Tunisian fighter, she became obsessed with "emigrating" to the Islamic State. Her role, she said, was to be a "housewife and camp nurse", producing the next generation of fighters while looking after those who had been wounded.[4]

Conley's case is both fascinating and disturbing. Not only because of her gender, unusual background and online conversion, or the willingness to entrust her life to a man she'd never met. But also because she knew that she was under FBI surveillance and seemed completely unfazed. In December 2013, she joined the US Army Explorers, a military cadet programme, which she hoped would provide her with the skills and training needed for violent jihad. When FBI agents confronted her that same month, she openly stated that "Jihad must

FIG. 6.1 Shannon Conley was radicalized via the internet and wanted to become a nurse in the Islamic State

be waged to protect Muslim nations". In the following months, the FBI tried to convince her to become involved in humanitarian work (which she rejected, saying it "does not solve the problem"). Eventually, the agents alerted her parents – to no avail.[5]

Instead, she became more deeply committed to her virtual boyfriend. When she eventually told her father that she wanted to "go marry a soldier", he refused permission, knowing that Islamic rules required the parents' consent. Conley's response was that she "disagreed with Islam on the issue and was going to travel and marry anyway".[6]

THE UNITED STATES VS EUROPE

Shannon Conley's story illustrates the weird and seemingly random ways in which Americans have connected to the jihadist movement. At the core of American home-grown jihadism is what appears to be a contradiction. Jihadists view America as the country whose global dominance and military aggression is the principal cause of all Muslim suffering. Yet those who are closest to the "head of the snake" – American Muslims – are less susceptible to jihadist ideology and violence than their European brethren. In the post-9/11 period, there have been fewer cases of home-grown radicalization in the United States than in Europe. Jihadist countercultures – like the ones described in the previous chapter – are practically unknown. And those who nevertheless become radicalized are often isolated loners and outcasts – like Conley or indeed Omar Mateen (1986–2016), who killed 49 people in a nightclub in Orlando, Florida, in June 2016 – who join the global movement via "virtual milieus" and act without being part of a structure or organization. In fact, the nine home-grown jihadist attacks in the United States since 11 September 2001 were all carried out by lone operators.[7]

For most of the post-9/11 period, home-grown jihadism in the United States was a tiny phenomenon. From 2001 to 2011, 205 US citizens or residents were charged with jihadist-related activities.[8] That's 20 people a year – far fewer than in Britain, for example, where the average was more than 40.[9] Less than half (90) wanted to carry out attacks within the United States. The majority (115) were involved in fundraising and propaganda, or wanted to become foreign fighters (especially in Somalia and Afghanistan). And of the 90 who wanted to attack at home, nearly a third resulted from so-called "sting operations" – a controversial FBI practice whereby informants assist would-be jihadists in plotting attacks they wouldn't otherwise be interested in or capable of.[10] All in all, the full extent of the home-grown threat in the decade after September 11 may have amounted to no more than 60 people.

How can this be explained? For Marc Sageman, a former CIA operative turned scholar, the principal reason lies in America's "national myths" and cultural values that make it easier for immigrants to become part of society. At their heart is the idea of the "melting pot" – the narrative that America is a nation of immigrants in which everyone's ancestors have, at some point, come from another country. Closely related is the concept of the American Dream – the promise of unlimited opportunity for those who work hard and play by the rules. None of these narratives are necessarily "true" for everyone in a factual or statistical sense – though they are "true enough" to be believed:

> The reality is that social mobility is probably not as great as advertised in the United States and is greater than advertised in Europe. But when dealing with perceptions, the promise of the American Dream still shines bright for most immigrants.[11]

According to Sageman, belief in the "American Creed" – "melting pot, the American Dream, individualism, and grassroots voluntarism" – explains why the jihadist narrative of "America at war with Islam" has failed to resonate more strongly.[12] More so than Europeans, American Muslims regard themselves as part of the national project. They choose to come to America because they want to be part of it. And the vast majority see no difficulty in reconciling their American and Muslim identities.[13]

Another, related, argument is that American jihadists have found it difficult to organize and build structures. For one, that's because of geography and the history of Muslim immigration. American Muslims aren't as homogeneous as their European counterparts: they didn't all arrive at the same time, and their countries of origin differ widely. Unlike their European counterparts, they haven't all clustered in the same places. Outside New York, Los Angeles, Dearborn, Michigan and Minneapolis, Muslim communities are spread across the country. And with the exception of the Somali community, Muslim "ghettos" – like those in the suburbs of Paris, Brussels or the north of England – are virtually unheard of.[14] This has produced a population that is more prosperous, more aspirational, and harder to reach – both physically and ideologically – for extremists whose message is built on grievance and rebellion.

Finally, Sageman believes that American Muslims' exposure to America – and Americans – makes them less willing to accept the jihadists' narrative and portrayal of their country. Unlike Muslims in Europe, they can distinguish between the US government, some of its policies and interests, and ordinary Americans whose views may be different – if not fundamentally opposed – to their government. They understand that it is possible to be patriotic without supporting the government, or blaming the people who carry out its policies. And they realize that turning against their country will have consequences for their families and their community. In Sageman's words, "It seems easier to be anti-American from afar than from within."[15]

FROM 9/11 TO BOSTON

The pattern of home-grown jihadist plots in the United States illustrates the movement's lack of space and ideological resonance: not only has the number of plots been small, there also is little evidence of organized structures or countercultures. For what little success they have had, American jihadists have relied on lone actors, people with extensive connections abroad, or – indeed – the internet, which enabled the American–Yemeni preacher Anwar al-Awlaki to be influential from abroad.

The two potentially most devastating plots were connected to Afghanistan and Pakistan. In September 2009, Najibullah Zazi (*1985) and two of his high-school friends wanted to blow themselves up on the New York City Subway – a plot that could have killed dozens of people. Zazi was an Afghan–American who had grown up in Queens but maintained deep ties to the place in eastern Afghanistan where he was born. From what is known, his radicalization didn't take place in America but during a trip to his country of birth from which he returned profoundly transformed: hostile to the Western lifestyle, angry at the United States, and with ties to al-Qaeda, whose head of external operations helped him plan the attack.[16]

Faisal Shahzad (*1979), who nearly succeeded in setting off a car bomb in New York's Times Square in May 2010, had turned against America over the course of several years. With a house in Connecticut, a secular wife and a career as a financial analyst, he seemed like an advertisement for the American Dream. Yet during trips to Pakistan, he connected with jihadists and eventually trained with the Pakistani Taliban.[17] What the two cases have in common is the lack of support structures within the United States: both Shahzad and Zazi had to go abroad in order to connect with the jihadist movement. And they actively hid their involvement from their local communities.

The one exception to the pattern of comparatively isolated and externally inspired attacks was the Somali community. Of the nearly 40 US citizens or residents who have been charged with supporting the jihadist group al-Shabaab between 2007 and 2014, three-quarters were ethnic Somalis who had been recruited in Little Mogadishu, the predominantly Somali neighbourhood of Minneapolis. Their intention wasn't to blow themselves up on the New York Subway but to join the group in Somalia. As a result, the first three Americans who became suicide bombers didn't die in the United States but as combatants in the Somali Civil War.[18] That so many of them came from Little Mogadishu was no coincidence. With high unemployment, low-paying jobs and few chances to move up or out, the area is more similar to the tightly knit, mono-cultural "ghettos" of Europe than the American melting pot.[19] This offered jihadist recruiters the perfect breeding ground in which to embed themselves, radicalize and recruit others.

The third – and probably most significant – cluster began as an actual group but migrated online when it failed to attract supporters and lost many members to infighting and arrests. It started in 2004 as the (pretentiously named) Islamic Thinkers Society and consisted of a dozen or so people who copied the "megaphone" tactics of al-Muhajiroun in Britain (see previous chapter). Based in New York City, they staged provocative protests, called for the nuclear destruction of Israel and praised jihadist terrorists wherever they could be found.[20] Like al-Muhajiroun, they invested much effort into their online presence, which became the group's main vehicle and attracted "fans" from across the country. Among their most gifted and prolific bloggers was Samir Khan (1985–2011), a Pakistani–American from Brooklyn, who started *Jihad Recollections* – the first online jihadist magazine in English.[21]

During the same period, al-Awlaki was becoming the most influential al-Qaeda promoter in the English language. Based in Yemen, he communicated with his American followers through online lectures, sermons, and via email, calling on them to take matters into their own hands. The strategy worked – but only to a limited extent. There remained a huge gap between the number of people who listened to al-Awlaki's lectures and those willing to take action. His most successful year was in 2009, when two of his supporters attacked the US military: Carlos Bledsoe (*1985), an African American convert, shot dead a soldier in Arkansas, and Major Nidal Hasan (*1970), an Army psychiatrist, killed 13 at Fort Hood, Texas.[22]

From 2010, the campaigns of al-Awlaki and whatever was left of the Islamic Thinkers Society began to merge. The physical link was Khan, who joined al-Awlaki in Yemen and launched al-Qaeda's online magazine *Inspire*. Though initially dismissed as "just another piece of propaganda",[23] *Inspire* became popular among English-speaking jihadists and set the tone for al-Qaeda's online campaign. It combined al-Awlaki's charisma and spiritual authority with Khan's talent for editing, presentation and catchy headlines ("what to pack for jihad", "how to build a bomb in your mom's kitchen"). The result was a powerful package that influenced would-be jihadists long after the two propagandists' death in a drone strike in September 2011. They had created the virtual milieu from which a majority of American jihadists during the coming years was going to emerge. This included the Tsarnaev brothers, Dzhokhar (*1993) and Tamerlan (1986–2013), who were fans of al-Awlaki. The instructions from *Inspire* enabled them to build the pressure-cooker bomb that killed three people and wounded over 200 at the Boston Marathon in April 2013.[24]

AMERICANS AND THE SYRIAN JIHAD

Like other Muslim communities, many American Muslims were outraged by the Syrian conflict and the plight of the country's Sunni population, whom they regarded as victims of a brutal campaign by the Syrian government. Although President Obama sided with the Sunni opposition and committed to overthrowing Assad, he was ultimately reluctant to become involved. Many American Muslims felt betrayed, but very few decided to participate in the conflict.[25] The principal reason for the lack of mobilization, especially compared to Europe, was that those American Muslims who may have wanted to fight in Syria didn't have the opportunity to turn intention into reality. The groups that were recruiting fighters in Europe and sent them on their way to Syria didn't have a presence in the United States. Foreign fighter recruitment in America relied on self-mobilization – principally the internet – which yielded limited returns.

Like their European brethren, American Muslims were exposed to a steady stream of news about atrocities and brutal violence from Syria. Like in Europe, the conflict came to be seen in increasingly sectarian terms. And there were Salafist preachers too who were fanning the flames, dehumanizing religious minorities and portraying the confrontation as an "existential threat" to Sunni Muslims. A prominent example is Ahmad Musa Jibril (*1972), a Palestinian–American cleric based in Dearborn, Michigan. When he got kicked out of his local mosque, Jibril embraced the internet and started publishing his sermons online. Many of them were "angry rants" directed at Western governments, Jews and Shi'as.[26] When the Syrian conflict started, he became one of the earliest cheerleaders of foreign fighting:

> If your heart doesn't melt to what's happening in Syria, then your faith is in doubt. Has the internet not carried through the genocide of what the *rafida* [derogatory term for Shi'as] are doing to your brothers? Are there no heroic souls with lofty ambitions? Are there no helpers and defenders of the righteous?[27]

But unlike his European counterparts, Jibril wasn't connected to any actual organization. He didn't run a group that could have channelled people's anger into action. Nor did he host meetings or have people who would have organized the trip to Syria, provided references or bought tickets. As a result, his impact remained limited – however popular his sermons may have been with "fanboys" on the internet.[28]

The total number of US citizens or permanent residents who have made it into Syria may be no more than 100. Prior to the emergence of the Islamic State, they often looked like Eric Harroun (1982–2014), a white convert from Colorado with a receding hairline and a winning smile who spent two months with the Free Syrian Army (FSA) and Jabhat al-Nusra in early 2013. He had served in the US Army, then worked in various dead-end jobs, converted to Islam, and eventually decided to travel the world. When the Syrian conflict broke out, he happened to be in Egypt and got caught up in the revolutionary spirit of the period. Following travels to Lebanon and Turkey, he ventured into Syria, where his previous military training made him an ideal recruit for the FSA.[29]

From what we know, Harroun had no connections with jihadists in the United States. He wasn't part of any jihadist scene, nor is there any indication that he became particularly pious during his time in Syria. On the contrary, his Facebook profile, which he regularly updated, was filled with jokes, links to music videos and references to Western popular culture, including pictures of what he claimed was his girlfriend (who had no Muslim name and wore no Islamic dress). What made him famous was a series of videos that showed him standing on pickup trucks, handling weapons or sitting among FSA fighters giving passionate – and occasionally funny – speeches against Assad's henchmen.[30] His association with al-Nusra lasted for just two weeks.

During a brief trip to Turkey in February 2013, he decided to quit fighting. After news broke that he had died in battle, he told a journalist: "Syrian media must be smoking something because I am alive and well chilling in Istanbul having a Martini."[31] When he flew back to the United States, he had no intention of attacking his country or immersing himself in the jihadist scene. Nor did he have the opportunity: upon arrival at Washington Dulles Airport, the FBI arrested and charged him. Following his trial and release, he became depressed, started taking drugs and died of a heroin overdose. Having survived one of the world's most vicious wars, Harroun still couldn't cope with being a nobody.

THE RISE OF THE ISLAMIC STATE

This is not to say that all American fighters were harmless buffoons. Abdullah Ramo Pazara (1976–2014) from St Louis, Missouri, rose through the ranks and led a unit of Islamic State fighters from the Balkans. Though it remains unclear quite how important he became (there are unconfirmed rumours that he served as deputy to Islamic State commander Omar al-Shishani), the pictures that he posted on Facebook show him taking part in numerous battles and attending a mass execution of Iraqi soldiers. In one message to a friend in America, he boasted that his unit had captured a prisoner who, he said, was going to be "slaughtered" the next day.[32]

Like other foreigners who were allowed to play meaningful military roles in the Islamic State, Pazara had received military training and is reported to have fought during the Bosnian War in the 1990s.[33] But his radicalization didn't happen until after he arrived in America in the early 2000s. Following the failure of a trucking company, which he started in 2004, he became more and more isolated, moved to various places, and eventually ended up in St Louis, where he befriended a tiny group of Bosnian Salafists who continued to raise money for him after he had left for Syria in early 2013.[34] Like many others, he died in the battle for Kobane in the fall of 2014.

Unlike Pazara, many American would-be jihadists never made it to Syria. By the end of January 2016, US prosecutors had charged 80 Americans with Islamic State related offences, especially fund-raising and attempting to join. More than three-quarters (61) were indicted in 2015 alone.[35] Part of this may have been a greater willing-ness by prosecutors to step in and bring charges. But it also reflected a real and significant increase in radicalization, which followed the group's caliphate declaration and rapid expansion in the second half of 2014. From the perspective of would-be jihadists, making *hijrah* now involved becoming part of a new, exciting and seemingly all-powerful project – a utopia that was open to men, women and even families.

Most important, the rise of the Islamic State spurred the crea-tion of a virtual counterculture through which most of the American would-be jihadists connected with the movement. The story of Mohammed Hamzah Khan, a 19-year-old engineering student from Chicago, and his younger sister and brother is typical. Over the course of several months, the three siblings became immersed in Islamic State propaganda, spending many hours a day watching videos and chatting with "fanboys". One day, Mohammed connected with a man who introduced himself as Abu Qaqa and offered to facilitate their journey to Syria. Following his instructions, the Khans applied for passports, bought tickets and wrote down phone numbers, which Abu Qaqa told them to ring once they had arrived in Istanbul.[36] By September 2014, they were ready to go.

What attracted Khan and his siblings was no longer the Syrian conflict but the caliphate as a perfect Islamic society. Writing to his parents, he explained:

[A]n Islamic State has been established and it is thus obligatory upon every able bodied male and female to migrate there... I want to be ruled by the shariah, the best law for all mankind...

I [also] do not want my progeny to be raised in a filthy environment like this. We are all witness that the Western societies are getting more immoral day by day.

Lastly... I extend an invitation to [you, my parents] to join me in the Islamic State. True, it is getting bombed, but let us not forget that we didn't come to this world for comfort.[37]

Needless to say, none of the Khans ever reached their "Promised Land".[38] Like the journeys of Shannon Conley and others, their trip to Syria ended at their local airport.

The only face-to-face grassroots cluster in the United States emerged – once again – among the Somali community in Minneapolis. Starting in 2014, the networks that had facilitated travel to Somalia during the late 2000s were now used to recruit people for the Islamic State. And again, the dynamics were more similar to those in Europe

FIG. 6.2   Mohammed Hamzah Khan spent many hours a day watching jihadist videos and chatting to "fanboys"

than the "virtual" recruitment that happened in much of the rest of the United States: one or two left for Syria, stayed in touch with their friends, and successively brought them over. Within less than two years, more than 15 Somali-Americans had tried to make their way into the caliphate. They weren't random acquaintances who had connected on social media. As Lorenzo Vidino and Seamus Hughes point out, they "grew up in the same community, attended the same schools, and worshiped at the same mosque".[39]

THREATS TO THE HOMELAND

Despite the ongoing threat, Americans have reason to be confident. The next wave of terror will affect them less severely than the Europeans. The number of Americans who have succeeded in joining the Islamic State is comparatively small. With few exceptions, there are no formalized structures and networks, no "real world" clusters and megaphone jihadists, that facilitate recruitment. And the reason those structures don't exist is because American Muslims are less receptive to the jihadist narrative, better integrated into the American mainstream, and – generally – more at ease with being Western and Muslim than their European brethren. America, therefore, remains the exception.

The bad news is that, even in America, there exists a virtual counter-culture that has drawn citizens and residents into the Islamic State's orbit. The internet may not be as powerful as a recruitment tool as many claim, but it has inspired and mobilized a (small) number of Americans who consider themselves part of the Islamic State – and are willing to fight and die for it.

The risk of complex, externally organized attacks is smaller than in Europe: there are only a few Americans who have joined the Islamic State, and therefore just a tiny number of returnees that US security agencies need to worry about. Also, the United States are harder to reach for Islamic State fighters from Syria and Iraq than Europe. As Peter Bergen put it:

> You can drive from France to Syria and back. You can't drive from Syria to New York City. That presents a hurdle for terrorists trained in Syria, who would have to board a plane to the States and who might well be on a watch list.[40]

Even so, there remains a risk that home-grown terrorists will strike as lone operators, that is, without being part of a jihadist command and control structure. Indeed, other than attacks against American citizens and interests abroad, the danger of home-grown, Islamic State inspired attacks is the most immediate threat to the United States.

Some of this threat has materialized already. In May 2015, two gunmen attempted to attack a community centre in Garland, Texas, which hosted a Prophet Mohammed cartoon exhibition. One of the attackers, Elton Simpson (1985–2015), had previously tried to travel to Somalia and had been convicted for lying to the FBI. In early 2015, he reached out to Islamic State fighters via social media and discussed the operation. Just before it was launched, he and his partner sent messages from their Twitter account, declaring their allegiance to the caliph and announcing the operation. In the end, they were shot dead by a police officer before they could do any harm.[41]

Far more dramatic was the shooting in San Bernardino, California, in December 2015. The attackers, Syed Rizwan Farook (1987–2015) and Tashfeen Malik (1986–2015), a married couple of Pakistani descent, killed 14 people at a function at a public health centre. During a search of their house, investigators found nearly 20 self-made bombs, suggesting that this wasn't going to be their only target. Like the would-be shooters at Garland, they had declared their allegiance to the Islamic State, which – in turn – claimed their attack and referred to them as "soldiers" who had achieved "martyrdom".

Six months later, in early June 2016, Omar Mateen, a 29-year-old security guard from Orlando, Florida, carried out the most deadly attack of the current "wave". Late on a Saturday night, he entered a gay nightclub and shot dead 49 people. Like in all the previous cases, the information that is currently available suggests that he had no formal connection to the Islamic State, but was radicalized online and declared his allegiance to the group only minutes before the attack – via a phone call to the local police department.

In some respects, these stories are perfect illustrations of the nature of American home-grown jihadism. Malik, for example, failed to find jihadists in her local community.[42] She reached out to fighters and jihadist groups via social media, but was turned down repeatedly.[43] In the end, becoming a lone wolf appeared to be the only option in a country where the security agencies are (hyper) vigilant and Muslim communities resilient.

7

Al-Qaeda

TWO WEEKS BEFORE CHRISTMAS 2013, INSTEAD OF WRAPPING presents in England or Germany, I was sitting under a tree in sweltering heat in the provincial Somalian town of Baidoa. That morning I had arrived by helicopter from Mogadishu with a team from the United Nations. We were there to inspect a new facility built for former al-Shabaab militants.

The jihadist group, which has been officially allied with al-Qaeda since 2012, had been pushed back from large parts of the country in the preceding months, which meant that thousands of fighters were suddenly out of a job – and no one knew whether they were still dangerous or not. The purpose of this facility was to reintegrate these fighters into civilian life.

I found the project interesting, but what had really brought me here was the opportunity to speak to young men who had been fighting for al-Shabaab only a few weeks earlier. After lunch it was time: five former members sat down with me under the tree and I had two hours in which to get a better idea of who they were and what motivated them.

Of course I was aware how little could be discovered in such a brief time, and that my interlocutors were being closely watched.

I was not hoping for a comprehensive interview, but for a first impression.

Four of the five were what the Australian author David Kilcullen calls "accidental guerrillas":[1] simple people without jobs or education who'd suddenly become part of an army in which they fought for an ideological agenda that they neither really knew nor fully understood. What motivated them were the "two dollars a day" that al-Shabaab paid them, or they had simply been caught up in the turmoil of Somalia's apparently endless – and endlessly complicated – civil war. To the Americans they were terrorists and "members of al-Qaeda", but in reality none of them was a "global jihadist" like bin Laden or many of the Europeans who go to war in Syria.

They represent an aspect of the jihadist phenomenon often over-looked in the media: wherever jihadists participate in civil wars, con-trol territory and pay wages, there are local recruits who fight for them but have little to do with their global objectives – war against America, "crusaders and Zionists". Only the fifth former fighter I was sitting with in Baidoa was familiar with al-Shabaab's ideology and had actu-ally met a foreign fighter. "I wanted to join al-Shabaab because they promised to introduce Sharia," he said.

The fact that global jihad has two faces – a global and a local face – has become more apparent than ever since the Arab Spring and the resultant upheaval in the Middle East, because there are now more Muslim countries in a state of tumult, where conflicts are playing out or uncertainty dominates, and therefore more opportunities for jihadists to establish themselves, take territory and build up state structures. This local foundation is why al-Qaeda has survived the rise of the Islamic State in countries like Somalia and why the "old jihadists" still have a role to play in the fifth wave of terrorism.

It is true, however, that al-Qaeda has lost support in many places and is being challenged by the Islamic State even in strongholds like

Yemen. Al-Qaeda has lost its role as the vanguard and leader of global jihad and even jihadists are discussing whether the group should continue to exist.[2] The competition between various groups has created an important new dynamic that could lead to attacks in Europe – whether because local groups like al-Nusra provide a base for their internationalist comrades; because effective al-Qaeda subsidiaries like al-Qaeda in the Arabian Peninsula (AQAP) successfully carry out attacks on the West; or because rivalry with the Islamic State forces al-Qaeda to reassert itself.

AL-NUSRA

The break between the Islamic State and al-Nusra that took place in spring 2013 was dramatic and deeply scarring. Al-Baghdadi's claim that al-Nusra was merely a subsidiary of ISIS (see Chapter 3) was vehemently rejected by al-Julani, the group's leader. In a speech in April he argued that al-Nusra had been an independent project since the outset and went on to "renew" his oath of loyalty to al-Qaeda's chief, al-Zawahiri.[3] Al-Baghdadi accused him of desertion and added that, according to this opinion, ISIS and its Iraqi predecessor, the Islamic State in Iraq, had been separate from al-Qaeda since 2006 (something that al-Julani, who was a member of the group throughout, had apparently not realized).[4] Several mediation attempts failed and, in February 2014, al-Zawahiri lost patience, came down on the side of al-Nusra and announced that ISIS was being ejected from al-Qaeda. For its part, ISIS blocked attempts at reconciliation by renaming itself the Islamic State and proclaiming the caliphate, which meant that in the event of a reconciliation with al-Nusra, the latter would have to submit to al-Baghdadi's authority. In short, it is now practically impossible for them to merge as equals. From al-Nusra's perspective – and from that of al-Qaeda as a whole – the Islamic State is arrogant and lacking in respect. "It's like a cancer," one of al-Qaeda's chief ideologues said recently.[5]

The "irreconcilability" of the two groups is also due to how much blood has been shed on both sides. While al-Nusra and ISIS were still cooperating on various fronts in summer 2013, they had turned against each other almost everywhere by that autumn. In January 2014 open war broke out. The most costly battles were in the Syrian provinces of Aleppo and Idlib, where hundreds of jihadists who had fought side by side only a year earlier were killed. The conflict has never formally ended, but its intensity and the frequency of actual fighting have gone up and down since late summer 2014. Both groups have consolidated their own territory and now often stay out of the other's way.[6] At the end of May 2015, around 10 per cent of the Syrian population was living in territory controlled by al-Nusra either on its own or in collaboration with other groups, most of them in the two strongholds of Idlib in the north-west and Daraa in the far south.[7]

But what difference is there between the two groups and why is al-Nusra often considered less dangerous? The main disparity is not ideological: both are jihadist groups with a Salafist agenda based on the same ideologues, even though al-Nusra appears to be less strict on implementation and has so far refrained from the more gruesome elements of life under the Islamic State: beheadings, enslavement, sexual violence and the mass displacement and execution of religious minorities. The biggest difference is in strategy: while al-Nusra considers itself a Syrian group whose chief priority is to bring down the Assad regime, the Islamic State has been a global, transnational project from the very beginning. This is why it is the Islamic State that presents an immediate threat to Europe, although that is not to say that al-Nusra is harmless, let alone a potential Western ally. Al-Nusra, too, ultimately wants a caliphate, has recruited European fighters, sees itself as part of a global movement and could easily mobilize its forces for a conflict with the West.

LOCAL AGENDA

Until now, al-Nusra has concentrated exclusively on the conflict in Syria. The prima facie – and perhaps most important – reason for that lies in the group's structure. Unlike the Islamic State, al-Nusra is 70 per cent Syrian and is also led and dominated by Syrians.[8] The story of Bashar and Hisham, two fighters from near Palmyra, is typical. We met them in a café in the Turkish border town Reyhanli, where they were recuperating from fighting in Syria. They had been among the first activists, taking to the streets against Assad at the start of 2011, filming the demonstrations and posting the videos on YouTube. When the conflict escalated, they wanted to fight. Al-Nusra was not the first group they got involved with, but in their opinion it is the best: "In contrast to the Free Syrian Army, al-Nusra is honest and treats the population well," Hisham told us. Bashar added: "They are the bravest, the best fighters: real lions." It doesn't bother them that al-Nusra is a jihadist organization. "When Bashar [al-Assad] murdered our families, no one came to help us. Only the [jihadists] fought beside us, and we're grateful," explained Bashar.

They said Islam was their religion and that a free Syria should be governed Islamically. Precisely how that would work they didn't know, but they didn't want to have anything to do with the "foreigners" of the Islamic State. "We're for democracy, but an Islamic, Syrian one," said Hisham.[9] In their ideological indifference they resemble the Somalian al-Shabaab fighters I met in Baidoa: for them, it is not primarily about the West, America or Europe, but about "their" country, "their" village and "their" family. Al-Qaeda's "global jihad" does not interest them and they do not consider themselves a part of it.

Another important factor is the group's coalition strategy. Having learnt from the failure in Iraq, where local tribes turned against al-Qaeda in the mid-2000s (see Chapter 3), al-Nusra has emphasized local alliances – even when the other groups are not fully on board with the Salafist agenda. Unlike the Islamic State, al-Nusra has never intended to dominate the uprising, but considers itself one partner in it, or better yet: the first among equals. In the internecine war against ISIS, al-Baghdadi's troops found themselves facing not just al-Nusra but also a coalition of Islamist and Salafist groups – the Syrian Islamic Front. And in the city of Idlib, an al-Nusra stronghold, the group does not govern alone, but in collaboration with the Islamic Front.

Even though al-Nusra has recently been undertaking more solo efforts, the group values this coalition, which makes it stronger and protects it against external attacks.[10] When the United States bombed al-Nusra training camps in autumn 2014, al-Nusra's partners supported them. "We are all al-Nusra" appeared as a slogan on posters and the internet.[11] The other side of this coin is that the group has to subordinate its ambitions beyond Syria to the interests of its coalition partners. They and their sponsors – many of them in Gulf states – have no interest in a war against America and Europe, and as long as that remains the case, it probably won't happen.[12]

GLOBAL POTENTIAL

But the strategic straitjacket that al-Nusra's local alliances have tied it into is no guarantee that the group will not act as an incubator for terrorist attacks in the West. Foreign fighters are one of the main dangers here. Granted, al-Nusra has fewer of them and they do not exercise the same influence on the group's character or direction as they do for ISIS. Moreover, al-Nusra's foreigners are usually of higher "quality" – there are hardly any "gangstas", failures or confused newcomers who've just discovered Islam and are "doing jihad".[13] But ideologically, al-Nusra's foreign fighters can hardly be distinguished from those of the Islamic State. They, too, are ultimately fighting not for the Syrians or their own families, school friends or compatriots, but for the abstract idea of the *Ummah*, the global community of Muslims – and some of their number fall into the category of "dangerous", just as some are "disillusioned" and some will simply disappear after their return to Europe (see Chapter 4).

One of those who can certainly be categorized as "dangerous" is Ismail Jabbar, from Middlesex on the outskirts of London, whom my team has been following for some time. The 22-year-old was a retail trainee in a big London department store before he set off for Syria in autumn 2013.[14] He has already taken part in numerous operations with al-Nusra and posted several pictures of himself with dead Syrian soldiers. He has little time for al-Nusra's restraint when it comes to beheadings: "All the brothers want to behead someone, but no one gets a chance," he explained in spring 2014 on the website Ask.fm. In his opinion, the focus on Syria is also wrong: "Someone needs to just grab a knife and do some damage outside subway just inspiring the believers," he wrote on Twitter. And shortly afterwards: "Just blow a petrol station up. How hard is it?"[15] Statements like this have nothing to do with al-Nusra's official strategy, but people like Jabbar – who've learnt their "trade" under al-Nusra – could go on to join other, more radical groups, or pursue their objectives on their own initiative.

Al-Nusra's connections with jihadists in other parts of the world are equally worrying. The group's leaders consider them "brothers" despite their strategic differences; they give them shelter and so act as accomplices in the others' terrorist campaigns. In summer 2014, for example, it emerged that AQAP bomb makers were guests in Syria, where they were developing new explosive charges that could be hidden in phones and laptops. The subsequent heightening of security at Western airports had nothing to do with the Islamic State, but was because of al-Nusra, in whose territory the Yemeni "delegation" was staying.[16] Less than two months later, the Americans bombed al-Nusra positions, claiming their target was a training camp for a new group called Khorasan. In truth, there was no such group. "Khorasan" consisted of al-Qaeda envoys from the tribal areas of Pakistan who had been invited to Syria to share their expertise in making booby traps and suicide vests with their Syrian "brothers".[17] This connection was neither surprising nor coincidental: al-Nusra remains part of the "jihadist international" and anyone who believes it represents a "moderate alternative"[18] to the Islamic State is playing with fire.

AQAP

From a European perspective, one of the most important – and most dangerous – al-Qaeda groups at the moment is AQAP, which was founded by a merger of the Saudi and Yemeni al-Qaeda subsidiaries. In the mid-2000s, the Saudis had come under so much pressure in their homeland that dozens fled over the border just as a spectacular prison break put the entire Yemeni leadership back in circulation. At the start of 2009, they created an organization that included the most experienced and dedicated jihadists in the world. Many were compatriots of bin Laden, knew him personally and had become fighters because of him.[19]

The group's long-standing leader, the Yemeni Nasir al-Wuhayshi (1976–2015), killed by an American drone strike in June 2015, was a bin Laden loyalist. He met the al-Qaeda chief when he was only 21, gained his trust and became one of his personal assistants. In 2001, when bin Laden was surrounded by American and Afghan troops in the mountains of Tora Bora, al-Wuhayshi was one of his bodyguard. After that, their paths diverged: while bin Laden stayed in

Pakistan, al-Wuhayshi fled to Iran, was imprisoned there and, after a few months, deported to Yemen.[20]

In prison, al-Wuhayshi had time to plan, reflect and – most importantly of all – to succeed in establishing himself as leader of the group. His relationship with bin Laden was not his only asset; he was also effective, humble and charismatic – personal qualities that made him popular among ordinary foot soldiers. "I was fascinated by him," admitted Morten Storm, a Danish former jihadist who spent several days with al-Wuhayshi. "He had the same softly spoken humility as his mentor bin Laden, and exuded the same charisma. His fighters loved him and would do anything for him."[21]

While in prison, al-Wuhayshi closely followed the collapse of al-Qaeda in Iraq (AQI) and drew the same conclusions as al-Julani (see Chapter 3). The organization he created in Yemen prioritized displaying a Yemeni face. Al-Wuhayshi and AQAP implemented the concept of "Islamic statehood" before the Islamic State did it. He spent lots of time with tribal leaders and married dozens of his fighters to their daughters.[22] He had no interest in foreign fighters for a long time and would send them on to Somalia or Pakistan. In areas controlled by AQAP, he founded Sharia courts to provide law and order, but exercised restraint in imposing "Islamic" punishments. Instead, his men repaired damaged roads, dug wells and connected villages to the electrical grid. "Taking care of things like food, electricity and water has a great effect," he wrote later. "We won a lot of sympathy that way."[23]

Indeed, two years after it was founded, AQAP had risen to become an important player in the Yemeni Civil War, occupying territory in three provinces, controlling two mid-sized cities and commanding thousands of tribal fighters in addition to its own troops. In March 2011, al-Wuhayshi proclaimed the province of Abyan to be a quasi-independent state with himself as emir.

But despite all his successes in Yemen, al-Wuhayshi had not lost sight of the "global jihad". On the contrary, the foundations he had laid domestically were to support the pursuit of his global ambitions. That was the difference between him and al-Julani. For al-Wuhayshi it was not a case of either/or: he considered the local and global dimensions of jihad to be complementary, two sides of the same coin.

So in parallel to his local expansion, he built up a foreign operations unit to carry out attacks abroad. He also supported the Yemeni–American preacher Anwar al-Awlaki and his online magazine *Inspire*, which was actually produced in Yemen. One of his most important associates was Ibrahim Hassan al-Asiri (*1982), a Saudi who studied chemistry and made bombs for AQAP. In August 2009, al-Asiri sent his own brother on a suicide mission with explosives hidden in his rectum. Al-Asiri built the explosive charges for underwear- and

FIG. 7.1 The Yemeni jihadist Nasir al-Wuhayshi, leader of AQAP and member of the al-Qaeda high command until his death in June 2015

parcel-bomb plots aiming to blow up aeroplanes in the skies above America. And he was behind the phone and laptop bombs developed in Syria in the summer of 2014. He was considered so dangerous that he spent years on the FBI's Most Wanted list.[24]

Al-Wuhayshi had no great liking for the Islamic State. He was a proponent of bin Laden's vision and al-Zawahiri's probable successor as head of al-Qaeda. From his perspective, al-Baghdadi was a renegade who had distorted and betrayed his mentor's legacy. But even AQAP, the most successful and aggressive of the al-Qaeda groups, has been put under pressure by the rise of the Islamic State. Two of its units have deserted since summer 2014 and declared their loyalty to al-Baghdadi.[25] That does not present an existential problem for al-Wuhayshi's successor, because the group is strong enough to survive breakaways of this sort. But for the first time since it was founded, AQAP is facing competition from a more extreme organization that is successfully luring away its members.[26]

For the past two years, the group has consciously positioned itself as Yemen's "moderate alternative" to the Islamic State and condemned beheadings and attacks on Shi'i mosques[27] – in the knowledge that those actions are opposed by the tribes and local groups with which it is allied. But external pressure has mounted on AQAP to take the lead in the jihadist cause and – even more importantly – to prove that al-Qaeda still has a role to play in it.

COMPETITION

For the first time since the war in Afghanistan in the 1980s, the movement is deeply divided. Of course there have always been a variety of groups and tendencies with differing aims, strategies and tactics. But al-Qaeda was the first – and for a long time, the only – group that made itself a global champion of jihad and claimed to lead the fight against the West. The collaboration between local groups, which strove to overthrow their own countries, and al-Qaeda, which fought against the West, often appeared such a matter of course that Osama bin Laden was seen as the "leader" of the jihadist movement and "jihadism" and "al-Qaeda" were used interchangeably.

The American counterterrorism strategy of June 2011 referred to the entire movement as "al-Qaeda" and differentiated merely between the (al-Qaeda) leadership, (al-Qaeda) subsidiaries and (al-Qaeda) supporters.[28] The notion that there were jihadist groups with no connection to al-Qaeda – and who didn't want any connection – was unimaginable in Washington at the time. That was why many Western governments overlooked the internal tensions and ruptures caused by the Arab Spring and failed to either realize or take seriously that the Islamic State was becoming a new locus of power with a strategy of its own. As late as February 2014, when the Islamic State already controlled a third of Syria and was storming one Iraqi town after another, President Obama compared the group to a bunch of amateurs.[29]

In reality, the two groups became rivals in 2013, with the Islamic State – not al-Qaeda – directing the tempo and the tone of the conflict. That was most markedly the case in the Middle East, where it had been practically impossible for al-Qaeda to operate openly before the Arab Spring. For the first time in decades, jihadists in countries like Egypt, Tunisia and Libya had an opportunity to come out publicly for their cause. And although many of the new groups did not initially commit themselves one way or the other, the majority tended towards the Islamic State. Even in long-established al-Qaeda subsidiaries there was conflict between opponents and supporters of al-Baghdadi, with the older generation – often Afghanistan veterans who had known bin Laden personally – staying loyal to al-Qaeda while the younger generation wanted to join the newer, more dynamic and (seemingly) more successful Islamic State (see Appendix B). Bin Laden's successor, al-Zawahiri, is playing only a bit part in this power struggle: he controls no troops, is far from the action (probably in Pakistan) and can exert influence solely because some of the movement's leaders feel morally obligated to him by their oath of loyalty. "There is no organisation, only a few channels of communication and loyalty," explained Muhammad al-Maqdisi, one of the group's most important ideologues. "Al-Qaeda today is based on the loyalty principle."[30]

INCORPORATION, SPLIT, TAKEOVER

There are three models for the expansion of the Islamic State, and the first is the wholesale *incorporation* of other groups. This is what happened with Boko Haram, the Nigerian group that developed out of a Salafist sect in the 2000s and has been fighting for an Islamic state since 2009 by carrying out attacks on Christians, non-Salafist Muslims, government officials and the military. Boko Haram was never an official affiliate of al-Qaeda but was courted for years by bin Laden. The Nigerians received support from al-Qaeda in the Islamic Maghreb (AQIM) and from al-Shabaab in Somalia. Bin Laden wrote its leaders several letters from his hideout in Pakistan.[31] For a long time, most experts assumed that Boko Haram had some kind of "relationship" with al-Qaeda, even though it was often said that the group was "too brutal even for al-Qaeda".[32]

As late as May 2014, the UN Security Council comprehensively described the connections between Boko Haram and AQIM.[33] But less than two months later, Boko Haram released a video showering praise on al-Baghdadi. And in March 2015, its leader announced Boko Haram's incorporation into al-Baghdadi's caliphate. In less than a year, al-Qaeda had lost Boko Haram to the internal competition.

More common than the incorporation of entire groups, however, is that these groups *split*, for example the Pakistani Taliban, whose official name is Tehrik-i-Taliban Pakistan (TTP). Already in 2013 there was a lot of upheaval within the group after its leader was killed by an American drone strike. The group could not agree on a replacement who would be acceptable to all its factions and regional subgroups.[34] So from mid-2014 onwards, the Islamic State – through no effort of its own – began to attract frustrated and disappointed jihadists who were looking for a new, more exciting project. In October, five regional leaders from the Pakistani tribal areas declared that they had switched allegiance to the Islamic State. They were followed by several hundred foot soldiers. As a result, a movement that was still relatively unified a few weeks beforehand now consisted of two rival – if not hostile – camps.[35] In January 2015, al-Baghdadi formalized the split, officially recognized the deserters' group, accepted them into the Islamic State and put them under his own command as the province of Khorasan.[36]

This does not mean that the Islamic State's triumph in Pakistan is inevitable. In March 2015, a splinter group that had left the Pakistani Taliban in 2014 returned to the fold. And at the end of May, the group published a confident statement in which it explained to its supporters why it had rejected al-Baghdadi's caliphate. Attacks on Shi'as and other "heretics" might be ideologically justified, the group said, but they were "unwise" because they were condemned by the population. There was also no point in fighting too many enemies at the same time and even the Prophet had counselled against doing so.[37] It would therefore be premature to completely write off the Pakistani Taliban. The most likely outcome is a long and (for outsiders) complicated power struggle in which the rival groups and leaders steal one another's followers and try to grab attention through ever larger and more spectacular operations.[38]

The third model is that of the *hostile takeover*. The best example is in Libya, where al-Qaeda initially seemed to have the upper hand. Immediately after the fall of Gaddafi in autumn 2011, al-Zawahiri called on his fellow campaigners to establish Libya as a new base for al-Qaeda. An envoy was sent to drive forward the setting up of a new organization. Al-Qaeda's starting point was the port city of Derna, which had always been a stronghold of the jihadist movement and had provided al-Qaeda with hundreds of fighters in Iraq during the war.[39] There and in Benghazi, branches of the jihadist group Ansar al-Sharia were formed in 2012 and 2013 – carrying out the attack on the US consulate in 2012. Most experts at the time assumed that they were closely linked to al-Qaeda. An official American report, which appeared before the attack on the consulate, argued that although Ansar al-Sharia was not an al-Qaeda subsidiary, it "embodied the al-Qaeda presence in Libya".[40]

The situation abruptly changed when the Islamic State also turned its attention to Libya. In April 2014, 200 Libyans who had fought for the Islamic State in Syria returned to Derna and founded a new group, Majlis Shura Shabab al-Islam ("Shura Council for Islamic youth"), in direct competition with Ansar al-Sharia.[41] The pattern was the same as in Syria and Iraq. The group established a court, founded a religious police, dominated first one part of the city, then several, made alliances with some groups and went into battle against others. Members of Ansar al-Sharia were invited to join the Shura Council and those who refused were mercilessly persecuted.[42] Six months later, al-Baghdadi sent an envoy that has led the group since then and is pushing its expansion into other parts of the country. In the meantime, the three provinces carved out by the Islamic State in Libya have absorbed hundreds of members of Ansar al-Sharia, mounted attacks in every major city and trained as many as 3,000 foreign fighters, most of them Tunisian and Algerian.[43] Among them were the perpetrators of the attacks on the Bardo Museum and the Sousse beach resort in Tunisia.[44]

It is not for nothing that Libya has become a magnet for jihadist groups, first al-Qaeda and now the Islamic State. Just as in other countries, the jihadists have profited from instability and chaos. In the absence of a functioning government, they can act openly and attract people to their cause. Moreover, their totalitarian vision of society becomes appealing because it promises "total order" (see Chapter 3) in a country previously ruled arbitrarily.

This connection between chaos and the desire for order is one of the most important explanations for why jihadist groups have gained in popularity since 2011, as the Arab Spring has brought not the greater peace, prosperity and stability many originally hoped for, but, above all, a high degree of uncertainty.[45] Libya is the most extreme example of this. A report by the US State Department in 2013 summed up the situation there in the following terms:

> [A] central government with weak institutions and only tenuous control over its expansive territory; the ubiquity of uncontrolled weapons and ammunition; porous and inaccessible borders; heavily armed militias and tribes with varying loyalties and agendas; high unemployment among young males along with slow-moving economic improvement; divisions between the country's regions, towns, and tribes; political paralysis due to infighting and distrust among and between Libya's political actors; and the absence of a functioning police force or national army.[46]

Experts consider each and every one of these points to be a risk factor for the emergence of extremist groups.[47] The presence of so many of these factors in a single country indicates that Libya – just like Yemen, Iraq or Syria – will continue to provide a base for jihadists for years to come.

EUROPE

Neither the Islamic State nor al-Qaeda is fighting for territory in Europe, but Europe is an important theatre of war for both. Al-Qaeda has never altered its strategy of focusing on the West and the Islamic State, too, has come to see the continent as enemy territory, where attacks are legitimate while the West drops bombs in Syria and Iraq. Although the attack on *Charlie Hebdo* was claimed by AQAP, the hostage siege in a kosher supermarket in Paris, the three further attacks in Paris and the attack in Copenhagen (see Chapter 5) were all carried out by supporters of the Islamic State. It is conceivable that the two groups' foot soldiers will come together in an ad-hoc way for future European operations, but it is more likely that they will compete against each other, since al-Qaeda in particular has an interest in mounting spectacular attacks on the West to strengthen its profile.

COOPERATION

After the January 2015 attacks on *Charlie Hebdo* and a kosher supermarket, there was much speculation that they had been a collaboration between al-Qaeda and the Islamic State. The media reported that the attacks – each of which was claimed by one or the other – had been "coordinated" on the principle that "the enemy of my enemy is my friend".[48] All that was lacking from this theory was the proof: neither al-Qaeda nor the Islamic State took responsibility for the other organization's attack. And there was no other evidence that the leaders of the two groups had made an agreement. On the contrary, the Islamic State and al-Qaeda are hostile to each other in practically every Middle Eastern country, steal each other's supporters and are pursuing different aims in their European operations. Why would they be working together?

The answer lies – as so often – in the jihadist counterculture. The three perpetrators were radicalized in Paris during the Iraq War in 2003, knew one another from the jihadist scene and had become close friends. Chérif (1982–2015) and Saïd (1980–2015) Kouachi, the two brothers responsible for the attack on *Charlie Hebdo*, had come into contact with a radical preacher who convinced Chérif to go to Iraq as a fighter. He ended up not in Iraq, however, but in a French prison, where he got to know Amedy Coulibaly (1982–2015), the hostage-taker in the kosher supermarket.[49] In the late 2000s, all three were part of the jihadist milieu in Paris, supported al-Qaeda and dreamt of fighting for AQAP. But only Chérif and his brother – not Coulibaly – made it to Yemen, where they trained with AQAP and were instructed by al-Awlaki to carry out an attack in Europe.[50] When the time came – almost four years later – Coulibaly had already thrown in his lot with the Islamic State. But that changed nothing about his friendship with the Kouachis. It didn't matter that the brothers had started to work for "the competition"; he supported their operation and wanted to help them with an attack of his own.

What happened in Paris is symptomatic of the situation all over Europe. The jihadist milieus are split between supporters of al-Qaeda and the Islamic State, but there has not yet been any open hostility

FIG. 7.2 The *Charlie Hebdo* attackers Chérif and Saïd Kouachi, who trained with AQAP in Yemen

between them. The old fighters in particular, those who were radicalized before the war in Syria and have been supporters of al-Qaeda for a long time, have no fear of collaboration. Friendships and personal relationships are more important to them than membership of a group. It remains to be seen whether this position will remain tenable if the two groups start to fight each other more intensively in countries like Syria, Yemen or Libya.

RIVALRY

The converse dynamic is what the American political scientists Andrew Kydd and Barbara Walter call "outbidding", something they first observed among Palestinian groups during the so-called Second Intifada at the start of the 2000s. There, too, several groups were competing for attention, support and recruits, and they tried to outbid one another with ever more spectacular attacks. As a consequence, the frequency of terrorist operations increased and the tempo was set by neither the political situation nor Israeli actions, but by this internecine rivalry. Ultimately, say Kydd and Walter, even non-religious groups began to employ Islamic rhetoric and recruit suicide bombers – more so even than Hamas, who had introduced the tactic.[51]

Today, there are signs of a similar contest for attention and recruits. In February 2015, al-Shabaab released a video in which it threatened to commit attacks on North American shopping malls. Many experts were surprised, because until then al-Shabaab had operated exclusively in East Africa. Nor could any actual plot be connected to the video. Even the FBI declared that the threat was empty.[52] Many experts therefore came to the conclusion that for al-Shabaab it was chiefly a matter of attracting attention, since the group had lost out through the rise of the Islamic State: fewer recruits, less publicity and – presumably – less money.[53] Even ethnically Somalian jihadists from Norway or Denmark would rather go to fight in Syria or Iraq than in their parents' own country.[54] What could be more obvious than to get back into the conversation by making spectacular threats?

No one knows whether or when the next al-Qaeda attack in Europe will take place. But the pressure to carry out a spectacular operation in the West is higher than ever. Al-Qaeda has to prove that it continues to lead the global jihad and deserves the jihadist movement's support. Bin Laden became the leader of the global jihad by mounting attacks in the West and groups like AQAP are working flat out to follow his example.

8

Counterterrorism

IN EARLY SEPTEMBER 2014, I SPENT AN ENTIRE DAY IN A BASE-
ment meeting room belonging to the United States Mission to the
UN in New York. America's UN ambassador Samantha Power had
invited me to contribute to a Security Council resolution that President
Obama and the entire UN Security Council was to approve three
weeks later. The document was about jihadist foreign fighters and
the effects of the conflicts in Syria and Iraq on global terrorism. This
meeting was for the Americans to brief the other 14 ambassadors
in the Security Council, who would then discuss the nearly completed draft.[1] I was surprised by how little disagreement there was.
Even Russia and the United States, who regularly tear into each
other at Security Council sessions, were of one mind when it came
to foreign fighters. More than a year before the November 2015
attacks in Paris, everyone already understood how extraordinary
and significant the phenomenon was – and that its consequences
would affect them all.

On 24 September 2014, the Security Council unanimously passed
resolution 2,178, making it binding for all of the UN's 193 member
states.[2] It obliges every country to prevent "terrorist foreign fighters"
from travelling abroad, to exchange relevant information and to make

membership of foreign terrorist groups a criminal offence. For the first time, a Security Council resolution also obliged member states to take preventive action – something I had especially emphasized in the American Mission's basement. The document is a practical building block in the war against jihadist terror, but it also symbolizes a new approach in dealing with it. Cooperation is given the same importance as punishment, and the military and police are not seen as the only means of getting the terrorist threat under control. Almost everyone has now accepted that the fifth wave is a challenge not just to the security services – the police, intelligence services and the military – or just to the state, but also to our society and politics.

But not everything about the fifth wave is new. The Islamic State's roots lie in al-Qaeda, and what we are seeing now in the Middle East is the transition from one generation to another. The fifth wave is thus also a continuation of the fourth – and of the pattern that Rapoport discovered and described after the 9/11 attacks. The strategies and tactics of terrorism have not fundamentally changed: Pisacane's propaganda of the deed, Most's "lone wolves", Marighella's strategy of provocation, Fanon's argument about the liberating – even "purifying" – effects of violence, and the mass mobilization of foreign fighters have all been seen before. Nor is it new for terrorist groups to be anchored in political movements, to recruit from sympathetic milieus or to capture the fantasies of a generation. The Prussian general Carl von Clausewitz (1780–1831) said long ago that every war "has its own grammar, but not its own logic".[3] The same goes for terrorism.

And yet the fifth wave is not merely a repeat of the previous one. To a greater degree than the fourth, it is unfolding in a globalized world: what happens in Syria and Iraq has direct consequences for security in Europe.[4] Even comparatively small operations – a beheading, say – have global repercussions, because the terror they communicate can be globally disseminated by the perpetrators. In the Middle East, jihadists are implementing a state-building project to which its opponents do not yet have any response. And in Europe there is a risk of polarization – not only of a conflict between terrorists and the state, but also that radicals at opposite ends of the political spectrum will drive each other to further extremes that would threaten the peace of our societies, the harmonious coexistence of people from different backgrounds and religions, and therefore our democracies in their entirety.

The fifth wave is not least a quantitative challenge, especially in Europe. The political movements and milieus from which the third and fourth waves recruited their members comprised thousands of people, but the number of terrorists and those willing to commit acts of violence was relatively small. The core of the Red Army Faction numbered several dozen and even al-Qaeda in the 1990s and 2000s had only a few hundred active supporters. In this fifth wave, the number is several times higher. In the German city of Karlsruhe, to take just one example, the state prosecutor has opened more than 500 cases against jihadists in the past two years. The situation is similar in the United Kingdom, France, Scandinavia and Belgium, where the demands placed on the authorities have long exceeded their ability to handle them. As one senior Belgian official told me a year before the attacks in Brussels, "We've been running flat out since 2013."[5]

As with every new wave, the security services and the state will have to scrutinize their methods and assumptions. It is not enough to simply say, "keep at it", when the nature and extent of the threat have changed so dramatically. Nor will the traditional appeal for more money, more staff and more powers solve the problem by itself. A new, comprehensive approach is necessary – and that includes not only the traditional tools of foreign and domestic security, but also a credible and strategic policy on prevention, intervention and deradicalization.

EXTERNAL SECURITY

Journalists, politicians and terrorism specialists tend to treat the rise of the Islamic State as an isolated problem. To do so is to forget that the group is a part and consequence of a historical transformation in the Middle East, which began with the Arab Spring in 2011 and whose ending no one can predict. Commentators argue about whether this is the Arab world's Thirty Years' War or its Reformation.[6] Regardless of which historical comparison is more accurate, we are in the middle of it, and going back to the Sykes–Picot system as it existed in 2011 is practically impossible. Too much blood has flowed for that; too many institutions lie in rubble; the trust between ethnic and sectarian groups has been too deeply shattered. The Islamic State has capitalized on this and there will be no truly lasting "solution" to its existence as long as there is chaos in the Middle East.[7]

Those who believe the solution lies in a return to the "strong men" of the Arab world – the Mubaraks, Gaddafis and Saddams – have not understood that it was these supposedly strong men, their corrupt regimes and the decades of political, economic and social paralysis they engendered that were the main reason the Arab Spring happened in the first place.[8] The stability they purported to guarantee was an illusion, because problems were never solved, only ever swept under the carpet.[9] That someone like Assad – who has the lives of tens of thousands of his own people on his conscience and who directly and indirectly supported the rise of the Islamic State[10] – is now again being seen as an ally in the struggle against terrorism, is grotesque.[11] Nor does it make either political or military sense because the fear that he will regain control is the main reason many Syrian Sunnis tolerate the Islamic State. As unbelievable as it may sound, for many Syrians the Islamic State is the lesser of two evils.

Doing nothing – that is, staying out of the conflict in the hope that the extremists will kill each other off – would be just as problematic.[12] The Islamic State is the product and beneficiary of sectarian tensions that have heightened since the Americans' disastrous war in Iraq, but it also stokes them up further, exporting its hate-filled ideology into neighbouring states, radicalizing the discourse and so undermining the coexistence of different ethnicities and religious groups throughout the region. "Only ten years ago," said the former US ambassador Alberto Fernandez, "no one was talking about *jizya* [the "protection tax" that Christians have to pay in the Islamic State]. Most Arabs wouldn't even have known what *jizya* was. Today you're hearing the idea everywhere."[13] The same goes for slavery: "Not even the strictest, most backward-looking Salafists would have defended slavery a couple of years ago. But the Islamic State has reintroduced it. Just like that."[14]

The war waged by the Islamic State – including in places far removed from its heartland in Syria and Iraq – destabilizes countries everywhere in the region, forces minorities to flee and has triggered an unprecedented exodus of refugees. Not least, it also presents a threat to the security of Europe and the West: the Islamic State today is already more powerful and strategically significant than the "Islamic Emirate of Afghanistan" from which bin Laden organized the 9/11 attacks. Large-scale attacks in the West do not (yet) interest the Islamic State, but its strategic calculations could change at any time.

So what is to be done? The most important thing is to realize that there is no simple, quick solution – and certainly no purely military one – to the problem of the Islamic State. When American generals and politicians like Senator John McCain loudly demand the deployment of Western troops, they are making the same error in reasoning that led to the Iraq War, a real case of "Back to the Future".[15] Al-Baghdadi, whose predecessor almost drove the Americans to defeat in Iraq, would like nothing better than a repeat of that conflict. A direct confrontation with the Americans would give his forces the opportunity to portray themselves as anti-imperialist resistance fighters. Moreover, the renewed occupation of "liberated areas" would not only cost an enormous amount of money, claim too many victims and be hard to sustain politically, it would also lend credence to the narrative of a Western war against Islam, which the Islamic State uses to attract sympathizers and support. And instead of solving the political, sectarian and social problems in Iraq and Syria, it would further exacerbate those tensions. The result: more chaos, not less – and an even more successful Islamic State.

The only realistic solution consists of a systematic, long-term and comprehensive strategy of aggressive containment, as advocated by the Council on Foreign Relations scholar Steve Simon. A state that – like the Islamic State – depends on continuous expansion will ultimately fail of its own internal dynamics. If the Islamic State wins no more military victories and is no longer in a position to meet the needs of its population, and its internal contradictions and tensions become obvious, it will gradually collapse in on itself – taking with it the ideological project that it represents. Containment is thus neither passive nor pacifist: it requires training, weapons, intelligence work, special forces and targeted air strikes to support local forces on the ground. But other things are just as important: diplomacy and politics, that is, a "New Deal" for the Iraqi Sunnis and a change of regime in Syria; an ideological counter-argument on- and offline; support for neighbouring countries struggling to accommodate huge numbers of refugees, and active conflict prevention in the countries into which the Islamic State is trying to expand.

DOMESTIC SECURITY

The next essential component is counterterrorism in the narrow sense. The central challenge is the same in every free society, since almost all terrorists come out of a counterculture, a "scene", but not everyone involved in these scenes is a future terrorist (see Chapter 5). It may make things easier for the authorities that they don't have to scour the entire population for terrorists, but the problem of differentiation – who is prepared to commit violence, who isn't? – exists nevertheless. Even in a relatively hidden milieu the proportion of terrorists to non-terrorists is often 1 to 100 – or even 1 to 1,000. The success of counterterrorism depends on how well the security services can distinguish between (actual) terrorists, the counterculture and the rest of the population, and on how efficient and precisely targeted their measures are for each of those groups (see Fig. 8.1).

For authoritarian states, the answer is simple: instead of racking your brains about who's dangerous and who isn't, treat everyone in the counterculture as a potential terrorist. That some are innocent people who would never have become terrorists and that some are actively *opposed* to violence, is unimportant – and in many instances even a desirable outcome.[16] But those who equate fighting terrorism

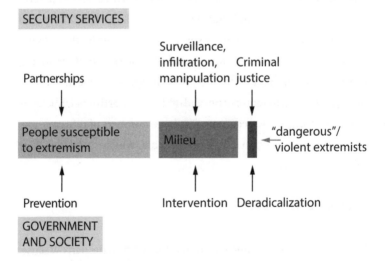

FIG. 8.1 The division of responsibilities in counterterrorism

with fighting the counterculture are acting not just unethically, but inefficiently. Locking up 3,000 people because 30 of them might be terrorists makes no sense and would require a massive security apparatus that only authoritarian states can afford. The greatest problem with this attitude is that in almost all cases, harsh repression doesn't work. It radicalizes those who previously weren't prepared to commit acts of violence and is often precisely what the terrorists are hoping for (see Chapter 1).[17]

MUSLIMS, SALAFISTS, TERRORISTS

The milieu that will be in the forefront of the security services' minds during the fifth wave is the Salafist counterculture. It is the social and ideological incubator for the jihadists who join al-Qaeda and the Islamic State. It can be found on- and offline, in universities, prisons, radical mosques, Islam seminars, community centres and town centres. In Europe, it now has tens of thousands of supporters – and gains more every day. As in other countercultures, there are different groups and tendencies among the Salafists; not all lean towards violence, but for some it is the last stop before going over to outright terrorism. The security services' task is to watch the supporters and understand how the scene works, who exercises influence within it and which members are dangerous or potentially violent. It is just as important for them to win over informants and deploy them so that the "dangerous" among the Salafists lose influence within the counterculture itself. Repressive tactics directed against the scene *as a whole* strengthen the "dangerous" position and are therefore usually not only ineffective, but also highly counterproductive.

The same applies to the 99 per cent of European Muslims who are not part of the Salafist scene. To harass or criminalize them on the basis of their religion is illegal and an enormous waste of time, money and resources, which would be better spent on dealing with Salafists.

Of course, deeply problematic views continue to exist within Muslim communities in Europe.[18] Attitudes such as anti-Semitism, antipathy towards democracy and rejection of gender equality must be tackled, but that is down to civil society and politics, not to the security services and least of all to the police. Treating Muslims as potential terrorists and candidates for surveillance, which the FBI has done in the past, would do severe damage to our society and squander the opportunity to win them as partners.[19]

The target group that the security services should actively pursue consists of the dangerous and potentially violent people within the Salafist counterculture. This is a matter of criminal prosecution, disrupting terrorist networks and preventing attacks. It is absurd that the authorities in many Western countries are still not allowed full access to the communication data of potentially highly dangerous terrorists. And the constant questioning of whether or not to cooperate with foreign partners – especially the United States – only makes counterterrorism harder.[20]

The security services' demands for more staff, money and powers are justified, but they have to be properly accounted for and their use has to be effectively controlled. The security services should also do more to explain to a sceptical public why more resources and more powers are needed, what will be done with them and how misuse will be prevented. That is why the fifth wave is a challenge to the authorities themselves: how open are they to new ideas? How ready are they to call received wisdom into question? How capable are they of innovation and change? Giving the public the impression that it is simply about building bigger and more powerful bureaucracies would be no help to anyone – least of all those fighting terrorism.

PREVENTION

Equipping the security services with new staff, money and powers – in other words, matching their size and capabilities to the scale of the threat – is only one of two possibilities for coping with the fifth wave. Coming at it from the other side – making sure there are fewer cases for the security services to investigate in the first place – is just as crucial. The two approaches do not preclude each other. On the contrary. A comprehensive modern approach to counterterrorism requires both: strong, able, well-equipped security services and also a systematic, adequately resourced policy for terrorism prevention, intervention and deradicalization. The people involved, the target groups, the methods and the tools all differ, but prosecution and prevention are two sides of the same coin. Our government and society must conduct both with the same attention and energy.

The ultimate test for whether a government is serious about preventive counterterrorism is the existence – and implementation – of a transparent, well-financed strategy. In no other field would it be acceptable for various actors and projects to work on a matter of such significant national interest more or less on their own – without any coherence, common goals or coordination. If this were education, health or transport, the government would be accused of incompetence and negligence. But when it comes to the politics of prevention, many countries still display a lack of interest in or understanding of what needs to be done. That is fatal, since it is in this sphere, of all places, that resources have to be joined up, duplications avoided and lessons shared from successes (and failures), while separate ministries and different levels of government need to be coordinated to be effective. Transparency is just as important, because preventive counterterrorism requires the NGOs and civil society organizations to know who's doing what and how their own activities fit into the whole.

Internationally, the preventive approach is becoming ever more firmly established. The Netherlands became the first country to formulate a national prevention strategy, in 2004 – followed by Britain, Norway, Denmark and Sweden. Outside Europe, there are strategies in place in Australia, Canada and the United States. The Obama administration, in particular, has made prevention a priority. In February 2015, the White House organized a global prevention summit attended by prime and interior ministers from more than 60 countries. And even the general secretary of the UN now thinks the subject is important: his recently released Global Strategy calls on every member state to develop its own national action plan. Even Germany and France, which had long resisted the idea, are now rhetorically committed to this idea (though actions haven't yet followed words).

BUILDING BLOCKS OF A NATIONAL STRATEGY

If you study other countries' prevention strategies, what quickly becomes apparent is that the most important elements are very similar wherever you look. The first is prevention in the narrow sense. By that I mean the programmes and initiatives aimed not at extremists and radicals, but at people who are susceptible to extremist influence. That includes, for example, a demographic of young people from unstable backgrounds and socially deprived areas who are often also – though not always – first or second-generation immigrants. The overwhelming majority will never become extremists or commit a crime, but they belong to the target group from which the Salafists do their recruiting. The aim of prevention is to get to them first: to make young people aware of extremism, anticipate the extremists' arguments, offer alternatives, stabilize the young people's circumstances and so "inoculate" them against attempted recruitment.

These programmes are organized in places where young people spend their time and can be engaged with – in schools, youth centres, sports centres and on the internet. Parents and teachers also play a part in prevention, because they have a great deal of influence and are often the first to notice their children or pupils drifting towards extremism. These kinds of programmes have nothing to do with criminal justice or police work and should be kept strictly separate from them, because criminalizing young people and treating them as potential terrorists only strengthens the sense of marginalization that extremists exploit for radicalization.

The second building block consists of so-called interventions. These are for people who have already been radicalized and are on the verge of becoming extremists – or even terrorists. The idea of an intervention is to hinder that process through intensive engagement with the individual. In the British programme, called "Channel", for example, everyone involved sits down together, analyses the case and decides what is needed to stop the radicalization. Led by the police, this group can include theologians, psychologists, teachers, social workers and even the security services.[21] In Germany, most of the responsibility is assigned to parents. The Federal Office for Migration and Refugees maintains a hotline that puts parents in touch with the relevant NGOs.[22] The idea is good, because parents are often the ones with the most influence on radicalized young people: many of the fighters we've tracked during our research say that leaving their families was the hardest part.[23] But the NGOs are chronically under-funded and find themselves having to fight for every employee despite the dramatic rise in the number of cases they're trying to deal with.[24]

The third building block comprises deradicalization and exit programmes. These, too, are individually tailored measures, but in contrast to classic interventions, they are for people who have already been members of extremist and terrorist groups and now want to break away from them. Many of the initiatives and processes this entails are identical to those for intervention and include consultation with parents. The greatest difference is the – often very arduous – process of moving the defectors out of their social environment, because those who've been in an extremist group for years usually have only very few friends or contacts left outside the scene and often find it difficult to shake off the extremists' ongoing influence. Denmark,[25] Sweden and Germany already have defector programmes, albeit on a small scale and, in Germany's case, with inadequate funding.[26] Systematically instituting programmes like this for disillusioned returnees from Syria could free up the security services to concentrate on the really dangerous fighters.[27]

Another essential element consists of cooperation with Muslim communities, because they represent the faith that the jihadists claim as their own and cite as their justification. In theory, non-Salafist Muslims provide a counterweight to extremism, embody religious diversity and can reach people to whom the state has no access. But in practice, this cooperation is often very difficult. That is partly because mainstream Muslim communities are just as helpless and clueless about Salafism as the rest of society. Their leaders tend to be old men with no insight into the realities of life for young Muslims and who would rather avoid the controversial questions about identity, drugs and sex that the Salafists actively address. Moreover, they are fed up of politicians and the media holding them responsible for the actions of a small minority and believe that the tone of the media's reporting on Islam, the Islamic State and terrorism is fomenting a growing Islamophobia.

This attitude is understandable, at least in part, but these mainstream communities and their associations are making a mistake if they avoid the subject, because extremism is ultimately a threat to them, too, and to the millions of Muslims living peacefully in the

West. A functioning prevention strategy will need Muslim communities to aggressively and credibly engage with extremists, and the state not to communicate with Muslim citizens only via Homeland Security and "security partnerships", but to truly accept them as fellow citizens and offer them real participation in society.

Moreover, a national prevention strategy must look at all forms of extremism. Concentrating solely on Muslims and the jihadist threat, as has been the case in Britain and the United States, makes it harder to collaborate with Muslim communities.[28] And even more importantly, it overlooks the danger posed to European societies by the prospect that jihadists and Far Right radicals will drive each other to further extremes. Jihadist terrorism is bad, but the political polarization that could result from a confrontation between extremist Muslims and extremists on the Far Right would be an even more serious strategic threat. Anyone wanting to preserve Western democracy and the capacity for people from different backgrounds to live together peacefully will need a prevention policy that understands the connection between all forms of radicalization.

PROS AND CONS

The first – and perhaps most important – objection raised to a national prevention strategy is that prevention doesn't work. But in truth there is any amount of evidence to show that is does. In May 2015, Charles Farr, the then head of the British Office for Security and Counterterrorism, explained to a German audience that 70 per cent of participants in Britain's "Channel" deradicalization programme never came to their attention again – a huge decrease in workload, said Farr, because it meant the security services only had to deal with those left over.[29] Of course, the earlier an intervention takes place, the harder it is to demonstrate that it has been effective: a 13-year-old who has gone through a prevention programme will be exposed to many other influences in the following years and it is hard to prove that he (or she) did *not* become a terrorist because of the programme.[30] But criticism on these lines questions the entire logic of prevention in any field and must explain the presence of the large-scale – and long-established – prevention programmes for alcohol, Aids and youth violence.

Another argument seeks to cast doubt on whether national prevention programmes or strategies are practical because in most countries the programmes and initiatives they would consist of are scattered across the entire government apparatus. Add to that the differences between various levels of government – national, state and local – as well as the need for cooperation with NGOs, and you have a bureaucratic nightmare. But the fragmentation of responsibilities and budgets is not an argument *against* having a national prevention strategy; it is an argument *for* having one. A strategy of this type would make it possible to bring everyone involved to the table, to set priorities, assign tasks and compare results. Particularly federal countries like Germany and the United States surely must have an interest in clearly demarcating the responsibilities of the national and state governments. It is already working in Canada and Australia.[31]

The weakest argument against it is that terrorism prevention costs money. Most governments are already spending a lot on terrorism prevention – just without any overall strategy, coordination or control. In Germany, for example, there are programmes and funding allocations in at least three federal ministries: family, interior and justice. Then there are 16 federal states with their own initiatives as well as a long list of state and federal agencies – from the Federal Agency for Civic Education and the Office for Migration and Refugees through to the Federal Office for Protection of the Constitution – that all take it upon themselves to do prevention work. A national strategy would show how much money is already flowing into terrorism prevention, which allocations make sense and where more money is needed. The absence of such a strategy means that money is wasted, synergies remain unexploited and programmes doing good work are chronically underfinanced. Additional funding is urgently needed, but it is equally important that the money already available is spent in a more targeted way. Without a clear policy, overview and strategy, that will not be possible.

I suspect that resistance to a national prevention strategy has little to do with these arguments. An effective plan would require officials to shed light on their bureaucracy's entrenched interests, question them and innovate – something that many countries' leaders are not (yet) willing to do. Elsewhere in Europe the story has often been the same: prevention has not been taken seriously in many places. Politicians and senior officials have been happy to pay lip service to the idea, but have done little about it. The introduction of a national strategy has almost always followed a crisis or terrorist attack: the murder of the film-maker Theo van Gogh in the Netherlands; the attacks on 7 July 2005 in the United Kingdom or the publication of the Mohammed cartoons in Denmark.

The prospect that a coordinated national strategy will only be recognized as important when it is too late is not typical of any country's mentality or institutions in particular, but it is undoubtedly a grave mistake whose consequences will come home to roost during the fifth wave of terrorism.

APPENDIX A

Fighters from Western Europe (January 2015)

COUNTRY	ABSOLUTE NUMBER	PER MILLION INHABITANTS
Austria	100–150	17
Belgium	440	40
Denmark	100–500	27
Finland	50–70	13
France	1,200	18
Germany	500–600	7.5
Ireland	30	7
Italy	80	1.5
The Netherlands	200–250	14.5
Norway	60	12
Spain	50–100	2
Sweden	40	5
United Kingdom	500–600	9.5

Source: Peter R. Neumann, "Foreign fighter total in Syria/Iraq now exceeds 20,000; surpasses Afghanistan conflict in the 1980s", *ICS. Insight*, 26 January 2015; available at http://icsr.info/2015/01/foreign-fighter-total-syriairaq-now-exceeds-20000-surpasses-afghanistan-conflict-1980s/, accessed 1 July 2016.

APPENDIX B

Relationship with the Islamic State (as of 1 May 2016)

Source: Aymenn Jawad al-Tamimi

COUNTRY	GROUP	BACKGROUND	SYMPATHETIC	DECLARED LOYALTY	PLEDGE ACCEPTED
ALGERIA	Wilayat al-Jaza'ir	Emerged from Jund al-Khilafah and other AQIM splinters. Pledges of allegiance accepted in November 2014.	Yes	Yes	Yes
EGYPT	Wilayat Sinai	Emerged from Jamaat Ansar Bayt al-Maqdis. Pledges of allegiance accepted in November 2014. Claimed attacks in mainland Egypt.	Yes	Yes	Yes
	Majlis Shura al-Mujahideen fi Aknaf Bayt al-Maqdis	Issued statement of support for IS in October 2014, but no pledge of allegiance. Sympathies divided between al-Qaeda and IS.	Yes	No	No
	Ajnad Misr	Al-Qaeda aligned. Carrying out attacks in mainland Egypt.	No	No	No
	Jamaat al-Murabiteen	Al-Qaeda aligned. Break-off from Jamaat Ansar Bayt al-Maqdis. Based in exile in Libya.	No	No	No
	Jamaat Jund al-Islam	Al-Qaeda aligned. Based in the Sinai.	No	No	No
GAZA	Jaysh al-Ummah fi Aknaf Bayt al-Maqdis	Al-Qaeda aligned.	No	No	No
	Pro-IS groups	Currently too small and internally divided to be accepted as official affiliates. Includes: For example: Jamaat Ansar al-Dawla al-Islamiya, Saraya Sheikh Omar Hadid.	Yes	Yes	No
INDIA/ BANGLADESH	Tanzim Ansar al-Tawheed fi Bilad al-Hind	Pledged allegiance to IS in October 2014, but no indication of acceptance.	Yes	Yes	No
	Al-Qaeda in the Indian Subcontinent	Al-Qaeda affiliate. Bangladesh division known as Ansar al-Islam.	No	No	No
	Pro-IS operatives in Bangladesh	No collective name, but have engaged in assassinations in Bangladesh. Claimed by IS.	Yes	Yes	Yes
IRAQ	Jama'at Ansar al-Islam	Iraqi branch largely merged with IS. Syria branch remains active.	Yes	Yes	Yes

COUNTRY	GROUP	BACKGROUND	SYMPATHETIC	DECLARED LOYALTY	PLEDGE ACCEPTED
LEBANON	Abdullah Azzam Brigades	Al-Qaeda aligned.	No	No	No
	Jabhat al-Nusra in Lebanon	Al-Qaeda aligned.	No	No	No
	IS operatives	No collective name, but have claimed attacks in Lebanon, most notably targeting Shi'a population in Dahiya suburb of Beirut.	Yes	Yes	Yes
LIBYA	Wilayat Barqa	Emerged from Majlis Shura Shabab al-Islam in Derna. Pledges of allegiance accepted in November 2014. Currently consists of towns to the east of Sirte (Harawa, Nofaliya, Bin Jawad).	Yes	Yes	Yes
	Wilayat Tarabulus	Emerged from splinters of Ansar al-Sharia. Has maintained covert presence in Sabratha to the west of Tripoli.	Yes	Yes	Yes
	Wilayat Fezzan	Limited claims of operations. No evidence of territorial control.	Yes	Yes	Yes
	Ansar al-Sharia Libya	Al-Qaeda aligned.	No	No	No
	Mujahideen Shura Council of Derna	Al-Qaeda aligned.	No	No	No
MAGHREB/ SAHEL	Al-Qaeda in the Islamic Maghreb (AQIM)	Al-Qaeda affiliate.	No	No	No
	Ansar Dine	Al-Qaeda aligned.	No	No	No
	Al-Mourabitoun	Al-Qaeda aligned.	No	No	No
	MUJAO	Pledged allegiance to IS. Has likely merged into IS West Africa Province network.	Yes	Yes	Yes
NIGERIA	Wilayat Gharb Ifriqiyah (West Africa)	Emerged from Boko Haram's pledge of allegiance in March 2015. Claimed attacks in Nigeria and Chad.	Yes	Yes	Yes
	Ansaru	Al-Qaeda aligned.	No	No	No

COUNTRY	GROUP	BACKGROUND	SYMPATHETIC	DECLARED LOYALTY	PLEDGE ACCEPTED
PAKISTAN–AFGHANISTAN	Wilayat Khorasan	Emerged from Pakistani and Afghan Taliban splinters. Pledges of allegiance accepted in January 2015. Has since incorporated Islamic Movement of Uzbekistan.	Yes	Yes	Yes
	Islamic Emirate of Afghanistan	Aligned with Afghan Taliban. Serves as source of authority for al-Qaeda leadership.	No	No	No
	Tehrik-i-Taliban	Pakistani Taliban. Al-Qaeda aligned.	No	No	No
RUSSIA/CAUCASUS	Wilayat al-Qawqaz	Emerged from Caucasus Emirate splinters. Province declared in June 2015. Now dominates Caucasus Emirate.	Yes	Yes	Yes
	Caucasus Emirate	Al-Qaeda aligned.	No	No	No
SAUDI ARABIA	Wilayat Najd	Emerged from declaration of provinces in November 2014. Formally announced in May 2015. Covers central part of the country, occasionally reaching into neighbouring countries such as Kuwait.	Yes	Yes	Yes
	Wilayat al-Hijaz	Announced in August 2015. Covers western part of the country.	Yes	Yes	Yes
	Wilayat al-Bahrain	Announced in October 2015. Covers eastern part of the country.	Yes	Yes	Yes
SOMALIA	Al-Shabaab	Al-Qaeda affiliate.	No	No	No
	IS contingent	Emerged in October 2015. Splinters from Al-Shabaab.	Yes	Yes	Yes
SOUTHEAST ASIA	IS contingents in the Philippines	Splinters from Abu Sayyaf. Claimed by IS media.	Yes	Yes	Yes
	IS contingents in Indonesia	Pledges of allegiance by leaders of Jamaah Ansharut Tauhid and Ikhwan Man Ta'a Allah. Claimed Jakarta attack in January 2016.	Yes	Yes	Yes
	Jama'ah Ansharusy Syari'ah	Emerged from Jamaah Ansharut Tauhid.	No	No	No
	Jemaah Islamiyah	Al-Qaeda aligned.	No	No	No

COUNTRY	GROUP	BACKGROUND	SYMPATHETIC	DECLARED LOYALTY	PLEDGE ACCEPTED
SUDAN	Jama'at al-Itisam Bil Kitab wa al-Sunna	Declarations of support, but no pledge of allegiance. Activities limited.	Yes	No	No
	Jabhat al-Nusra	Al-Qaeda affiliate.	No	No	No
	Jama'at Ansar al-Islam	Al-Qaeda aligned.	No	No	No
	North Caucasian-led groups	Al-Qaeda aligned. Includes: Ajnad Kavkaz (Abd al-Hakim al-Shishani's group), Junud al-Sham (Muslim Shishani's group), Caucasus Emirate in al-Sham, and Salah al-Din al-Shishani's contingent.	No	No	No
	Jabhat Ansar al-Din	Al-Qaeda aligned. Coalition of Harakat Fajr al-Sham al-Islamiya (Syrian group in Aleppo) and Harakat Sham al-Islam (Moroccan-led group in Latakia).	No	No	No
	Jund al-Aqsa	Al-Qaeda sympathetic.	No	No	No
SYRIA	Jaysh Muhammad in Bilad al-Sham	Al-Qaeda aligned, though some defections to IS.	No	No	No
	Turkistan Islamic Party	Al-Qaeda aligned.	No	No	No
	Yarmouk Martyrs Brigade	IS sympathies. Based in south-west Deraa (Yarmouk Valley) on the border with the Golan Heights.	Yes	No	No
	Islamic Muthanna Movement	Aligned with Yarmouk Martyrs Brigade.	N/A	No	No
	Imam Bukhari Battalion	Aligned with Afghan Taliban. Mostly Uzbek.	No	No	No
	IS factions	Includes: Lions of the Caliphate, Omar al-Shishani's contingent of Jaish al-Muhajireen wal-Ansar, Liwa Dawood.	Yes	Yes	Yes

COUNTRY	GROUP	BACKGROUND	SYMPATHETIC	DECLARED LOYALTY	PLEDGE ACCEPTED
TUNISIA	Uqba ibn Nafi Battalion	Aligned with al-Qaeda and Ansar al-Sharia Tunisia, though some defections to IS.	No	No	No
	Ansar al-Sharia Tunisia	Al-Qaeda aligned, though splits between IS and al-Qaeda supporters.	No	No	No
	IS contingents	Emerged from splinters of Uqba ibn Nafi' and Ansar al-Sharia Tunisia.	Yes	Yes	Yes
YEMEN	Al-Qaeda in the Arabian Peninsula (AQAP), Ansar al-Sharia Yemen	Al-Qaeda affiliate.	No	No	No
	IS provinces in Yemen	Emerged from AQAP splinters. Officially announced in November 2014. Includes: Wilayat San'a, Wilayat Hadhramaut, Wilayat Lahij, Wilayat Aden-Abyan, Wilayat Shabwa and Wilayat Ma'arib.	Yes	Yes	Yes

Names and Organizations

ADAMS, GERRY (*1948) Irish nationalist. Leader of the Irish Republican Army's political wing

ADNANI, ABU MOHAMMED AL- (*1977) Syrian jihadist and Islamic State spokesman

AHRAR AL-SHAM Salafist rebel group in Syria. Part of the Syrian Islamic Front

AL-QAEDA Jihadist terror network founded by Osama bin Laden

AL-QAEDA IN THE ARABIAN PENINSULA (AQAP) Al-Qaeda subsidiary in Yemen

AL-QAEDA IN IRAQ (AQI) Al-Qaeda subsidiary in Iraq. Predecessor of the Islamic State in Iraq (ISI)

AL-QAEDA IN THE ISLAMIC MAGHREB (AQIM) Al-Qaeda subsidiary in North Africa and the Sahel

ANAS, ABDULLAH (*1958) Algerian Islamist. Former foreign fighter and comrade of Azzam's in Afghanistan

ANSAR AL-SHARIA Jihadist groups in Tunisia and Libya. Emerged after the Arab Spring. The name is also used by AQAP

ARAFAT, YASSER (1999–2004) Palestinian nationalist. Leader of the Palestinian Liberation Organization (PLO)

ARIFI, MOHAMMED AL- (*1970) Saudi-Arabian Salafist and popular preacher

ARMED ISLAMIC GROUP (GROUPE ISLAMIQUE ARMÉ; GIA) Algerian jihadist group. Fought against the Algerian government in the 1990s

ARMY OF GOD American network of Christian fundamentalists. Responsible for attacks on abortion clinics

ASIRI, IBRAHIM HASSAN AL- (*1982) Saudi jihadist. AQAP bomb maker

AUM SHINRIKYO Japanese doomsday cult. Sprayed nerve gas into the Tokyo Metro in 1995

AWLAKI, ANWAR AL- (1971–2011) Yemeni–American jihadist and preacher. Joined AQAP in 2009

AYERS, BILL (*1944) American Far Left extremist. Leader of the Weathermen

AZZAM, ABDULLAH (1941–89) Palestinian jihadist. Mobilized Arab fighters for the Afghanistan conflict in the 1980s

BAADER, ANDREAS (1943–77) German Far Left extremist. Co-founder of the Red Army Faction

BAGHDADI, ABU BAKR AL- (*1971) Iraqi jihadist. "Caliph" and leader of the Islamic State

BAKR, HAJI (CA. 1958/64–2014) Iraqi jihadist. The Islamic State's military strategist in Syria

BANNA, HASSAN AL- (1906–49) Egyptian jihadist. Founder of the Muslim Brotherhood

BIN LADEN, OSAMA (1957–2011) Saudi jihadist. Founder and long-standing leader of al-Qaeda

BOKO HARAM Jihadist group from the north-east of Nigeria. Joined the Islamic State in 2015

BREIVIK, ANDERS (*1979) Norwegian Far Right extremist. In July 2011, he attacked a government building and a holiday camp run by the youth wing of the Norwegian Labour Party

COULIBALY, AMEDY (1982–2015)   French jihadist. Took hostages in a kosher supermarket in Paris in January 2015. Had sworn loyalty to the Islamic State

CUSPERT, DENIS   *See* Deso Dogg

DESO DOGG (1975–2015)   German jihadist and former rapper. Foreign fighter in Syria. Originally called Denis Cuspert

EGYPTIAN ISLAMIC GROUP   Egyptian jihadist group. Absorbed Afghanistan fighters after the end of the conflict in the 1980s

FIGHTING VANGUARD   Jihadist group in Syria. Fought against the Syrian government in the 1970s and early 1980s

FREE SYRIAN ARMY   Umbrella organization for non-Salafist Syrian rebels

GUEVARA, ERNESTO "CHE" (1928–67)   Argentinian Marxist. Fought alongside Fidel Castro in Cuba

HAMAS   Palestinian Islamist insurrectionary group. Subsidiary of the Muslim Brotherhood

HILL, PAUL (1954–2003)   American Christian fundamentalist. Anti-abortionist and member of the Army of God

HEZBOLLAH   Lebanese Shi'i militia. Currently fighting in Syria alongside Bashar al-Assad

IRISH REPUBLICAN ARMY (IRA)   Nationalist insurrectionary group in Northern Ireland. Fought for the province's unification with the Republic of Ireland

ISLAMIC STATE (IS)   Successor organization to the Islamic State in Iraq and (Greater) Syria (ISIS). Declared itself the caliphate in summer 2014

ISLAMIC STATE IN IRAQ (ISI)   Successor organization to al-Qaeda in Iraq (AQI). Predecessor of ISIS

ISLAMIC STATE IN IRAQ AND THE LEVANT (ISIL)   Another name for ISIS

ISLAMIC STATE IN IRAQ AND (GREATER) SYRIA Successor organization to Islamic State in Iraq (ISI). Renamed itself the Islamic State in mid-2014

JABHAT AL-NUSRA Al-Qaeda subsidiary in Syria

AL-JIHAD Jihadist group in Egypt. Also the name of magazine published by Azzam during the 1980s Afghanistan conflict.

JULANI, ABU MOHAMMAD AL- (CA. *1975) Syrian jihadist. Leader of Jabhat al-Nusra

KHOMEINI, RUHOLLAH (1902–89) Iranian revolutionary leader and spiritual head of Iran from 1979 to 1989

KHORASAN Network of al-Qaeda members from Pakistan who are part of al-Nusra. Also the name of the Islamic State's Pakistani "province"

KOËNIGSTEIN, FRANÇOIS CLAUDIUS (1859–92) French anarchist who called himself Ravachol. Responsible for a series of attacks on the police and judiciary

KOUACHI, CHÉRIF (1982–2015) AND SAÏD (1980–2015) French jihadists who attacked the satirical magazine *Charlie Hebdo* in January 2015. Trained with AQAP

KROPOTKIN, PJOTR (1842–1921) Russian anarchist and revolutionary theorist

MAJLIS SHURA SHABAB AL-ISLAM IS subsidiary in the Libyan city of Derna

MAQDISI, ABU MOHAMMED AL- (*1959) Jordanian jihadist. Influential ideologue and supporter of al-Qaeda. Al-Zarqawi's mentor

MARIGHELLA, CARLOS (1911–69) Brazilian communist. Revolutionary theorist and leader of the Brazilian Communist Party

MEINHOF, ULRIKE (1934–76) German Far Left extremist. Co-founder of the Red Army Faction

MOST, JOHANN (1846–209)   German–American anarchist

MUSLIM BROTHERHOOD   Islamist organization founded in Egypt in 1928

MUSSOLINI, BENITO (1883–1945)   Italian fascist and dictator from 1922 to 1943

NAJI, ABU BAKR (*1961)   Egyptian jihadist and author of *The Management of Savagery*

NARODNAYA VOLYA   Anarchist terrorist group in Russia. Murdered Tsar Alexander II

NATIONAL LIBERATION FRONT (FRONT DE LIBÉRATION NATION-ALE, FLN)   Nationalist insurrectionary group. Successfully fought for Algeria's independence from France

NEMMOUCHE, MEHDI (*1986)   French jihadist and former fighter in Syria. Attacked a police station in a suburb of Tours in December 2014. Supporter of the Islamic State

PALESTINIAN LIBERATION ORGANIZATION (PLO)   Umbrella organization for Palestinian insurrectionary groups

PISACANE, CARLO (1818–57)   Italian anarchist who developed the concept of the propaganda of the deed

RAMDANE, ABANE (1920–57)   Algerian nationalist. Military strategist and commander of the FLN

RAVACHOL   *See* François Claudius Koënigstein

RED ARMY FACTION (RAF)   Far Left German terrorist group that carried out attacks between 1970 and 1997

QUTB, MOHAMMED (1919–2014)   Egyptian jihadist. In exile in Saudi Arabia, he promoted the ideas of his brother Sayyid

QUTB, SAYYID (1906–66)   Egyptian member of the Muslim Brotherhood. Formulated the ideological foundations of revolutionary jihadism

SHISHANI, ABU OMAR AL- (1986–2016)   Georgian jihadist and important Islamic State commander

AL-SHABAAB Jihadist group in Somalia. Declared itself an al-Qaeda subsidiary in February 2012

SIBA'I, MUSTAFA AL- (1957–64) Syrian Islamist. Leader of the Muslim Brotherhood in Syria

SURI, ABU MUSAB AL- (1958) Syrian jihadist and revolutionary strategist

SYRIAN ISLAMIC FRONT Association of Salafist rebel groups in Syria

TAYMIYYAH, IBN (1263–1328) Syrian theologist still influential among Salafists

TEHRIK-I-TALIBAN (TTP) Network of jihadist groups in Pakistan. Also called the "Pakistani Taliban"

WAHHAB, MOHAMMED IBN 'ABD AL- (1703–92) Arab religious leader and creator of the "Wahhabist" doctrine

WEATHERMEN American terrorist group of the 1970s

WUHAYSHI, NASIR AL- (1976–2015) Yemeni jihadist. Founder and leader of AQAP

ZARQAWI, ABU MUSAB AL- (1966–2006) Jordanian jihadist and founder of al-Qaeda in Iraq (AQI)

ZAWAHIRI, AYMAN AL- (*1951) Egyptian jihadist and bin Laden's successor as head of al-Qaeda

ZEDONG, MAO (1893–1976) Chinese revolutionary leader and head of the Chinese Communist Party

Notes

FOREWORD

1 See, for example, Stephen M. Walt, "What should we do if the Islamic State wins?", *Foreign Policy*, 10 June 2015; Juan Cole, "One year after the fall of Mosul, is Iraq winning the war against ISIS?", *The Nation*, 11 June 2015; Rukmini Callimachi, Alissa J. Rubin and Laure Fouquet, "A view on ISIS's evolution in new details of Paris attacks", *New York Times*, 19 March 2016.

2 Harry S., letter to Chris Vallance, *BBC Radio 4*, January 2016.

3 Ibid.

4 Callimachi, "A view on ISIS's evolution", op. cit.

5 "Interview with Abu Umar al-Baljiki", *Dabiq*, February 2015.

6 See Jon Henley, "Abdelhamid Abaaoud, suspected Paris attacks ringleader, was killed in raid", *Guardian*, 19 November 2015.

7 See Peter R. Neumann, *Old and New Terrorism: Late Modernity, Globalization and the Transformation of Political Violence* (Cambridge: Polity Press, 2009).

INTRODUCTION

1 David Schanzer, Charles Kurzman and Ebrahim Moosa, "Anti-terror lessons of Muslim-Americans", *National Institute of Justice*, 6 January 2010, p. 16.

2 Leon Panetta, quoted in Craig Whitlock, "Panetta: U.S. 'within reach' of defeating al-Qaeda", *Washington Post*, 9 July 2011.

3 Seth G. Jones, *A Persistent Threat: The Evolution of al Qa'ida and Other Salafi Jihadists* (Santa Monica, CA: RAND, 2014), p. 27.

4 See Alex P. Schmid, "Terrorism: the definitional problem", *Case Western Reserve Journal of International Law*, 36(2–3) (2004), pp. 375–419.

1. ANARCHISM, ANTI-COLONIALISM AND THE NEW LEFT

1 David C. Rapoport, "The four waves of rebel terrorism and September 11", *Anthropoetics*, 8(1) (2002); available at: http://www.anthropoetics.ucla.edu/apo801/

terror.htm, accessed 1 July 2016. David. C. Rapoport, "The four waves of modern terrorism", in: Audrey Kurth Cronin and James M. Ludes (eds), *Attacking Terrorism: Elements of a Grand Strategy* (Washington DC: Georgetown University Press, 2004), pp. 46–73.

2   Carlo Pisacane, "On revolution", in: Robert Graham (ed.), *Anarchism: A Documentary History of Libertarian Ideas* (Tonawanda, NY: Black Rose Books, 2005), p. 68.

3   The phrase "propaganda of the deed", however, was coined not by him but by a French anarchist who published an article with that title in 1877. See Walter Laqueur, *A History of Terrorism* (New Brunswick, NJ: Transaction, 2002), p. 49.

4   Pyotr Kropotkin, "Expropriation", in: Graham, *Anarchism*, p. 154.

5   Charles Townshend, *Terrorism: A Very Short Introduction* (Oxford: Oxford University Press, 2002), p. 57.

6   Bruce Hoffman, *Inside Terrorism*, 2nd edition (New York: Columbia University Press, 2006), pp. 5–6.

7   Kropotkin, quoted in Jean Maitron, "The Era of the Attentats", in: Walter Laqueur and Yonah Alexander (eds), *The Terrorism Reader: A Historical Anthology* (New York: New American Library, 1987), p. 99.

8   Johann Most, *Revolutionäre Kriegswissenschaft. Ein Hand-büchlein zur Anleitung betreffend Gebrauches und Herstellung von Nitroglycerin, Dynamit, Schießbaumwolle, Knallquecksilber, Bomben, Brandsätzen, Giften usw., usw.* Neudruck der Ausgabe New York 1885. (*The Science of Revolutionary Warfare: A Little Handbook of Instruction in the Use and Preparation of Nitroglycerine, Dynamite, Gun-Cotton, Fulminating Mercury, Bombs, Fuses, Poisons, Etc., Etc.* Reprint of the 1885 New York Edition) (Berlin: Rixdorfer Verlagsanstalt, 1980).

9   Ibid., p. 56.

10   Johann Most, "Advice for terrorists", in: Laqueur and Alexander (eds), *The Terrorism Reader*, p. 100.

11   John Merriman, *The Dynamite Club: How a Bombing in Fin-de-Siècle Paris Ignited the Age of Modern Terror* (London: JR Books, 2009), pp. 69–87.

12   Vaillant, quoted in Alex Schmid and Janny de Graaf, *Violence as Communication: Insurgent Terrorism and the Western News Media* (London: Sage, 1982), p. 11.

13   Émile Henry, "A terrorist's defence", in: George Woodcock (ed.), *The Anarchist Reader* (London: Fontana Press, 1977), p. 195.

14   Ibid.

15   Cf. Martin A. Miller, "The intellectual origins of modern terrorism in Europe", in: Martha Crenshaw (ed.), *Terrorism in Context* (University Park, PA: Pennsylvania State University Press, 1995), pp. 39–41, 50, 56–7; David Miller, *Anarchism* (London: J.M. Dent & Sons, 1984), pp. 119–23.

16   Wilson, quoted in Marc Frey, "*Selbstbestimmung und Zivilisationsdiskurs in der amerikanischen Außenpolitik, 1917–1950*" ("Self-determination and Civilization Discourse in American Foreign Policy 1917–1950"), in: Jörg Fisch (ed.), *Die Verteilung der Welt: Selbstbestimmung und das Selbstbestimmungsrecht der*

Völker (*The World Divided: The People's Right to Self-Determination*) (Munich: Oldenbourg, 2011), p. 160.

17 Cf. "The Atlantic Charter: Declaration of principles issued by the president of the United States and the prime minister of the United Kingdom, 14 August 1941", *North Atlantic Treaty Organization;* available at http://www.nato.int/cps/en/natohq/official_texts_16912.htm, accessed 1 July 2016.

18 Frantz Fanon, *Die Verdammten dieser Erde* (*The Wretched of this Earth*) (Suhrkamp: Frankfurt am Main, 1966), p. 72.

19 Peter R. Neumann and M.L.R. Smith, *The Strategy of Terrorism* (London: Routledge, 2008), pp. 73–4.

20 Randall D. Law, *Terrorism: A History* (Cambridge: Polity Press, 2009), pp. 199–212.

21 Ibid., p. 214.

22 Cf. Alistair Horne, *A Savage War of Peace: Algeria 1954–1962* (Basingstoke: Macmillan, 1977), Chapter 20.

23 Neumann and Smith, *The Strategy*, p. 71.

24 Cf. Peter R. Neumann, *Britain's Long War: British Strategy in the Northern Ireland Conflict, 1969–98* (Basingstoke: Palgrave Macmillan, 2003), Chapter 1.

25 Adams, quoted in Peter R. Neumann, "The bullet and the ballot box: the case of the IRA", *Journal of Strategic Studies*, 28(6) (2005), p. 957.

26 See Donatella Della Porta and Mario Diani, *Social Movements: An Introduction* (Oxford: Wiley-Blackwell, 2005), Chapter 4.

27 "Carlos Marighela: Handbuch des Stadtguerillero" ("Carlos Marighella: The Urban Guerillero's Handbook") [sic!], *Nadir;* available at http://www.nadir.org/nadir/initiativ/rli/handbuch.html, accessed 1 July 2016.

28 Marighella, quoted in Neumann and Smith, *The Strategy*, p. 42.

29 Bill Ayers, *Fugitive Days: A Memoir* (Boston: Beacon Press, 2001), p. 121.

30 Ibid., p. 265.

31 Cf. Bryan Burrough, *Days of Rage: America's Radical Underground, the FBI, and the First Age of Terror* (New York: Penguin, 2015), Chapter 22.

32 Herfried Münkler, "Guerillakrieg und terrorismus" ("Guerrilla warfare and terrorism"), in: Wolfgang Kraushaar (ed.), *Die RAF und der linke Terrorismus* (*The RAF and Leftist Terrorism*) (Hamburg: Hamburger Edition, 2006), p. 91.

33 Cf. Tobias Wunschik, "Die zweite generation der RAF" ("The second generation of the RAF"), in: ibid., pp. 472–88; Alexander Straßner, "Die dritte generation der RAF" ("The third generation of the RAF"), in: ibid., pp. 489–510.

34 Mussolini, quoted in Walter Laqueur, *A History of Terrorism* (New Brunswick, NJ: Transaction, 2002), pp. 71–2.

35 Cf. Michael R. Ebner, *Ordinary Violence in Mussolini's Italy* (Cambridge: Cambridge University Press, 2011), p. 26.

36 Donald Sassoon, *Mussolini and the Rise of Fascism* (London: HarperCollins, 2007), p. 20.

37 Steve Bruce, "The problems of 'pro-state terrorism': Loyalist paramilitaries in Northern Ireland", *Terrorism and Political Violence*, 4(1) (1992), pp. 67–88.

38 Cf. Steve Bruce, *The Red Hand: Protestant Paramilitaries in Northern Ireland* (Oxford: Oxford University Press, 1992).

39 Anders Behring Breivik, "2083 – A European declaration of independence", July 2011, p. 1412.

2. THE RELIGIOUS WAVE

1 Hill, quoted in the documentary *Soldiers in the Army of God*, directed by Daphne Pinkerson and Marc Levin (Los Angeles: HBO, 2000).

2 Hill, quoted in John-Thor Dahlburg, "Amid storm, abortion foe is executed", *Los Angeles Times*, 4 September 2003.

3 Cf. National Abortion Federation, "Violence statistics & history"; available at http://prochoice.org/education-and-advocacy/violence/violence-statistics-and-history/, accessed 1 July 2016.

4 Bray, quoted in Mark Juergensmeyer, *Terror in the Mind of God: The Global Rise of Religious Violence,* 2nd edition (Los Angeles: University of California Press, 2000), p. 23.

5 Neal Horsley, quoted in *Soldiers in the Army of God.*

6 Bruce Hoffman, "Holy terror: the implications of terror motivated by a religious imperative" (RAND Corporation, 1993), p. 2.

7 Rapoport, "The four waves", p. 61.

8 François Burgat, *Face to Face with Political Islam* (London: I.B.Tauris, 2005); Gilles Kepel, *Jihad: The Trail of Political Islam* (London: I.B.Tauris, 2002).

9 Bernard Lewis, *The Crisis of Islam* (London and New York: Random House, 2003).

10 Roel Meijer, "Introduction", in: Roel Meijer (ed.), *Global Salafism: Islam's New Religious Movement* (London: Hurst, 2009); Shadi Hamid, "The roots of the Islamic State's appeal", *The Atlantic,* 31 October 2014.

11 Al-Banna, quoted in John Calvert, *Sayyid Qutb and the Origins of Radical Islamism* (London: Hurst, 2010), p. 81.

12 Lorenzo Vidino, *The New Muslim Brotherhood in the West* (New York: Columbia University Press, 2010), pp. 18–25; Richard P. Mitchell, *The Society of the Muslim Brothers* (Oxford: Oxford University Press), Chapters 2 and 6.

13 Qutb, quoted in Calvert, *Sayyid Qutb*, p. 217.

14 Ibid., pp. 221–7.

15 Meijer, "Introduction", pp. 3–7.

16 Kepel, *Jihad*, p. 51.

17 Cf. Joshua Teitelbaum, "The Muslim Brotherhood in Syria, 1945–1958: founding, social origins, ideology", *The Middle East Journal*, 65(2) (2011); Itzchak Weismann, "Sa'id Hawwa and Islamic revivalism in Ba'thist Syria", *Studia Islamica*, 85 (1997).

18 Cf. Umar F. Abd-Allah, *The Islamic Struggle in Syria* (Berkeley, CA: Mizan, 1983); Alison Pargeter, *The Muslim Brotherhood: From Opposition to Power* (London: Saqi, 2010), pp. 81–2.

19 Guido Steinberg, *Der nahe und der ferne Feind: Die Netzwerke des islamistischen Terrorismus* (*Near and Far Enemies: The Networks of Islamic Terrorism*) (Munich: C.H. Beck, 2005), p. 31.

20 Cf. Kepel, *Jihad*, p. 137.

21 Thomas Hegghammer, "Abdullah Azzam, the Imam of Jihad", in: Gilles Kepel and Jean-Pierre Milelli (eds), *Al Qaeda in its Own Words* (Cambridge, MA: Harvard University Press, 2008), pp. 81–93.

22 Abdullah Azzam, "The defense of Muslim territories constitutes the first individual duty", in: ibid., pp. 107–9.

23 Abdullah Azzam, "Join the caravan", in: ibid., p. 120.

24 Azzam, "The defense", in: ibid., p. 106.

25 Lawrence Wright, *The Looming Tower: al Qaeda's Road to 9/11* (London: Penguin, 2006), p. 107; Hegghammer, "Abdullah Azzam", p. 101.

26 Thomas Hegghammer, "The rise of the Muslim foreign fighters", *International Security*, 35(3) (2010), p. 61.

27 David Malet, *Foreign Fighters: Transnational Identity in Civil Conflicts* (Oxford: Oxford University Press, 2013), pp. 167–71.

28 Wright, *The Looming Tower*, p. 102.

29 Ibid., p. 119.

30 Malet, *Foreign Fighters*, pp. 172–80; interview with the former head of the secret service in Islamabad, 28 April 2015.

31 Wright, *The Looming Tower*, pp. 104–9.

32 Hegghammer, "Abdullah Azzam", pp. 96–7.

33 Quoted ibid., p. 81.

34 William McCants and Jarret Brachman, *Militant Ideology Atlas: Research Compendium* (Westpoint, NY: Combating Terrorism Center, U.S. Military Academy, 2006), p. 287.

35 Interview with the former head of the secret service in Islamabad, 28 April 2015.

36 Wright, *The Looming Tower*, pp. 131–6.

37 Cf. Mustafa Hamid and Leah Farrall, *The Arabs at War in Afghanistan* (London: Hurst, 2015).

38 Mary Anne Weaver, "Blowback", *The Atlantic*, 1 May 1996.

39 Cf. Peter R. Neumann, *Old and New Terrorism: Late Modernity, Globalization and the Transformation of Political Violence* (Cambridge: Polity Press, 2009), p. 38.

40 Cf. Jason Burke, *Al Qaeda: The True Story of Radical Islam* (London: Penguin, 2003), pp. 148–50.

41 Hegghammer, "The rise", p. 61.

42 Evan F. Kohlmann, *Al-Qaida's Jihad in Europe: The Afghan-Bosnian Network* (Oxford: Berg, 2004), pp. 16–19.

43 Jonathan Bronitsky, *British Foreign Policy and Bosnia: The Rise of Islamism in Britain, 1992–1995* (London: ICSR, 2010), p. 18; available at http://icsr.info/2010/11/british-foreign-policy-and-bosnia-the-rise-of-islamism-in-britain-1992-1995-2/, accessed 1 July 2016.

44 Quoted by Robert Sam Anson, "The journalist and the terrorist", *Vanity Fair,* August 2002.

45 Cf. Robert Fisk, "Anti-Soviet warrior puts his army on the road to peace", *Independent,* 6 December 1993.

46 "Bin Laden's Fatwa", PBS. 23 August 1996; https://azelin.files.wordpress.com/2010/08/usama-bin-laden-1996-declaration-of-war-against-the-americans.pdf, accessed 22 August 2016. "Al Qaeda's second Fatwa", PBS. 23. February 1998; http://fas.org/irp/world/para/docs/980223-fatwa.htm, accessed 22 August 2016.

47 "The war of unintended consequences: four years after 9/11", *Guardian,* 12 September 2005.

48 Bruce Hoffman and Fernando Reinares (eds), *The Evolution of the Global Terrorist Threat: From 9/11 to Osama bin Laden's Death* (New York: Columbia University Press, 2014).

49 "Zawahiri's letter to Zarqawi (English Translation)", *Combating Terrorism Center at West Point,* undated, available at https://www.ctc.usma.edu/posts/zawahiris-letter-to-zarqawi-english-translation-2, accessed 1 July 2016.

50 Quoted in Lawrence Wright, "The rebellion within", *New Yorker,* 2 June 2008.

51 Research by Alexander Meleagrou-Hitchens, 19 May 2015.

52 Peter Bergen, "A gripping glimpse into bin Laden's decline and fall", *CNN,* 11 March 2015.

53 Cf. "US 'within reach of strategic defeat of al-Qaeda'", *BBC News,* 9 July 2011.

54 Al-Zawahiri, quoted in Shiraz Maher and Peter R. Neumann, *Al-Qaeda at the Crossroads: How the terror group is responding to the loss of its leaders & the Arab Spring* (London: ICSR, 2012), pp. 9–10; available at http://icsr.info/wp-content/uploads/2012/10/ICSR_Maher-Neumann-Paper_For-online-use-only1.pdf, accessed 1 July 2016.

55 Attiya Allah al-Libi, quoted ibid., p. 12.

56 Al-Awlaki, quoted ibid., p. 14.

3. THE ISLAMIC STATE

1 Interview with Abdullah Anas, 8 April 2015.

2 Cf. Steve Contorno, "What Obama said about Islamic State as a 'JV' team", *PolitiFact,* 7 September 2014.

3 Cf. Volker Perthes, quoted in Thorsten Herdickerhoff, "Neue grenzen in Nahost" ("New borders in the Middle East"), *Vorwärts,* 18 November 2014, available at http://www.vorwaerts.de/artikel/neue-grenzen-nahost, accessed 1 July 2016.

4 Guido Steinberg, *Kalifat des Schreckens: IS und die Bedrohung durch den islamistischen Terror (Caliphate of fear: IS and the threat of Islamist terror)* (Munich: Knaur, 2015), pp. 52–8.

5 Ibid., p. 138.

6 Quoted in "Zarqawi: Our eyes are on Jerusalem", *Associated Press*, 26 April 2006.

7 Steinberg, *Kalifat des Schreckens*, p. 5.

8 Cf. *Iraq Body Count*; available at https://www.iraqbodycount.org/, accessed 1 July 2016.

9 "Zawahiri's letter to Zarqawi (English Translation)", *Combating Terrorism Center at Westpoint*, undated, available at https://www.ctc.usma.edu/posts/zawahiris-letter-to-zarqawi-english-translation-2, accessed 1 July 2016.

10 Derek Harvey and Michael Pregent, "The lessons of the surge: defeating ISIS requires a new Sunni awakening", *New America Foundation*, June 2014, p. 2.

11 Qassim Abdul-Zarah, "Al-Qaeda making comeback in Iraq, officials say", *Associated Press*, 9 October 2012.

12 Michael Weiss and Hassan Hassan, *Inside ISIS: Inside the Army of Terror* (New York: Regan Arts, 2015), Chapter 9.

13 Cf. Peter R. Neumann, "Suspects into collaborators", *London Review of Books*, 3 April 2014.

14 Cf. Hassan Hassan, "A jihadist blueprint for hearts and minds is gaining traction in Syria", *The National*, 4 March 2014.

15 Cf. Noman Benotman and Roisin Blake, "Jabhat al-Nusra: a strategic briefing", Quilliam Foundation, January 2013; available at http://www.quilliamfoundation.org/wp/wp-content/uploads/publications/free/jabhat-al-nusra-a-strategic-briefing.pdf, accessed 1 July 2016.

16 Cf. Amir Musawy, Georg Mascolo and Volkmar Kabisch, "Auf der Spur des IS-Anführers al-Baghdadi" ("On the trail of IS leader al-Baghdadi"), *NDR*, 18 February 2015; available at https://www.ndr.de/nachrichten/investigation/Auf-der-Spur-des-IS-Anfuehrers-al-Baghdadi,baghdadi104.html, accessed 1 July 2016.

17 Richard Barrett, "The Islamic State", *The Soufan Group*, November 2014, p. 25.

18 Martin Chulov, "Isis: the inside story", *Guardian*, 11 December 2014.

19 Andrew Thompson, quoted in Jessica Stern and J.M. Berger, *ISIS: The State of Terror* (New York: William Collins, 2015), p. 35.

20 Interview with Aymenn Jawad al-Tamimi, 1 April 2015.

21 Al-Baghdadi, quoted in Steinberg, *Kalifat des Schreckens*, p. 78.

22 The jihadists in the Syrian border town al-Bukamal are a good example of this. Interview with Aymenn Jawad al-Tamimi, 1 April 2015.

23 Joas Wagemakers, *The Quietist Jihadi: The Ideology and Influence of Abu Muhammad al-Maqdisi* (Cambridge: Cambridge University Press, 2012), pp. 60–7.

24 Shaykh-ul-Islaam Ibn Taymiyyah, undated blog; available at https://shaykhulislaam.wordpress.com/2009/08/13/ruling-on-the-nu-sayrialawi-sect/

25 Abu Bakr Naji, *The Management of Savagery: The Most Critical Stage Through Which the Umma Will Pass* (Translated by William McCants) (Boston: John M. Olin Institute, 2006); https://azelin.files.wordpress.com/2010/08/abu-bakr-naji-the-management-of-savagery-the-most-critical-stage-through-which-the-umma-will-pass.pdf, accessed 1 July 2016.

26 Weiss and Hassan, *Inside ISIS*, p. 41.

27 Naji, *The Management of Savagery*, pp. 28–50.

28 Interview with William McCants, 2 March 2015.

29 Ibid.

30 Cf. Giles Fraser, "To Islamic State, Dabiq is important – but it's not the end of the world", *Guardian*, 10 October 2014; John Gray, "Isis: an apocalyptic cult carving a place in the modern world", *Guardian*, 26 August 2014.

31 Zarqawi, quoted in "Why Islamic State chose town of Dabiq for propaganda", *BBC News*, 17 November 2014.

32 Interview with William McCants, 2 March 2015.

33 Cf. William McCants, quoted in Zack Beauchamp, "ISIS is really obsessed with the apocalypse", *vox.com*, 6 April 2015, available at http://www.vox.com/2015/4/6/8341691/isis-apocalypse, accessed 1 July 2016.

34 Interview with Aymenn Jawad al-Tamimi, 1 April 2015.

35 "Jihadi John", quoted in "Why Islamic", *BBC News*.

36 Interview with Aymenn Jawad al-Tamimi, 1 April 2015; Weiss and Hassan, *Inside ISIS*, pp. 154–5.

37 Jürgen Todenhöfer, "'Islamischer Staat' – 7 Eindrücke einer schwierigen Reise" ("'Islamic State' – seven impressions of a difficult journey"), *Jürgen Todenhöfer*, 22 December 2014; available at http://juergentodenhoefer.de/7-eindruecke-einer-schwierigen-reise/, accessed 1 July 2016.

38 Ross Keith, "How many fighters does ISIS have", *Vocativ*, 19 February 2015; available at http://www.vocativ.com/world/isis-2/how-big-is-isis/, accessed 1 July 2016.

39 Interview with Aymenn Jawad al-Tamimi, 1 April 2015.

40 Barrett, "The Islamic State", p. 23.

41 David Siddharta Patel, "ISIS in Iraq: what we get wrong and why 2015 is not 2007 redux", *Middle East Brief*, January 2015; available at http://www.brandeis.edu/crown/publications/meb/MEB87.pdf, accessed 1 July 2016.

42 Barrett, "The Islamic State", p. 20.

43 Weiss and Hassan, *Inside ISIS*, pp. 153–65.

44 Interview with Aziz al-Hamza, 6 May 2015.

45 Peter R. Neumann, "Foreign fighter total in Syria/Iraq now exceeds 20,000; surpasses Afghanistan conflict in the 1980s", *ICS. Insight*, 26 January 2015; available at http://icsr.info/2015/01/foreign-fighter-total-syriairaq-now-exceeds-20000-surpasses-afghanistan-conflict-1980s/, accessed 1 July 2016.

46 Hegghammer, quoted in Joshua Holland, "Why have a record number of Westerners joined the Islamic State?", *Moyers & Company*, 10 October 2014; available at http://billmoyers.com/2014/10/10/record-number-westerners-joined-islamic-state-great-threat/, accessed 1 July 2016.

47 Cf. Mohammed M. Hafez, "Suicide terrorism in Iraq: a preliminary assessment of the quantitative data and documentary evidence", *Studies in Conflict and Terrorism* 29(8) (2006), pp. 591–619.

48 Patrick Cockburn, *The Rise of Islamic State: ISIS and the New Sunni Revolution* (London: Verso, 2015), p. 15.

49 Interview with Aymenn Jawad al-Tamimi, 1 April 2015.

50 Cockburn, *The Rise*, p. 64.

51 Christoph Reuter, "The terror strategist: secret files reveal the structure of the Islamic State", *Spiegel Online*, 18 April 2015; available at http://www.spiegel.de/international/world/islamic-state-files- show-structure-of-islamist-terror-group-a-1029274.html, accessed 1 July 2016.

52 Barrett, "The Islamic State", p. 31–2.

53 According to recent reports, Western air strikes have forced ISIS troops to move in smaller groups and use civilian vehicles. See Raniah Salloum, "Mit neuer Terror-Taktik zum Erfolg" ("New terror tactics bring success"), *Spiegel Online*, 31 May 2015; available at http://www.spiegel.de/politik/ausland/is-islamischer-staat-mit-neuer-taktik-in-syrien-a-1036435.html, accessed 1 July 2016.

54 But Western air strikes have made this more difficult for the Islamic State. Cf. Daveed Gartenstein-Ross, "The Islamic State's Anbar offensive and Abu Umar al-Shishani", *War on the Rocks*, 9 October 2014, available at http://warontherocks.com/2014/10/the-islamic-states-anbar-offensive-and-abu-umar-al-shishani/, accessed 1 July 2016.

55 Reuter, "The terror strategist".

56 90 per cent of the Ansar al-Sunna members who fought alongside the Islamic State at Mosul have now actually switched allegiance to the group. Interview with Aymenn Jawad al-Tamimi, 1 April 2015.

57 Cf. Cockburn, *The Rise*, Chapter 4.

58 Ministry of Information, "Information prize", 11 May 2013; administrative committee in the government of Baghdad North, undated list of goods.

59 "The Islamic State", *Vice News*, 13 August 2014; https://news.vice.com/video/the-islamic-state-part-4, accessed 1 July 2016.

60 Naji, *The Management of Savagery*, p. 28.

61 Zaid al Fares, "Frontline ISIS. How the Islamic State is brainwashing children with Stone Age school curriculum", *International Business Times*, 1 September 2014.

62 Abu Rumaysah al Britani, *A Brief Guide to the Islamic State (2015)* (Raqqa: ISIS, 2015).

63 Gilgamesh Nabeel, "The Islamic State's plan for universities", *Al-Fanar*, 25 November 2014.

64 Borzou Daragahi and Erika Solomon, "Fuelling Isis inc", *Financial Times*, 21 September 2014.

65 Georg Mascolo, "Der IS sitzt auf dem Trockenen" ("IS has run dry"), *Süddeutsche Zeitung*, 8 April 2015.

66 Charles Lister, "Cutting off ISIS cash flow", *Middle East Politics & Policy, Brookings Institution*, 24 October 2014.

67 Cf. "Financing of the terrorist organisation Islamic State in Iraq and the Levant (ISIL)", *Financial Action Task Force Report*, February 2015, pp. 15–18.

68 Aaron Y. Zelin, "The Islamic State's model", *Washington Post*, 28 January 2015; available at https://www.washingtonpost.com/blogs/monkey-cage/wp/2015/01/28/the-islamic-states-model/, accessed 1 July 2016.

69 Interview with Aymenn Jawal al-Tamimi, 1 April 2015.

70 Ibid.

71 Cf. Ishaan Tharoor, "Islamic State burned a woman alive for not engaging in 'extreme' sex act, U.N. official says", *Washington Post*, 22 May 2015.

72 The Islamic State's argument is that it is a state and can therefore do things that a group like al-Qaeda never could. Interview with Shiraz Maher, 11 April 2015.

73 Interview with William McCants, 15 March 2015.

74 Cf. Sinan Salaheddin, "Islamic State introduces new restrictions to prevent Mosul residents from fleeing city", *The Globe and Mail*, 13 March 2015.

75 Lizzie Dearden, "Isis advertises 10 jobs in the caliphate including press officers, bomb makers and teachers", *Independent,* 10 April 2015.

76 Interview with one of the founders of Raqqa Is Being Slaughtered Silently, 6 May 2015.

77 Sinan Salaheddin, "Islamic State introduces new restrictions to prevent Mosul residents from fleeing the city", *The Globe and Mail,* 13 March 2015; Jalal Zein Eddine, "ISIS is crumbling in Syria: here's why", *Now,* 31 March 2015.

78 Issa, quoted in "Voices from inside the 'giant prison' of Raqqa", *Syria Deeply*, 23 April 2015.

79 Interview with Aziz al-Hamza, 6 May 2015.

80 Issa, quoted in "Voices from inside".

81 Interview with Aziz al-Hamza, 6 May 2015.

4. FOREIGN FIGHTERS

1 Aaron Y. Zelin, "European fighters in Syria", *ICS. Insight,* 2 April 2013; available at http://icsr.info/2013/04/icsr-insight-european-foreign-fighters-in-syria-2/, accessed 1 July 2016.

2 Ibid.

3 Neumann, "Foreign fighter total".

4 Hegghammer, "The rise", p. 61.

5 Neumann, "Foreign fighter total".

6 Ibid.

7 Behnam T. Said, *Islamischer Staat: IS-Miliz, al-Qaida und die deutschen Brigaden (Islamic State: IS militia, al-Qaida and the German brigades)* (Munich: C.H. Beck, 2014), pp. 158–9.

8 Interview with a representative of the Belgian domestic intelligence service, 14 April 2015.

9 Many converts also have an immigrant background, e.g. Russian–Germans or Shi'as who convert to Sunni Islam. See interview with representatives of the Hamburg Constitution Protection Office, 23 March 2015.

10 Cf. "Analyse der den deutschen Sicherheitsbehörden vorliegenden Informationenüber die Radikalisierungshintergründe und-verlaufe der Personen, die aus islamistischer Motivation aus Deutschland in Richtung Syrien ausgereist sind" ("Analysis of information available to the German security services about the backgrounds and radicalization processes of people who have left Germany for Syria on an Islamic impetus"), Germany Ministry of the Interior, undated (ca. 2014).

11 Interview with Melanie Smith, 22 December 2014.

12 David Malet, *Foreign Fighters: Transnational Identity in Civil Conflicts* (Oxford: Oxford University Press, 2013). Chapter 1.

13 Cf. Interview with Shiraz Maher, 11 April 2015.

14 Ibid.

15 Ifthekar Jaman, quoted in Shiraz Maher, "From Portsmouth to Kobane", *New Statesman*, 31 October 2014.

16 Mohammed al-Arifi, "Oh Syria, the Victory is Coming", YouTube, 8 February 2012; available at https://www.youtube.com/watch?v=GE6En9e7dew, accessed 1 July 2016.

17 Ifthekar Jaman, quoted in "Briton Ifthekar Jaman 'killed in fighting in Syria', family says", *BBC News*, 17 December 2013.

18 Mary Anne Weaver, "Her Majesty's Jihadists", *New York Times Magazine*, 14 April 2015.

19 Ifthekar Jaman, quoted in Maher, "From Portsmouth".

20 Interview with Shiraz Maher, 11 April 2015.

21 Maher, quoted in Weaver, "Her Majesty's Jihadists".

22 David Thomson, *Les Français jihadistes* (*The French Jihadists*) (Paris: Éditions des Arènes, 2014), pp. 246–7.

23 The Facebook page belonging to Salahuddin Shabazz (Jean-Edouard).

24 Jean-Edouard, quoted in Thomson, *Les Français jihadistes*, p. 257.

25 The Facebook page belonging to Salahuddin Shabazz (Jean-Edouard).

26 Tweets from @AbouAyaat (Jean-Edouard).

27 Ibid.

28 Ibid.

29 Thomson told me in May 2015 that Jean-Edouard was preparing to carry out a suicide bombing. Emails with David Thomson, 2 May 2015.

30 Cf. Donatella Della Porta, "Recruitment processes in clandestine political organizations: Italian leftwing terrorism", *International Social Movement Research*, 1 (1988), pp. 155–69; Marc Sageman, *Understanding Terror Networks* (Philadelphia: University of Pennsylvania Press, 2004).

31 Interview with representatives of the Bremen Constitution Protection Office, 20 April 2015.

32 Hubert Gude, "Muslime gegen Muslime" ("Muslims versus Muslims"), *Spiegel Online*, 31 March 2014, available at http://www.spiegel.de/spiegel/print/d-126267969.html, accessed 1 July 2016.

33 Cf. "Gewaltorientierter Islamismus in Bremen" ("Violent Islamism in Bremen"), *Der Senator für Inneres und Sport*, 16 April 2015.

34 Notice from the Senator for Domestic Affairs and Sport to the "Culture and Families Association", 21 November 2014.

35 Interview with representatives of the Bremen Constitution Protection Office, 20 April 2015.

36 ARD interview with Ebrahim B., 10 July 2015.

37 Ibid.

38 "Hijra to the Islamic State", *Islamic State*, March 2015.

39 Ibid., p. 5.

40 Interview with a representative of the Belgian domestic intelligence service, 14 April 2015.

41 Interview with Schleuser Abdullah, 9 April 2014. For clips from this and other interviews, see Ahmet Senyurt, "Die infrastruktur der Gotteskrieger: reportage von der türkisch-syrischen grenze" ("The Holy Warriors' infrastructure: a report from the Turkish-Syrian border", *report München*, 22 April 2014; http://www.br.de/fernsehen/das-erste/sendungen/report-muenchen/syrien-grenzgebiet-al-kaida100.html, accessed 1 November 2015 (Link no longer working.)

42 Cf. Jan Rübel, "Auf einkaufstour im namen des bösen" ("Shopping in the name of evil"), *Yahoo! Deutschland*, 5 November 2014; available at https://de.nachrichten.yahoo.com/blogs/reingezoomt/auf-einkaufstour-im-namen-des-bösen-084158504.html, accessed 1 July 2016.

43 "Indictment", Public Prosecutor General of the Federal Court of Justice, file 2 *StE 4/14-8*, 23 May 2014.

44 "Hijra to", *Islamic State*, p. 6.

45 Interviews with Abdullah, Hisham and Bashar, 9–11 April 2014.

46 "Hijra to", *Islamic State*.

47 ARD interview with Ebrahim B., 10 July 2015.

48 Interview with Schleuser Abdullah, 9 April 2014.

49 "Indictment", Public Prosecutor General, pp. 54–7.

50 Cf. Andrew Zammit, quoted in Michael Safi, "Not all foreign fighters will pose a security threat to Australia, says expert", *Guardian*, 15 April 2015.

51 Cf. "A window into the Islamic State", *Dabiq*, October 2014, pp. 27–9.

52 Interview with Aziz al-Hamza, 6 May 2015.

53 Steve Rose, "The Isis propaganda war: a hi-tech media jihad", *Guardian*, 7 October 2014.

54 Interview with Aziz al-Hamza, 6 May 2015.

55 Cf. for example Anwar al-Awlaki, "The virtues of Ribaat & the one who dies in Ribaat", YouTube, 16 January 2015; https://www.youtube.com/watch?v=NQesjAIeats, accessed 1 November 2015. (Link no longer working.)

56 "The virtues of Ribat: for the cause of Allah", *Dabiq #9*, May 2015, pp. 8–13.

57 Interview with Shiraz Maher, 11 April 2015.

58 Interview with Aymenn Jawad al-Tamimi, 1 April 2015.

59 Interviews with Bashar and Hisham, 11 April 2014.

60 Cf. Mohammed M. Hafez, "Suicide terrorism in Iraq: a preliminary assessment of the quantitative data and documentary evidence", *Studies in Conflict and Terrorism*, 29(8) (2006), pp. 591–619.

61 Interview with Aymenn Jawad al-Tamimi, 1 April 2015.

62 This is confirmed by, for example, the Wolfsburg defector Ebrahim B. See ARD interview with Ebrahim B., 10 July 2015.

63 Cf. Richard Kerbaj, "Soft reception for returning Brits as Isis turns to chick lit", *Sunday Times*, 9 November 2014.

64 Jaak Raes, "Lessons learned from Verviers and European co-operation in the field of counter-terrorism", *Rede beim 12. Symposium des Bundesamtes für Verfassungsschutz (Speech at the 12 symposium of the Constitution Protection Office)*, 4 May 2015; available at http://www.verfassungsschutz.de/de/oeffentlichkeitsarbeit/symposium/symposium-2015, accessed 1 July 2016.

65 Cf. Daniel Bax, "Beihilfe zum Dschihad" ("Helping out in Jihad") *taz*, 5 October 2014.

66 Thomas Hegghammer, "Should I stay or should I go? Explaining variation in jihadists' choice between domestic and foreign fighting", *American Political Science Review*, 107(1) (2013), pp. 1–15.

67 Jytte Klausen and Adrienne Roach, "Western jihadists in the Syrian and Iraqi insurgencies", *Working Paper #4, The Western Jihadism Project*, August 2014, pp. 40–4.

68 Extract from a WhatsApp conversation with an English fighter, 26 August 2014.

69 Cf. Richard Kerbaj, "Jihadists from UK stuck in Turkey after deserting Isis", *The Sunday Times*, 5 October 2014.

70 "Isis 'executes 100 deserters' in Syria's Raqqa", *Al Arabiya*, 20 December 2014; available at http://english.alarabiya.net/en/News/middle-east/2014/12/20/ISIS-executes-100-deserters-in-Syria-s-Raqqa-report.html, accessed 1 July 2016.

71 Interview with Aziz al-Hamza, 6 May 2015.

72 Interview with Claudia Dantschke, 23 March 2015.

73 See Jana Simon, "Der Junge, der in den Krieg ging" ("The boy who went to war"), *Zeit Magazin*, 22 May 2015.

74 Interview with a representative of the Belgian domestic intelligence service, 14 April 2015.

75 Hegghammer, "Should I", p. 11.

76 Andrew Zammit, "List of alleged violent plots in Europe involving Syria returnees", *The Murphy Raid*, 25 January 2015; available at http://andrewzammit.org/2014/06/29/list-of-alleged-violent-plots-in-europe-involving-syria-returnees/, accessed 1 July 2016.

77 Interview with representatives of the Hamburg Constitution Protection Office, 23 March 2015.

78 Daniel Byman and Jeremy Shapiro, "Be afraid. Be a little afraid: the threat of terrorism from Western foreign fighters in Syria and Iraq", *Brookings Institution, Policy Paper #34*, November 2014.

5. SUPPORTERS

1 Tom Wyke, "Radical British Islamist who stabbed football fan in the head with a pen skips bail and joins Islamic State in Syria", *Daily Mail*, 20 January 2015.

2 Stefan Malthaner and Peter Waldmann, "Radikale milieus: das soziale umfeld terroristischer gruppen" ("Radical milieux: terrorist groups' social environment"), in: Stefan Malthaner and Peter Waldmann (eds), *Radikale Milieus: Das soziale*

Umfeld terroristischer Gruppen ("*Radical Milieux: Terrorist Groups' Social Environment*") (Frankfurt am Main: Campus, 2012), pp. 11–42.

3 Cf. Ulrich Kraetzer, *Salafisten: Bedrohung für Deutschland? (Salafists: A Threat to Germany?)* (Gütersloh: Gütersloher Verlagshaus, 2014).

4 A similar categorization can be found in: Götz Nordbruch, Jochen Müller and Deniz Ünlü, "Einfache antworten in schwierigen zeiten: was macht salafistische prediger attraktiv?" ("Simple answers in difficult times: what makes Salafist preachers attractive?", *Interventionen*, December 2013, pp. 15–18.

5 Aladin El-Mafaalani, "Salafismus als jugendkulturelle provokation" ("Salafism as a youth culture provocation"), in Thorsten Gerald Schneiders (ed.), *Salafismus in Deutschland: Ursprünge und Gefahren einer islamisch–fundamentalistischen Bewegung (Salafism in Germany: The origins and dangers of an Islamic-fundamentalist movement)* (Bielefeld: Transcript, 2014), p. 357.

6 Cf. Sinan Selen, "Foreign Fighters" conference, *Konrad-Adenauer-Stiftung*, 24 March 2015.

7 Quintan Wiktorowicz, "Anatomy of the Salafi movement", *Studies in Conflict and Terrorism*, 29 (2006), pp. 207–39.

8 More detailed distinctions can be found in, for example, Jarret M. Brachman, *Global Jihadism: Theory and Practice* (Abingdon and New York: Routledge, 2009), Chapter 2.

9 Cf. Nina Wiedl, "Geschichte des Salafismus in Deutschland" ("The history of Salafism in Germany"), in: Behnam T. Said and Hazim Fouad (eds), *Salafismus: Auf der Suche nach dem wahren Islam (Salafism: Searching for True Islam)* (Freiburg: Herder, 2014), pp. 428–31.

10 Nagie, quoted in Claudia Dantschke, "'Lasst Euch nicht radikalisieren!' – Salafismus in Deutschland" ("'Don't let yourselves be radicalised!' – Salafism in Germany"), in: Thorsten Gerald Schneiders (ed.), *Salafismus in Deutschland* (Bielefeld: Transcript, 2014), p. 176.

11 Said, *Islamischer Staat*, pp. 154–6.

12 Shiraz Maher and Peter R. Neumann, "German arrests: the rise of the megaphone Jihadists", *ICS. Insight,* 14 June 2012; available at http://icsr.info/2012/06/icsr-insight-german-arrests-the-rise-of-the-megaphone-jihadists-2/, accessed 1 July 2016.

13 Jytte Klausen, Eliane Tschaen Barbieri, Aaron Reichlin-Melnick and Aaron Y. Zelin, "The YouTube Jihadists: a social network analysis of al-Muhajiroun's propaganda campaign", *Perspectives on Terrorism*, 6(1) (2012); available at http://www.terrorismanalysts.com/pt/index.php/pot/article/view/klausen-et-al-youtube-jihadists/html, accessed 1 July 2016.

14 According to some reports, Bakri had already founded the group in the 1980s, but it is more likely that it was "re-founded" in 1990s London. See Quintan Wiktorowicz, *Radical Islam Rising: Muslim Extremism in the West* (Oxford: Rowman & Littlefield, 2005), p. 106.

15 Owen Bowcott, "Arrest extremist marchers, police told", *Guardian*, 6 February 2006.

16 *BBC Hardtalk*, BBC, 8 August 2005; available at https://www.youtube.com/watch?v=223gLcfCj_c, accessed 1 July 2016.

17 Colin Blackstock, "Taliban 'recruiter' questioned", *Guardian*, 4 December 2002.

18 Interview with Raffaello Pantucci, 14 May 2005.

19 The group also used the name *Forsane Alizza*. Cf. Peter R. Neumann and Scott Kleinmann, "Toulouse gunman's link to UK extremists", *ICS. Insight*, 21 March 2012; available at http://icsr.info/2012/03/icsr-insight-toulouse-gunmans-link-to-uk-extremists/, accessed 1 July 2016.

20 Ben Taub, "From ISIS to Belgium", *New Yorker*, 1 June 2015.

21 Cf. Jytte Klausen, quoted in "Is preacher Anjem Choudary a radicalising force?", *BBC News*, 13 May 2015; available at http://www.bbc.co.uk/news/uk-politics-32731177, accessed 1 July 2016.

22 Fouad Belkacem, quoted in Taub, "From ISIS"; interview with a representative of the Belgian domestic intelligence service, 14 April 2015.

23 Raes, "Lessons learned".

24 Pieter van Ostaeyen, "Belgian fighters in Syria and Iraq – April 2015", *pietervanostaeyen*, 4 May 2015; available at https://pietervanostaeyen.wordpress.com/2015/04/05/belgian-fighters-in-syria-and-iraq-april-2015/, accessed 1 July 2016.

25 Raes, "Lessons learned".

26 Even though one of Choudary's representatives, Abu Waleed, helped the Germans improve their online presence and integrated it into the English online network Salafimedia. Cf. Wiedl, "Geschichte des Salafismus", p. 428.

27 Cf. Guido Steinberg, *Al-Qaidas deutsche Kämpfer: Die Globaisierung des islamistischen Terrorismus* (*Al-Qaeda's German Fighters: The Globalisation of Islamist Terrorism*) (Hamburg: edition Körber-Stiftung, 2014), pp. 358–62.

28 Cf. Hendrik Rasehorn, "Ein Dutzend Wolfsburger kämpft für IS" ("A dozen Wolfsburgers are fighting for IS"), *Wolfsburger Nachrichten*, 7 November 2014.

29 Cf. Georg Mascolo, "Deutscher IS-Rekrut: Einer packt aus" ("German IS recruit: I've had enough"), *Süddeutsche Zeitung*, 16 July 2015.

30 Wolf Schmidt, *Jung, Deutsch, Taliban* (*Young, German, in the Taliban*) (Berlin: Christoph Links, 2012), p. 137.

31 Ibid., pp. 136–7.

32 Interview with a representative of the Belgian domestic intelligence service, 14 April 2015.

33 John Scheerhout, "Manchester terror twin who fled to Syria to become a 'jihadi bride' shows her support for Islamic State fighters on Twitter", *Manchester Evening News*, 7 September 2014.

34 Research by Melanie Smith, 8 May 2015.

35 Schmidt, *Jung, Deutsch, Taliban*, pp. 142–3.

36 Adam Bermingham, Maura Conway, Lisa McInerney, Neil O'Hare and Alan F. Smeaton, "Combining social network analysis and sentiment analysis to explore the potential for online radicalisation", *International Conference on Advances in Social Networks Analysis and Mining*, Athens, 20–22 July 2009.

37 Tweet by @ummuthmann, 7 January 2015.

38 Tweet by @baqiyah28, 7 January 2015.

39 Tweet by @jafarbritaniya, 7 January 2015.

40 Tweet by @bint_ibrah3m, 7 January 2015.

41 Interview with Melanie Smith, 19 May 2015.

42 Ibid.

43 Anonymous, "'Ich geriet an "Millatu Ibrahim", weil für mich damals alle Muslime gleich waren': Bericht einer Aussteigerin aus der Salafismus-Szene in Deutschland" ("'I got involved with "Millatu Ibrahim" because at that stage all Muslims were the same to me'; the account of one female defector from the Salafist scene in Germany"), in: Schneiders, *Salafismus*, pp. 456–7.

44 Tweets by @Bint_Mujahid, February 2015.

45 Erin Marie Saltman and Melanie Smith, *"Till Martyrdom Do Us Part": Gender and the ISIS Phenomenon* (London: IS. and ICSR, 2015).

46 Interview with Berna Kurnaz, 20 April 2015.

47 Patrick Kingsley, "Who is behind ISIS's terrifying online propaganda operation?", *Guardian*, 23 June 2014.

48 Spencer Ackerman, "ISIS online propaganda outpacing U.S. counter-efforts, ex-officials warn", *Guardian*, 22 September 2014.

49 J.M. Berger, "How ISIS games Twitter", *The Atlantic*, 16 June 2014. For a comprehensive overview of the Islamic State's official online presence, see Jessica Stern and J.M. Berger, *ISIS: The State of Terror* (New York: William Collins, 2015).

50 Cf. Jarret M. Brachman and Alix N. Levine, "You too can be Awlaki!", *The Fletcher Forum on World Affairs*, 35(1) (2011), pp. 25–46.

51 Morten S. Hopperstad, "Norsk islamist (25) tiltalt etter skyteepisode i Oslo", *VG Nyheter*, 1 February 2015; "Slik lever de Norske jihadestene i Syria", *NRK*, 31 March 2013.

52 Abul Hakim Ryding's Facebook page, post from 29 April 2013.

53 Joseph A. Carter, Shiraz Maher and Peter R. Neumann, *Greenbirds: Measuring Importance and Influence in Syrian Foreign Fighter Networks* (London: ICSR, 2014), pp. 18–28; available at http://icsr.info/wp-content/uploads/2014/04/ICSR-Report-Greenbirds-Measuring-Importance-and-Infleunce-in-Syrian-Foreign-Fighter-Networks.pdf, accessed 1 July 2016.

54 John Safran, "Musa Cerantonio: Muslim convert and radical supporter of the Islamic State", *Sydney Morning Herald*, 17 January 2015.

55 Musa Cerantonio's Facebook page, 24 February 2014.

56 Jarret M. Brachman, *Global Jihadism: Theory and Practice* (Abingdon and New York: Routledge, 2009), p. 39.

57 Rayat al-Tawheed, quoted in John Domokos and Alex Rees, "Jihad, Syria and social media", *Guardian*, 15 April 2014; available at http://www.theguardian.com/uk-news/video/2014/apr/15/jihad-syria-social-media-video, accessed 1 July 2016.

58 Interviews with Shiraz Maher, 11 April 2015, and Aymenn Jawad al-Tamimi, 1 April 2015.

59 Tweet by @ShamiWitness, 21 March 2014.

60 Cf. tweet by @Matthew_Barber, 21 August 2014 (and replies from Shami).

61 "Shami Witness unmasked: 'I will not resist arrest'", *Channel 4 News*, 12 December 2014; available at http://www.channel4.com/news/police-bangalore-islamic-state-twitter-shami-witness, accessed 1 July 2016.

62 "Who is Mehdi Masroor Biswas?", *The Times of India*, 13 December 2014.

63 Louis Beam, "Leaderless resistance", *The Seditionist*, February 1992; available at http://www.louisbeam.com/leaderless.htm, accessed 1 July 2016.

64 Cf. Brachman and Levine, "You too".

65 The most significant exceptions are the attacks in Fort Hood in July 2009 and in Boston in spring 2013. See "Homegrown extremism, 2001–2015", *New America Foundation;* available at http://securitydata.newamerica.net/extremists/analysis.html, accessed 1 July 2016.

66 "Roshonara & Taimour: followers of the borderless loyalty", *Inspire*, Winter 2010.

67 Shaky Abu Muhammad al-Adnani ash-Shami, "Indeed your lord is ever watchful", *Islamic State*, 22 September 2014.

68 Cf. interview with Nico Prucha, 24 May 2015.

69 Al-Baghdadi, quoted in "In new audio speech, Islamic State (ISIS) leader al-Baghdadi issues call to arms to all Muslims", *MEMRI*, 14 May 2015; available at http://www.memrijttm.org/in-new-audio-speech-islamic-state-isis-leader-al-baghdadi-issues-call-to-arms-to-all-muslims.html, accessed 1 July 2016.

70 "Joué-lès-Tours: Bertrand Nzohabonayo, de rappeur à apprenti jihadiste" ("Joué-lès-Tours: Bertrand Nzohabonayo: from rapper to apprentice jihadist"), *Le Parisien*, 21 December 2014.

71 Cf. Angélique Négroni and Jean-Marc Leclerc, "'Bilal', l'assaillant des policiers de Joué-lès-Tours, s'était autoradicalisé" ("'Bilal', who attacked policemen in Joué-lès-Tours, radicalized himself"), *Le Figaro*, 21 December 2014.

72 "Foreword", *Dabiq*, December 2014, p. 4.

73 "Foreword", *Dabiq*, March 2014.

74 This also applies to radicalization itself. Cf. Interview with Berna Kurnaz, 20 April 2015.

6. THE AMERICAN EXCEPTION?

1 See *United States of America v. Shannon Maureen Conley*, Case No. 14-mj-01045-KLM, Complaint (United States District Court for the District of Colorado, 9 April 2014.

2 "American teen wears hijab in court as she pleads guilty to charges she tried to join ISIS in Syria", *Daily Mail*, 10 September 2014.

3 *United States of America v. Shannon Maureen Conley*, op. cit.

4 Ibid.

5 Ibid.

6 Ibid.

7 "Deadly attacks since 9/11", *International Security, New America Foundation*; available at http://securitydata.newamerica.net/extremists/deadly-attacks.html, accessed 1 July 2016. Also Jerome Bjelopera, "American jihadist terrorism: combatting a complex threat", *Congressional Research Service*, January 2013; available at https://www.fas.org/sgp/crs/terror/R41416.pdf, accessed 1 July 2016.

8 "Deadly attacks", *International Security*, op. cit.

9 See Eliane Tschaen Barbieri and Jytte Klausen, "Al Qaeda's London branch: patterns of domestic and transnational network integration", *Studies in Conflict and Terrorism*, 35(6) (2012), pp. 411–31.

10 See "Terror plots", *International Security, New America Foundation;* available at http://securitydata.newamerica.net/extremists/terror-plots.html, accessed 1 July 2016. For details of some of these operations, see "Illusion of justice: human rights abuses in U.S. terrorism prosecutions", *Human Rights Watch,* July 2014: available at https://www.hrw.org/report/2014/07/21/illusion-justice/human-rights-abuses-us-terrorism-prosecutions, accessed 1 July 2016.

11 Marc Sageman, *Leaderless Jiihad: Terror Networks in the Twenty-First Century* (Philadelphia: Pennsylvania University Press, 2008), p. 96.

12 Ibid., p. 98.

13 See, for example, "American Muslim poll: politics, priorities, and prejudice in 2016", *Institute for Social Policy and Understanding*, March 2016; available at http://www.ispu.org/pdfs/repository/amp2016.pdf, accessed 1 July 2016. Also "Muslims in America: no signs of growth in alienation or support for extremism", *Pew Research Center*, August 2011; available at http://www.people-press.org/2011/08/30/muslim-americans-no-signs-of-growth-in-alienation-or-support-for-extremism/, accessed 1 July 2016.

14 See "Muslim Americans: middle class and mostly mainstream", *Pew Research Center*, May 2007; available at http://www.pewresearch.org/2007/05/22/muslim-americans-middle-class-and-mostly-mainstream/, accessed 1 July 2016.

15 Sageman, *Leaderless Jihad*, op. cit., p. 98.

16 Peter Bergen, *United States of Jihad: Investigating America's Homegrown Terrorists* (New York: Crown, 2016), pp. 113–17.

17 Ibid, pp. 123–7.

18 "Al Shabaab's American recruits", *Anti-Defamation League*, February 2015.

19 See Phil Mudd, quoted in Bergen, *United States of Jihad*, p. 175.

20 The Islamic Thinkers Society overlapped with "Revolution Muslim", another group and/or website that engaged in similar tactics and involved many of the individuals who had previously been active in the Islamic Thinkers Society. See communication with Lorenzo Vidino, March 2016. See also J.M. Berger, *Jihad Joe: Americans Who Go to War in the Name of Islam* (Washington DC: Potomac Books, 2011), Chapter 7.

21 "Samir Khan: American blogger and Al Qaeda propagandist", *Anti-Defamation League*, October 2011.

22 See Bergen, *United States of Jihad*, pp. 56–67, 68–84.

23 See, for example, "Return of Al Qaeda's Inspire Magazine", *Stratfor*, 4 May

2012, available at https://www.stratfor.com/sample/analysis/return-al-qaedas-inspire-magazine, accessed 1 July 2016.

24 Azmat Khan, "The magazine that 'inspired' the Boston Bombers", *PBS Frontline*, 30 April 2013.

25 In early 2016, the FBI cited a figure of 250 "travel attempts", which vastly overestimates the number of people who have successfully crossed into Syria.

26 Omar Sacirbey, "Extremism in our own communities?", *Beliefnet*, 2006; available at http://www.beliefnet.com/Faiths/Islam/2006/06/Extremism-In-Our-Own-Communities.aspx, accessed 1 July 2016.

27 Jibril lecture, cited in "Jihad, Syria, and social media: how foreign fighters have documented their war", *Guardian*, 15 April 2014: available at http://www.theguardian.com/uk-news/video/2014/apr/15/jihad-syria-social-media-video, accessed 1 July 2016.

28 See Joseph Carter, Shiraz Maher and Peter Neumann, *Greenbirds: Measuring Importance and Influence in Syrian Foreign Fighter Networks* (London: ICSR, 2014), pp. 20–3.

29 See Robert Young Pelton, "The All-American life and death of Eric Harroun", *VICE News*, 11 April 2014; available at https://news.vice.com/article/the-all-american-life-and-death-of-eric-harroun, accessed 1 July 2016.

30 Eric Harroun's Facebook page.

31 Harroun, cited in "U.S. soldier faces death penalty for fighting with al-Qaeda in Syria", *Daily Telegraph*, 9 April 2013.

32 *United States of America v. Ramiz Zijad Hodzic et al.*, Case No. 4:15CR00049 CDP/DDN, Indictment (United States District Court – Eastern District of Missouri), 5 February 2015.

33 See "Ramo Abdullah Pazara: Sprpski ratnik i islamski fanatik", *Slobodna Bosna*, 18 February 2015; available at http://www.slobodna-bosna.ba/vijest/19266/ramo_abdullah_pazara_srpski_ratnik_i_islamski_fanatik.html, accessed 1 July 2016.

34 *USA v. Ramiz Zijad Hodzic*, op. cit. See Robert Patrick, "Allegations of St. Louis terrorism support rooted back in Bosnian War", *St Louis Post-Dispatch*, 11 April 2015.

35 See Charles Kurzman, "Muslim-American involvement with violent extremism, 2015", *Triangle Center on Terrorism and Homeland Security*, February 2016.

36 *United States of America v. Mohammed Hamzah Khan*, Case No. 14CR564, Complaint (United States District Court – Northern District of Illinois), 4 October 2014.

37 "Letter prosecutors say Mohammed Hamzah Khan wrote to his parents", *Chicago Tribune*, 3 November 2014; available at http://www.chicagotribune.com/chi-letter-prosecutors-say-mohammed-hamzah-khan-wrote-to-his-parents-20141103-htmlstory.html, accessed 1 July 2016.

38 Bergen, *United States of Jihad*, op. cit. p. 2.

39 Lorenzo Vidino and Seamus Hughes, "ISIS in America: from retweets to Raqqa", *Program on Extremism*, December 2015, pp. 26–7.

40 Bergen, *United States of Jihad*, p. 259.

41 Vidino and Hughes, "ISIS in America", op. cit. p. 10.

42 Jessica Glenza, Tom Dart, Andrew Grumbel and Jon Boone, "Tashfeen Malik: who was the 'shy housewife' turned San Bernardino killer?", *Guardian*, 6 December 2015.

43 See Snejana Farberov, "Turned away: Tashfeen Malik tried to contact Islamic militant groups", *Daily Mail*, 12 December 2015.

7. AL-QAEDA

1 David Kilcullen, *The Accidental Guerrilla: Fighting Small Wars in the Midst of a Big One* (London: Hurst, 2009).

2 Cf. "Ayman al-Zawahiri: Al-Qaeda will be dissolved to strengthen ISIS", *Abna. com*, 5 April 2015, available at http://en.abna24.com/service/middle-east-west-asia/archive/2015/04/05/681278/story.html, accessed 1 July 2016.

3 Abu Mohammad al-Julani, "Concerning the Fields of al-Sham", April 2013; available at http://justpaste.it/jowlaniaprl2013, accessed 1 July 2016.

4 Cf. Aymenn Jawad al-Tamimi, "Comprehensive reference guide to Sunni militant groups in Iraq", *Jihadology*, 23 January 2014; available at http://jihadology.net/2014/01/23/musings-of-an-iraqi-brasenostril-on-jihad-comprehensive-reference-guide-to-sunni-militant-groups-in-iraq/, accessed 1 July 2016.

5 Abu Qatada, quoted in Shiv Malik, Ali Younes, Spencer Ackerman and Mustafa Kahlil, "How Isis crippled al-Qaeda", *Guardian*, 10 June 2015.

6 Interview with Aymenn Jawad al-Tamimi, 1 April 2015.

7 "Control of urban territory in Syria: May 20, 2015", *Institute for the Study of War*, 20 May 2015; available at http://www.understandingwar.org/backgrounder/control-urban-terrain-syria-may-20-2015, accessed 1 July 2016.

8 Interviews with Aymenn Jawad al-Tamimi, 1 April 2015, and Aziz al-Hamza, 6 May 2015.

9 Interview with Hisham and Bashar, 11 April 2014.

10 Interview with Aymenn Jawad al-Tamimi, 1 April 2015.

11 "Archive of Jabhat al-Nusra Billboards and Murals", *Aymenn Jawad al-Tamimi*, 24 March 2015; available at http://www.aymennjawad.org/2015/03/archive-of-jabhat-al-nusra-billboards-and-murals, accessed 1 July 2016.

12 Cf. David Blair and Richard Spencer, "How Qatar is funding the rise of Islamist extremists", *Telegraph*, 20 September 2014.

13 Peter R. Neumann, quoted in Mary Anne Weaver, "Her Majesty's Jihadists", *New York Times Magazine*, 14 April 2015.

14 Abul Taher and Amanda Perthen, "From shop assistant to the British Bin Laden", *Mail on Sunday*, 1 June 2014.

15 Jabbar, quoted ibid.

16 Cf. Howard Koplowitz, "Al Qaeda bomb plot? Obama urges European authorities to beef up airport security", *International Business Times*, 2 July 2014.

17 Al-Julani interviewed on al-Jazeera, 27 May 2015. Cf. Matt Levitt, "The Khorasan group should scare us", *Politico*, 25 September 2014.

18 Cf. Markus Bickel, "Moderate terroristen?" ("Moderate terrorists?"), *Frankfurter Allgemeine Zeitung*, 29 May 2015.

19 On the emergence of AQAP, see Gregory D. Johnsen, *The Last Refuge: Yemen, al-Qaeda, and America's War in Arabia* (New York and London: W. W. Norton, 2013), Chapter 3.

20 Cf. Eli Lake, "Meet al-Qaeda's new general manager: Nasser al-Wuhayshi", *The Daily Beast*, 8 September 2013.

21 Morten Storm, *Agent Storm: My Life Inside al-Qaeda* (London: Penguin, 2014), p. 286.

22 Ryan Evans, "From Iraq to Yemen: Al-Qaida's shifting strategies", *CTC Sentinel*, 1 October 2010.

23 Al-Wuhayshi, quoted in Storm, *Agent Storm*, p. 290.

24 Cf. Alexander Meleagrou-Hitchens and Peter R. Neumann, "Al Qaeda's most dangerous franchise", *Wall Street Journal*, 10 May 2012.

25 Cf. Oren Adaki, "AQAP official calls on rival factions in Syria to unite against West", *Long War Journal*, 1 October 2014; available at http://www.longwarjournal.org/archives/2014/10/aqap_leader_calls_on.php, accessed 1 July 2016.

26 Gregory D. Johnsen, "This man is the leader in ISIS's recruiting war against Al-Qaeda in Yemen", *Buzzfeed*, 6 July 2015, available at https://www.buzzfeed.com/gregorydjohnsen/this-man-is-the-leader-in-isis-recruiting-war-against-al-qae?utm_term=.auDPPY5gw#.ggyooWnzd, accessed 1 July 2016.

27 Tweet by @ccx667.

28 "National strategy for counterterrorism", *White House*, June 2011, pp. 3–5.

29 Cf. Glenn Kessler, "Spinning Obama's reference to Islamic State as a 'JV' team", *Washington Post*, 3 September 2014.

30 Al-Maqdisi, quoted in Malik, "How Isis crippled".

31 Virginia Comolli, *Boko Haram: Nigeria's Islamist Insurgency* (London: Hurst, 2015), pp. 98–101.

32 Tim Cocks, "Boko Haram too extreme for 'al Qaeda in West Africa' brand", *Reuters*, 28 May 2014.

33 Cf. "Security council Al-Qaida sanctions committee adds Boko Haram to its sanctions list", *UN Security Council*, 22 May 2014; available at http://www.un.org/press/en/2014/sc11410.doc.htm, accessed 1 July 2016.

34 Bill Roggio and Thomas Joscelyn, "Discord dissolves Pakistani Taliban coalition", *Long War Journal*, 18 October 2014; available at http://www.longwarjournal.org/archives/2014/10/discord_dissolves_pa.php, accessed 1 July 2016.

35 Bill Roggio, "Pakistani Taliban emir for Bajau joins Islamic State", *Long War Journal*, 2 February 2015; http://www.longwar-journal.org/archives/2015/02/pakistani_taliban_em.php, accessed 1 November 2015. (Link no longer working.)

36 Khorasan is an archaic name for a region encompassing Afghanistan, Pakistan and parts of Iran and central Asia. The Islamic State's "Khorasan province" is not equivalent to what the Americans called the "Khorasan group", which visited al-Nusra in summer 2014.

37 Thomas Joscelyn, "Pakistani Taliban rejects Islamic State's 'self-professed Caliphate'", *Long War Journal*, 27 May 2015; available at http://www.longwarjournal.org/archives/2015/05/pakistani-taliban-rejects-islamic-states-self-professed-caliphate.php, accessed 1 July 2016.

38 Cf. Interview with Michael Semple, *BBC World News*, 4 June 2015.

39 Cf. Brian Fishman and Joseph Felter, "Al-Qa'ida's foreign fighters in Iraq: a first look at the Sinjar records", *Combating Terrorism Center at West Point*, 2 January 2007.

40 "Al-Qaeda in Libya: a profile", *Library of Congress*, August 2012, p. 2; available at http://fas.org/irp/world/para/aq-libya-loc.pdf, accessed 1 July 2016.

41 Mohamed Eljarh, "A snapshot of the Islamic State's Libyan stronghold", *Foreign Policy*, 1 April 2015; available at http://foreignpolicy.com/2015/04/01/a-snapshot-of-the-islamic-states-libyan-stronghold-derna-libya-isis/, accessed 1 July 2016.

42 Aaron Y. Zelin, "The Islamic State's first colony in Libya", *Policywatch 2325, Washington Institute*, October 2014.

43 See Mark Hosenball, "US fears Islamic State is making serious inroads in Libya", *Reuters*, 20 March 2015.

44 Richard Spencer, "Tunisia attacker trained in Libya at the same time as Bardo Museum terrorists", *Telegraph*, 30 June 2015. Cf. Aaron Zelin, "The Tunisian-Libyan jihadi connection", *ICS. Insight*, 6 July 2015.

45 Cf. James Zogby, "The region disagrees on the Arab Spring's results", *The National*, 20 December 2014.

46 "Country reports: Middle East and North Africa overview", *U.S. Department of State, Country Reports on Terrorism 2013*; available at http://www.state.gov/j/ct/rls/crt/2013/224823.htm, accessed 1 July 2016.

47 Cf. Karin Von Hippel, "The roots of terrorism: probing the myths", *Political Quarterly*, 73(3) (2002), pp. 25–39.

48 Cf. Peter King, quoted in "Peter King: AQAP and ISIS worked together on Paris attacks", *Breitbart.com*, 17 February 2015, available at http://www.breitbart.com/video/2015/02/17/peter-king-aqap-and-isis-worked-together-on-paris-attacks/, accessed 1 July 2016.

49 Angelique Chrisafis, "*Charlie Hebdo* attackers: born, raised and radicalised in Paris", *Guardian*, 12 January 2015.

50 Paul Cruickshank and Barbara Starr, "U.S. working assumption: AQAP ordered Said Kouachi to carry out an attack", *CNN*, 21 January 2015; Thomas Joscelyn, "Paris terrorist reportedly claimed ties to Anwar al-Awlaki, AQ", *Long War Journal*, 9 January 2015.

51 Andrew H. Kydd and Barbara F. Walter, "The strategies of terrorism", *International Security*, 31(1) (2006), pp. 49–80.

52 Cf. Faith Karimi, Ashley Fantz and Catherine E. Shoichet, "Al Shabaab threatens malls, including some in U.S.; FBI downplays threat", *CNN*, 22 February 2015.

53 Ibid.

54 Stig Jarle Hansen, lecture at "jihadist insurgencies" conference, London, 28 May 2015.

8. COUNTERTERRORISM

1 Cf. Hayes Brown, "How Obama decided to make terrorist recruitment his U.N. priority", *thinkprogress.org*, 24 September 2014, available at http://thinkprogress.org/world/2014/09/24/3570460/obama-unsc-foreign-fighters/, accessed 1 July 2016.
2 See "Resolution 2178 (2014)", *United Nations Security Council*, 24 September 2014; http://www.un.org/en/sc/ctc/docs/2015/SCR%202178_2014_EN.pdf, accessed 1 July 2016.
3 Carl von Clausewitz, *Vom Kriege (On War)*, 2nd edition (Berlin: Ullstein, 1999), p. 683.
4 Cf. Peter R. Neumann, *Old and New Terrorism: Late Modernity, Globalisation and the Transformation of Political Violence* (Cambridge: Polity Press, 2009).
5 Interview with a representative of the Belgian domestic intelligence service, 14 April 2015.
6 Thomas Friedman, "The Arab quarter century", *New York Times*, 9 April 2013; "How Luther went viral", *The Economist*, 17 December 2011.
7 Cf. Aaron David Miller, "5 Reasons the U.S. cannot defeat ISIS", *Woodrow Wilson Center blog*, 6 June 2015, available at https://www.wilsoncenter.org/article/5-reasons-the-us-cannot-defeat-isis, accessed 1 July 2016.
8 See Jamie Dettmer and Mike Giglio, "Bring back Mubarak!", *Daily Beast*, 22 January 2013.
9 Cf. Jean-Pierre Filiu, *From Deep State to Islamic State: The Arab Counter-Revolution and Its Jihadi Legacy* (London: Hurst 2015).
10 Cf. Peter R. Neumann, "Suspects into collaborators", *London Review of Books*, 3 April 2014.
11 Matthew Holehouse, "Britain must talk to dictator Assad to defeat Isil, says former head of the Army", *Telegraph*, 22 August 2014.
12 See Daniel Pipes, "Wait out the war in Syria", *Washington Times*, 21 August 2012.
13 Alberto Fernandez, *U.S.-Islamic World Forum*, Doha (Qatar), 2 June 2015.
14 Cf. Anonymous, "The mystery of ISIS", *New York Review of Books*, 13 August 2015.
15 Rory Carroll, "McCain urges ground troops against Isis: 'They're winning, and we're not'", *Guardian,* 12 October 2014.
16 Cf. Peter R. Neumann and M.L.R. Smith, *The Strategy of Terrorism* (London: Routledge, 2008), pp. 69–70.
17 Cf. Peter R. Neumann (ed.), *Radicalization – Volume II: Issues and Debates* (London and New York: Routledge, 2015), Part 7 ("Conflict, repression and counterterrorism").
18 Cf. Katrin Brettfeld and Peter Wetzels, "Muslime in Deutschland: integration, integrationsbarrieren, religion sowie einstellungen zu demokratie, rechtsstaat und

politisch-religiös motivierter gewalt" ("Muslims in Germany: integration, barriers to integration, religion and attitudes to democracy"), *University of Hamburg and the Federal Ministry of the Interior*, July 2007; Munira Mirza, Abi Senthilkumaran and Zein Ja'far, "Living apart together: British Muslims and the paradox of multiculturalism", *Policy Exchange*, May 2007.

19 Cf. "Illusion of justice: human rights abuses in US terrorism prosecutions", *Human Rights Watch*, 21 July 2014; available at http://www.hrw.org/node/126101, accessed 1 July 2016.

20 Cf. Peter R. Neumann, "Algorithmen und agenten" ("Algorithms and agents"), *International Politik*, November/December 2014.

21 "Channel duty guidance: protecting vulnerable people from being drawn into terrorism", *Home Office*, 23 October 2012; available at https://www.gov.uk/government/uploads/system/uploads/attachment_data/file/425189/Channel_Duty_Guidance_April_2015.pdf, accessed 1 July 2016.

22 Interview with Daniel Köhler, 23 March 2015.

23 Cf. Carolyn Hoyle, Alexandra Bradford and Ross Frenett, *Becoming Mulan? Female Western Migrants to ISIS* (London: Institute for Strategic Dialogue, 2015), p. 16.

24 In the Bremen advice centre *kitab*, for example, two part-time workers are responsible for more than 150 cases across the whole of northern Germany. Interview with Berna Kurnaz, 20 April 2015.

25 Cf. "Prevention of radicalisation and extremism: action plan", *The Danish Government*, September 2014; available at http://www.justitsministeriet.dk/sites/default/files/media/Pressemeddelelser/pdf/2015/SJ20150422125507430%20%5BDOR1545530%5D.PDF, accessed 1 July 2016.

26 Interviews with Daniel Köhler and Claudia Dantschke, both on 23 March 2015.

27 Interview with Judy Korn, 24 March 2015.

28 Randeep Ramesh, "Anti-terror strategy is seen as intrusive and secretive by many Muslims", *Guardian*, 9 March 2015.

29 Charles Farr, "Terrorismusabwehr und deradikalisierung aus britischer sicht" ("Terrorism prevention and deradicalization from a British perspective"), *Speech at the 12th symposium of the German Constitution Protection Office*, 4 May 2015; available at http://www.verfassungsschutz.de/de/oeffentlichkeitsarbeit/symposium/symposium-2015, accessed 1 July 2016.

30 See Peter R. Neumann, "Preventing violent radicalization in America", *Bipartisan Policy Center*, June 2011, pp. 21–4; available at http://bipartisanpolicy.org/wp-content/uploads/sites/default/files/NSPG.pdf, accessed 1 July 2016.

31 Interview with Bremen senator for the interior Ulrich Mäurer, 20 April 2015.

Further Reading

BLOGS

Jihadica – Documenting the Global Jihad; available at http://www.jihadica.com/, accessed 1 July 2016.

Jihadology – A Clearinghouse for Jihadi Primary Source Material, Original Analysis and Translation Service; available at http://jihadology.net/, accessed 1 July 2016.

Aymenn Jawad al-Tamimi; available at http://www.aymennjawad.org/, accessed 1 July 2016.

BOOKS AND ARTICLES

Bergen, Peter, *United States of Jihad: Investigating America's Homegrown Terrorists* (New York: Crown, 2016).

Calvert, John, *Sayyid Qutb and the Origins of Radical Islamism* (London: Hurst, 2010).

Fishman, Brian M., *The Masterplan: ISIS, al-Qaeda and the Jihadi Strategy for Final Victory* (New Haven, CT: Yale University Press, 2016).

Hafez, Mohammed M., "Suicide terrorism in Iraq: a preliminary assessment of the quantitative data and documentary evidence", *Studies in Conflict and Terrorism*, 29(8) (2006), pp. 591–619.

Hamid, Mustafa and Leah Farrall, *The Arabs at War in Afghanistan* (London: Hurst, 2015).

Hegghammer, Thomas, "Should I stay or should I go? Explaining variation in Jihadists' choice between domestic and foreign fighting", *American Political Science Review*, 107(1) (2013), pp. 1–15.

Hoffman, Bruce, *Inside Terrorism*, 2nd edition (New York: Columbia University Press, 2006).

Hoffman, Bruce and Fernando Reinares (eds), *The Evolution of the Global Terrorist Threat: From 9/11 to Osama bin Laden's Death* (New York: Columbia University Press, 2014).

Jones, Seth G., *A Persistent Threat: The Evolution of al Qa'ida and Other Salafi Jihadists* (Santa Monica, CA: RAND, 2014).

Juergensmeyer, Mark, *Terror in the Mind of God: The Global Rise of Religious Violence*, 2nd edition (Los Angeles: University of California Press, 2000).

Kepel, Gilles, *Jihad: The Trail of Political Islam* (London: I.B.Tauris, 2002).

Klausen, Jytte and Adrienne Roach, "Western Jihadists in the Syrian and Iraqi insurgencies", *Working Paper #4, The Western Jihadism Project,* August 2014.

Law, Randall D., *Terrorism: A History* (Cambridge: Polity Press, 2009).

Lister, Charles, *The Syrian Jihad: Al-Qaeda, the Islamic State and the Evolution of an Insurgency* (London: Hurst, 2015).

Maher, Shiraz, *Salafi-Jihadism: The History of an Idea* (London: Hurst, 2016).

Malet, David, *Foreign Fighters: Transnational Identity in Civil Conflicts* (Oxford: Oxford University Press, 2013).

McCants, William, *The ISIS Apocalypse: The History, Strategy and Doomsday Vision of the Islamic State* (New York: St Martin's Press, 2015).

Meijer, Roel (ed.), *Global Salafism: Islam's New Religious Movement* (London: Hurst, 2009).

Moubayed, Sami, *Under the Black Flag: At the Frontier of the New Jihad* (London: I.B.Tauris, 2015).

Naji, Abu Bakr, *The Management of Savagery: The Most Critical Stage Through Which the Umma Will Pass* (Translated by William McCants) (Boston: John M. Olin Institute, 2006).

Nesser, Petter, *Islamist Terrorism in Europe: A History* (London: Hurst, 2016).

Neumann, Peter R., *Old and New Terrorism: Late Modernity, Globalisation and the Transformation of Political Violence* (Cambridge: Polity Press, 2009).

Neumann, Peter R. and M.L.R. Smith, *The Strategy of Terrorism* (London: Routledge, 2008).

Rapoport, David C., "The four waves of modern terrorism", in Audrey Kurth Cronin and James M. Ludes (eds), *Attacking Terrorism: Elements of a Grand Strategy* (Washington DC: Georgetown University Press, 2004), pp. 46–73.

Stern, Jessica and J.M. Berger, ISIS: *The State of Terror* (New York: William Collins, 2015).

Storm, Morten, *Agent Storm: My Life Inside al-Qaeda* (London: Penguin, 2014).

Warrick, Joby, *Black Flags: The Rise of ISIS* (London: Bantam Press, 2015).

Weiss, Michael and Hassan Hassan, *Inside ISIS: Inside the Army of Terror* (New York: Regan Arts, 2015).

Wiktorowicz, Quintan, "Anatomy of the Salafi movement", *Studies in Conflict and Terrorism,* 29 (2006), pp. 207–39.

Wright, Lawrence, *The Looming Tower: Al Qaeda's Road to 9/11* (London: Penguin, 2006).

Index

9/11 10, 45–52, 116, 130, 138–9, 141,
  173, 176

Abu Sayyaf 113
Abyan 160
Adams, Gerry 22
Adnani, Abu Mohammed al- 132,
  134
Adorno, Theodor W. 23
Afghanistan 40–8, 55, 57–8, 82, 87,
  105–6, 139, 141, 162–3, 176
Ahrar al-Sham 89
al-Qaeda 1–2, 5, 13, 16, 34, 44–52, 57,
  59–60, 64–6, 68–9, 80, 114, 118–19,
  130, 132–3, 135, 141–3, Chapter 7
  passim, 173–4, 179
al-Qaeda in the Arabian Peninsula
  (AQAP) 49, 50, 154, 159–62,
  168–9, 171
al-Qaeda in Iraq (AQI) 160
al-Qaeda in the Islamic Maghreb
  (AQIM) 49, 164
al-Shabaab 79, 142, 152–3, 156, 164,
  170
Albu Nimr 79
Aleppo 2, 68, 97, 155
Alexander II 12
Algeria 18–21, 24, 43, 46, 50, 55, 78
Algiers 19–21
Anas, Abdullah 55–6
al-Anbar 79

Ansar al-Sharia 166
Ansar al-Sunna 73
Ansar Bayt al-Maqdis 191
Ansaru 192
Antakya 99, 110–11
Antwerp 118
Arab Spring 2–4, 46, 51–2, 56, 58, 153,
  163, 167, 175
Arafat, Yasser 20
Arifi, Mohammed al- 91
Arkansas 143
Armed Islamic Group (Groupe
  Islamique Armé; GIA) 46
Army Explorers (US) 137
Army of God 32–4, 52
Arvada 136
Asiri, Ibrahim Hassan al- 161
Assad, Bashar al- 60–61, 79–80, 83,
  88, 90–1, 107, 144–5, 155–6, 175
Aum Shinrikyo 34
Australia 88, 127, 182, 186
Austria 10, 16, 88
Awlaki, Anwar al- 13, 50, 52, 126–7,
  130–1, 136, 141–3, 161, 169
Ayers, Bill 25–6
Azaz 99
Aziz, Abu Rahin 72, 111
Azzam, Abdullah 41–7, 55, 57, 105

Baader, Andreas 27
Baghdad 2, 50, 62, 71, 75

Baghdadi, Abu Bakr al- 56, 58, 62–6, 68, 71, 78–80, 88, 132–3, 154, 157, 162–6, 176
Baidoa 152–3, 156
Bakr, Haji 73–4
Bakri, Omar 115–16, 118
Balkans 47, 87, 146
Bangladesh 2, 91
Banna, Hassan al- 36–7, 39
Beam, Louis 130
Belgium 88–9, 98, 105, 117, 174
Benghazi 166
Bergen, Peter 150
Berlin 118
Bin Laden, Osama 1–2, 43–52, 55–9, 64, 68, 105, 153, 159–60, 164–4, 171, 176
Bismarck, Otto von 13
Biswas, Mehdi Masroor *see* Shami Witness
Bledsoe, Carlos 143
Boko Haram 2, 77, 164
Bosnia 47, 105
Boston 50, 141, 143
Brachman, Jarret 127
Brazil 24
Bray, Michael 33–4
Breivik, Anders 30
Bremen 96
Bruce, Steve 30, 34
Brussels 108, 117, 133, 140, 174
Byman, Daniel 108

Cairo 35–6, 39, 41, 51
Camp Bucca 62, 71
Canada 87, 133, 182, 186
Carter, Joseph 110
Castro, Fidel 24
Caucasus 2, 74
Cerantonio, Musa 126–7
Charlie Hebdo 130, 134–5, 168–9
Chicago 26, 147
China 19, 56, 87
Choudary, Anjem 115–16, 118, 125

Choudhry, Roshonara 122, 131
Churchill, Winston 17–18
CIA 139
Clausewitz, Carl von 173
Cockburn, Patrick 73, 75
Conley, Shannon 136–8, 148
Connecticut 141
Copenhagen 135, 168
Coulibaly, Amedy 169
Cuspert, Denis *see* Deso Dogg
Cyprus 18

Dabiq (online magazine) 68–9, 81, 101–3, 123, 129, 134–5
Damascus 41, 66, 71
Daraa 155
Dearborn 140, 144
Denmark 88, 96, 171, 182, 184, 187
Denver 136
Derna 166
Deso Dogg 102, 118
Dijon 134
Din, Nur ad- 58
Dinslaken 6, 118
Düsseldorf 98–9

Egypt 2, 35–7, 39–40, 43, 46, 51, 65, 112, 145, 163
Egyptian Islamic Group 46
Ensslin, Gudrun 28

Facebook 1, 55, 86–7, 94, 100, 103, 122, 124–5, 127, 129, 134, 145–6
Fanon, Frantz 18–19, 25, 173
Farook, Syed Rizwan 150
Farr, Charles 185
FBI 26, 136–9, 146, 150, 162, 170, 180
Fernandez, Alberto 176
Fighting Vanguard 39
Finland 88
Fort Hood 143
France 10, 13–14, 17, 19–21, 88–9, 94–5, 98, 108, 117, 150, 174, 182

Frankfurt 98, 108, 122, 136
Frankfurt School 23
Free Syrian Army 72, 88–9, 145, 156

Gaddafi, Muammar al- 1, 166
Garland 150
Gaulle, Charles de 20
Gaza 191
Gaziantep 98–9, 110
Gelowicz, Filiz 120–1
Germany 13, 17–18, 23, 27–8, 85, 88–9, 96–8, 101, 105, 108, 113, 115, 118–20, 136, 152, 182–4, 186
Gogh, Theo van 187
Great Britain 13, 17, 21–2, 36, 69, 91, 105, 111, 116, 120, 129, 183
Guevara, Ernesto Che 24
Gulf States 77, 89, 157

Haifa 9
Hakim, Abdul *see* Ryding, Kim Andre 125
Halane, Salma and Zahra 120
Hamas 34, 39, 170
Hamza, Aziz al- 72, 84
Harroun, Eric 145–6
Hasan, Nidal 143
Hassan, Hassan 36, 71–2, 161
Hayat 107
Hegghammer, Thomas 42, 45, 105, 107–9
Helfen in Not (Help in Need) 115
Help4Ummah 115
Henry, Emile 15
Herrmann, Joachim 105
Hezbollah 34, 88
hijrah 88, 132, 136, 147
Hill, Paul 32–3
Hitler, Adolf 30, 33
Hoffman, Bruce 34
Hughes, Seamus 149
Hussein, Saddam 58–9, 71, 79

Idlib 155, 157
Ikhwan Man Ta'a Allah 193
Imam Bukhari Bataillon 194
India 35, 129, 191
Indonesia 193
Inspire (online magazine) 13, 50, 130–31, 143, 161
Iran 40, 160
Iraq
  foreign fighters in 72, 74, 85, 87–9, 95, 96, 102, 105–6, 133, 150, 169, 171, 172
  Iraq War 49, 50, 56–7, 59, 61, 109, 119, 166, 169, 176
  Islamic State's territory in 58, 64, 68, 82
Ireland 20–2, 30, 88
Irish Republican Army (IRA) 21
Islamic Front 69, 157
Islamic Salvation Front 46
Islamic State (IS)
  character/philosophy 65, 69, 131–3
  economy 75, 77, 81, 176
  foreign fighters Chapter 4 *passim*, 111, 118, 119, 125–6, 149
  influences 66–8
  internet 123–7
  Islamic State in Iraq (ISI) 154
  Islamic State in Iraq and the Levant (ISIL) *see* Islamic State in Iraq and Syria (ISIS)
  Islamic State in Iraq and Syria (ISIS) 62–4, 92, 154, 155, 157
  "lone wolves" 129–31
  organization 70–3, 75–6, 78
  origins 49, 57–62
  problems 81–4
  relationship with al-Qaeda 65, 68, 69, 80, 153–4
  strategy/tactics 56, 70–3, 74, 79, 80, 122, 155, 163–6
  Western attacks 108, 130, 168–76
  women 119–22

Islamic Thinkers Society 142–3
Israel 21, 41, 58–9, 142
Issa, Ismail 83, 99, 101
Istanbul 96, 98–9, 125, 146–7
Italy 10–11, 16, 23, 28, 88

Jabbar, Ismail 158
Jabhat al-Nusra 61–4, 69, 72, 82, 85,
    89, 92, 145, 154–9
Jamaat Ansar al-Dawla al-Islamiya fi
    Bayt al-Maqdis 191
Jabhat Ansar al-Din 194
Jamaat al-Itisam bil-Kitab wa
    al-Sunna 194; see also Ansar
    al-Sunna
Jamaat Ansar al-Islam 191
Jaman, Ifthekar 90–2
Jaysh al-Ummah fi Aknaf Bayt
    al-Maqdis 191
Jaysh Muhammad in Bilad
    al-Sham 194
Jibril, Ahmad Musa 144–5
al-Jihad 44
al-Jihad (magazine) 44
Jihad Recollections 142
Jihadi John 131
Jones, Seth 2
Jordan 41, 58, 66

Kaldet til Islam (Call to Islam) 117
Karan, Burak 99
Kazakhstan 87
Kempten 118
Kenya 18, 48
Khan, Mohammed Hamzah 119,
    147–8
Khan, Mohammed Sidique 119
Khan, Samir 142–3
Khomeini, Ruhollah 40
Khorasan 159, 165
Kilcullen, David 153
Kilis 99, 101
Klausen, Jytte 106, 115
Kobane 75, 104, 147

Koënigstein, François Claudius 14
Kouachi, Cherif 169
Kouachi, Said 169
Kropotkin, Pjotr 11–12
Kurnaz, Berna 123
Kydd, Andrew 170

Léauthier, Léon-Jules 15
Lebanon 58, 145
Lewis, Bernard 35
Libya 52, 60, 78, 163, 166–7, 170
Lions of the Caliphate 194
Lister, Charles 77
London 13, 47, 49, 55, 111, 115–16, 119,
    122, 126, 130, 158
Los Angeles 140
Loyalists (Northern Ireland) 30

Madrid 49, 130
Mafaalani, Aladin El- 113
Maher, Shiraz 86, 91–3, 106, 110
Majlis Shura al-Mujahideen fi Aknaf
    Bayt al-Maqdis 191
Majlis Shura Shabab al-Islam (Shura
    Council for Islamic Youth) 166, 192
Malaysia 18
Malet, David 90
Malik, Tashfeen 150–1
Maliki, Nuri al- 80
Maqdisi, Abu Mohammed al- 58,
    164
Marcuse, Herbert 23
Marighella, Carlos 24–5, 27–8, 67,
    173
Mateen, Omar 138, 151
McCain, John 176
McCants, William 67
McKinley, William 16
Mecca 40, 43, 64
Medina 40, 64
Meinhof, Ulrike 28
Michigan 25, 140, 144
Millatu Ibrahim (Abraham's
    Way) 118, 122, 127

Minneapolis 140, 142, 148
Mogadishu 28, 46, 142, 152
Morocco 50, 72
Mosul 6, 64, 72–5, 77
Most, Johann 13–14
al-Mourabitun 92
Mubarak, Hosni 51, 65, 175
al-Muhajiroun 115–17, 142
MUJAO 192
Munich 21
Muslim Brotherhood 36–7, 39, 41, 46, 52, 55
Mussolini, Benito 29–30

Nagie, Ibrahim Abou 114
Naji, Abu Bakr 67–8, 76, 80
Nantes 6, 134
Narodnaya Volya (People's Will) 12
Nashville 1
Nasser, Gamal Abdel 37
National Liberation Front (Front de Libération Nationale; FLN) 19
NATO 52
Nemmouche, Mehdi 108
Netherlands, the 85, 88, 98, 117, 182, 187
New York 27, 51, 140–2, 150, 172
New Zealand 88
Nigeria 2, 77
Nobel, Alfred 13
Norway 88, 171, 182
Nzohabonayo, Bertrand 133

Obama, Barack 1, 93, 144, 163, 172, 182
Oberursel 108
Oklahoma City 130
Omar al-Shishani Group 194
Orlando 138, 151
Ottawa 133

Pakistan 40–1, 43–4, 47, 78, 87, 106, 116, 119, 130, 141, 159–60, 164–5
Palestine 19–21, 41

Palestine Liberation Organization (PLO) 20
Panetta, Leon 2
Paris 3, 15, 19, 93–4, 108, 121–2, 130, 133–4, 140, 168–9, 172
Pazara, Abdullah Ramo 146–7
Pearl, Daniel 47
Pennsylvania 51
Pensacola 32
Peshawar 41, 43, 45
Philippines 2, 193
Pisacane, Carlo 11, 173
Porta, Donatella della 95
Power, Samantha 172
Profetens Ummah (The Prophet's Community) 117, 125, 127
Punjab 34

Qutb, Mohammed 37–40, 44, 48
Qutb, Sayyid 37–40, 44, 48

Ramadi 75
Ramdane, Abane 19–20
RAND Institute 2
Rapoport, David 4–5, 9–10, 28, 31, 34, 173
Raqqa 6, 83, 107, 120
Raqqa Is Being Slaughtered Silently 107
Ravachol see François Claudius Koënigstein
Red Army Faction (RAF) 27, 174
Red Brigades 28
Reuter, Christoph 73
Reyhanli 156
Russia 56, 87, 172
Ryding, Kim Andre 125–6

Sadat, Anwar al- 44
Sageman, Marc 95, 139–40
Salafism 37–8, 58, 94, 99, 112–14, 184
Saltman, Erin 122
Samarra 62
San Bernardino 150
Şanlıurfa 99

Sartre, Jean-Paul 23
Saudi Arabia 37, 39–41, 72, 78
Schanzer, David 2
Schleyer, Hanns Martin 28
Schmidt, Wolf 119–20
Shahzad, Faisal 141
Shaitat 79
Shami Witness 129
Shapiro, Jeremy 108
Sharia4Belgium 117–18
Sharia4France 117
Sharia4Holland 117
Sheikh, Omar Said 47, 91
Shishani, Omar al- 74, 146
Siba'i, Mustafa al- 39
Simpson, Elton 150
Sinai 78
Smith, Melanie 121–2
Solingen 118
Somalia 2, 46, 79, 82, 85, 87, 106, 139,
    142, 148, 150, 153, 160, 164
Southampton 115
Soviet Union see Russia
Spain 16, 88
Steinberg, Guido 40
St Louis 146
Storm, Morten 36, 160
Stuttgart 28, 99, 101
Sudan 47
Suri, Abu Mussab al- 61, 68
Sweden 88, 104, 182, 184
Switzerland 88
Sydney 133
Sykes-Picot Agreement 64, 175
Syria
    conflict in 4, 114, 124, 168, 170, 172,
        176, 177
    foreign fighters in 72, 85–8, 90–9,
        101, 106–7, 111, 117, 118, 120, 123,
        129, 133, 144, 145, 171
    Islamic State expansion in 63, 64,
        74, 79, 82, 100, 163, 166
    origins of Islamic State in 60
Syrian Islamic Front 157

Tamimi, Aymenn Jawad al- 104
Tanzania 48
Tanzim Ansar al-Tawheed fi Bilad
    al-Hind 191
Tehrik-i-Taliban (Taliban Movement
    of Pakistan; TTP) 165
Thomson, David 94
Todenhöfer, Jurgen 74
Tsarnaev, Dzhokhar 143
Tsarnaev, Tamerlan 143
Tunis 51
Tunisia 2, 51, 72, 78, 163, 166, 167
Turkey 87, 92, 98–100, 105, 107,
    145–6
Turkistan Islamic Party 194
Turkmenistan 87
Twitter 86–7, 94, 100, 103, 123–4,
    129, 150, 158

United States of America 13, 18, 22–3,
    50, 51, 132, 138–44, 153, 162
Uwais al-Qarani Brigade 83
Uzbekistan 87

Vaillant, Auguste 15
Verviers 108
Vidino, Lorenzo 149
Vietnam 25
Vilvoorde 117–18
Vogel, Pierre 96

Wahhab, Mohammed ibn 'Abd
    al- 37
Walter, Barbara 170
Washington DC 51, 57, 146, 163
Weathermen 25–8
Weiss, Michael 71–2
Wilayat 78
Wilayat Najd 193
Wilson, Woodrow 17–18
Wolfsburg 97, 100, 118
Wright, Lawrence 43
Wuhayschi, Nasir al- 159–62

Yemen 2, 78, 142–3, 154, 160–2, 167,
  169–70

Zarqawi, Abu Musab al- 49, 57–62,
  64, 66–68, 79, 83, 131
Zawahiri, Ayman al- 44–6, 49–52, 59,
  64, 154, 162, 164, 166
Zazi, Najibullah 141
Zedong, Mao 19
Zelin, Aaron 85